Atlas of Interior Design

j

Atlas of Interior Design

Dominic Bradbury

Φ

North America
128 Interiors

Central America
21 Interiors

South America
19 Interiors

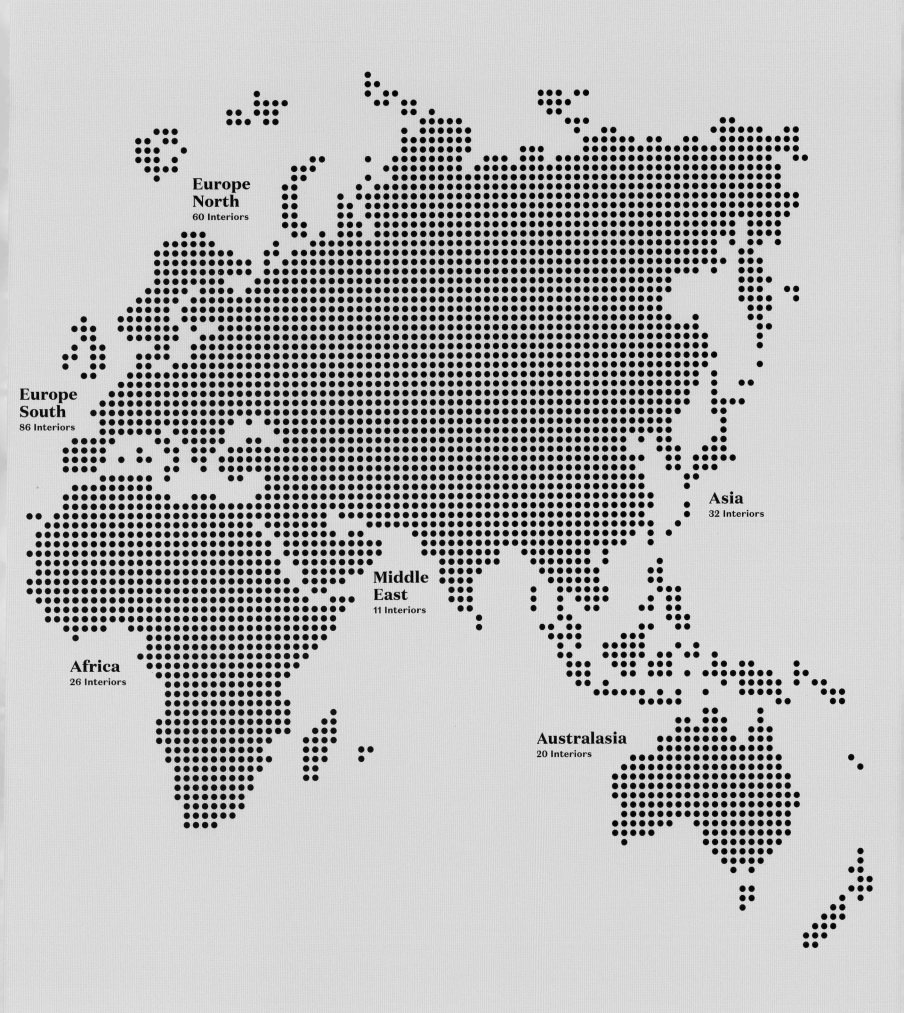

Europe North
60 Interiors

Europe South
86 Interiors

Africa
26 Interiors

Middle East
11 Interiors

Asia
32 Interiors

Australasia
20 Interiors

Introduction

Poetic Interiors

"Making a house is creating," the great French interior designer Madeleine Castaing once wrote. "I make houses like others write poetry, make music, or paint." Revered as one of the true originals in the design world, Castaing recognized the importance of the poetic, rather than the prosaic. Drawing on a wide range of influences, her work was inspired by both the past and the present, while embracing collaborations with artisans and artists, among them the painter, poet, and filmmaker Jean Cocteau with whom she worked a number of times—including on the interiors of Cocteau's own French country home in Milly-la-Forêt. There was a degree of playfulness, a touch of romance, and a spirit of adventure in Castaing's use of pattern and color. "Be audacious, but with taste," she advised. "You also need intuition, originality, vigor."

The results were not only poetic but characterful. Castaing avoided anything that spoke of reproduction or banality. The designer and her work became a key point of reference for younger generations of designers such as Jacques Grange, Mark Hampton, and Jacques Garcia, who suggested that Castaing "makes us feel emotions that, before her, we didn't know existed in interior design" while creating "a perfect balance between decoration, architecture, and landscape." "At a time when houses were sad," wrote Garcia, "she introduced poetry, a taste for life, and mystery."

Along with other true design originals, such as Billy Baldwin, David Hicks, and Renzo Mongiardino, Castaing reminds us of the value of poetry within the world of interiors, especially when it comes to the canvas of house and home. The designers featured within this book—and the residences that they have created around the world—adopt a poetic approach that treats interior design as an art or craft, rather than simply a profession. The *Atlas of Interior Design* is intended as a celebration of design artistry beginning in the postwar period and progressing to the present, covering all parts of the world. This inspirational journey includes an extraordinary diversity of styles ranging from Minimalism to maximalism with much in between, but essential to all styles is the elevation of house and home through true creativity and originality.

Design & Decoration

"Interior design is essentially the process of maximizing the potential of a space and what it contains," explained David Hicks in his textbook *Style and Design* (1998). "The best rooms also have something to say about the people who live in them, telling a story in colour, shape, texture and pattern, that others can appreciate and enjoy."

Rather like Castaing, Hicks was always interested in "in reconciling old with new, in combining different strands of interest in a harmonious whole." Hicks's enduring influence as a designer stems not only from his original approach to design, particularly his use of vivid colors and geometric patterns, but also his keen ability to communicate ideas and market his work not just in Britain—where he lived and worked—but also around the world. He became one of the first interior designers to turn himself into a brand, working across a spectrum of projects and creating collections of textiles, carpets, and furniture.

Along the way, Hicks wrote *Style and Design*, which is arguably one of the most useful and informative design textbooks ever published.

Interior design was, as Hicks suggested, a relatively new profession. Stepping back to the eighteenth century, architects and architectural designers tended to take control of the interiors, as well as the exteriors, of their buildings with the help of craftspeople and artisans. During the nineteenth century trades became increasingly dominant, with furniture designers and cabinetmakers, upholsterers, gilders, curtain makers, and other artisans all operating within a complex design hierarchy. Hicks points to Arts and Crafts master William Morris as one of the first true interior designers, whose work embraced many different aspects of design during the late nineteenth century, but also the importance of "talented amateurs" during the Thirties, such as Syrie Maugham and Elsie de Wolfe, who played a part in the growing recognition of interior design as a profession in its own right.

In Mark Hampton's landmark book, *Legendary Decorators of the Twentieth Century* (1992), Hampton, who began his career in the Sixties working with David Hicks, stresses the importance of the shift from "period rooms," designed and decorated within one clear aesthetic style, toward spaces with a more eclectic and individual character: "Where one or two points of view may have been popular before, an enormous range of styles became acceptable," Hampton argued. "If the nineteenth century successively loved all of its revivals—Greek, Gothic, and so on—the twentieth century pulled the cork. The genie got out; anything was possible (even in one room) and it still

is. Oftentimes the people who make it possible are called interior decorators."

Hicks makes a useful but perhaps contentious distinction between interior decoration and interior design, while also accepting a degree of crossover between the two. Decoration, he suggests, involves "re-covering, re-colouring, re-painting, re-lighting and rearranging an existing room with existing possessions," while "interior design is the creation of new interior architecture and form, whether in the conversion of an old building or in a completely new structure."

Others may disagree, but this differentiation does point to the relevance of architectural elements and spatial planning within interior design and the particular importance given to proportion and scale, and circulation and light. Many of the projects featured in this book certainly have a strong architectural dimension to them, whether new builds, renovations, or conversions, while the architects are credited throughout as well as interior designers.

Hicks, Hampton, and others stress the importance of the structural framework and organization of a space, or the "bones" of a room, which draw on long-established architectural design principles. Symmetry, scale, proportion, and balance are the cornerstones of the most successful spaces, but there are clearly other key considerations, such as clarity, functionality, and cohesion. There is generally a need for a focal point in a space, which might traditionally mean a fireplace, but could also be a key vista or an artwork, while the repetition of certain elements adds rhythm and possibly a touch of theater. Comfort is an often-underrated consideration, along with the need for well-conceived lighting, which encompasses functional lights, wall fixtures, and statement chandeliers.

While there is no set rule book for interiors, there is a commonly accepted set of design principles that lie behind the creation of thoughtful and well-conceived spaces. These principles add depth, discipline, rigor, and order to a house, or room, whatever its aesthetic style might be. When a designer chooses to break away from such principles then they should, at least, be aware of it and clear about the reasons why. In other words, as Hicks puts it, "rules are meant to be broken":

> The designer should not only recognize the importance of certain fundamental principles, but also be prepared to bend or even break rules creatively. Many of the most successful schemes derive their impact from a startling combination of colours or a novel conjunction of patterns which fly in the face of accepted practice. Rules give structure, but often at the expense of vitality.

Much of this vitality derives from what Hicks describes as the "designer's palette" and the way that it is used, rather than a process of undermining the underlying architectural design principles exhibited in a space. The way that a designer chooses to use this palette of color, texture, pattern, and form can clearly be transformative, even if its "bones" remain unchanged. A combination of design principles and creative self-expression such as this lies at the heart of truly thoughtful design and lends depth to interiors of all kinds.

Global Design

As well as depth, breadth is the other great strength of postwar and contemporary interior design. As a profession, interior design embraces a wide range of creative incomers who bring with them fresh ideas, left-field perspectives, and original ways of thinking and working.

As well as dedicated interior designers and architects, the *Atlas of Interior Design* features the work of original creatives of many different kinds. They include product and furniture designers such as Dieter Rams, Russel Wright, and Marc Newson, along with fashion designers from Laura Ashley to Bill Blass to Giorgio Armani, who have explored the world of interiors in their own way. Similarly, theater and set designers, such as Renzo Mongiardino and Oliver Messel, have famously overlapped with interior design, while the same is true today of artists and filmmakers, such as Julian Schnabel and Luca Guadagnino. In this respect, no other discipline of design is quite so democratic or open-minded, inviting the contributions of artists, antique dealers, artisans, and innovators.

During the mid-century period, in particular, there was a push toward multidisciplinary design studios that encouraged the process of cross-pollination between disciplines. Designers such as Gio Ponti, Alvar Aalto, and Arne Jacobsen, among others, saw few boundaries between disciplines and actively applied themselves to architecture, interiors, furniture, lighting design, and much else. Such multitasking may have fallen out of favor during the Eighties and Nineties, but it has increasingly made a comeback over recent years, as seen in the work of multifaceted designers and ateliers such as Anna Karlin, Faye Toogood, and Apparatus.

The *Atlas of Interior Design* encompasses the work of many talents and original voices, yet particularly seeks to explore the work of creative thinkers from around the world. The breadth and diversity of global interior design is evidenced by the broad spectrum of design styles, aesthetic choices, and ways of living. Cultural contexts and vernacular traditions along with factors such as climate and topography have shaped the evolution of interior design in various parts of the globe, which all have their own traditions and specialities.

Australia and South Africa, for instance, are well known for their beach houses and waterside homes. The West Coast of the United States and parts of Central and South America are celebrated for perfecting inside-outside living, with outdoor rooms and fresh-air retreats. The thatched *palapas* of Mexico and the *haciendas* of Brazil, with their broad verandas, have informed the evolution of indoor-outdoor connectivity as much as the steel-framed houses, curtain walls, and banks of sliding glass seen in Californian Desert Modernist residences.

Canada and Scandinavia provide a positive emphasis on organic architecture and design, informed by a tradition of island escapes and mountain huts, along with "warm" Modernists such as Alvar Aalto, Jørn Utzon, and Børge Mogensen. Russian *dachas*, Swiss chalets, Portuguese beach huts, Italian *masserias*, Indian *havelis*, London townhouses, and Greek island retreats all provide their own unique themes and variations, as well as multiple points of inspiration for designers and homemakers alike. North Africa, Turkey, and the Middle East offer vivid exemplars in terms of the use of color and geometric pattern as well as the creation of secret courtyard gardens and rooftop terraces.

Increasingly, designers across India, Sri Lanka, Japan, and other parts of Asia have established themselves on the international stage, bringing a fresh sensibility focused on the value of warm materials, crafted finishes, and artisanal detailing combined with a pared-down approach to the layering of a room. The *Atlas of Interior Design* seeks to celebrate such diversity, region by region, country by country, while pinpointing key themes within a broad range of showcased residences.

Twenty-first-century Interiors

The criteria for the interiors within the *Atlas of Interior Design* are not simply restricted to geography or chronology. The selection and editing process has also been guided by the search for "poetic" rather than prosaic projects and by the hunt for houses that have a true sense of character, personality, and individuality. Many familiar names are included, of course, but there are also a number of inventive and pioneering designers whose work might not be so familiar.

There are a number of broad themes within the evolution of twentieth- and early-twenty-first-century global residential interiors. These include the gradual shift toward more informal and open-plan living in the home, as well as the growing importance of general connectedness to outside space of one kind or another, with gardens, verandas, and terraces becoming an integral part of a residence. Kitchen design has been revolutionized as the kitchen itself has played a more central role within our houses and apartments, often forming a key part of an open-plan living space. Bathroom design, similarly, has been transformed over the years with more attention and space given to spalike retreats, partly shaped by the examples of hotels and resorts. Dedicated spaces for work, entertainment, and recreation have become a staple of many contemporary homes. Sustainability has become a key priority for both architects and interior designers, with the need to conserve energy and resources now informing all parts of the design process when it comes to house and home, as in other aspects of daily life.

The wealth of exceptional twenty-first-century interior design projects suggests comparisons to the mid-century Modern period of the Fifties and Sixties, defined too by its spirit of experimentation. Certain parallels can be drawn between these two periods of time, including a cross-pollination between design disciplines and an enthusiasm for a more expressive approach to interiors, including the use of color, texture, pattern, and form. Beyond this, there is also an educated and well-informed acceptance of eclecticism, with a growing appreciation of the idea that old and new can coexist quite happily along with design from many different parts of the world.

The *Atlas of Interior Design* is intended, therefore, not only as a resource of information but as a source of inspiration. The marked sophistication of so much contemporary residential design adds a new layer of breadth and depth to the case studies and landmark homes of the mid- to late twentieth century. In a post-pandemic age, the ideal of a thoughtfully and beautifully conceived house, or apartment,

has fresh resonance. The hope is that this book can help inform the design of our forthcoming personal retreats, safe havens, and escape pods by encouraging us to express our own ideas and personalities within the spaces that we live in. With this in mind, we should circle back to Madeleine Castaing and her words of wisdom: "A secret: love your house," she said. "Love makes miracles."

North America

Eppich House

Arthur Erickson & Francisco Kripacz
West Vancouver (CA), 1979–1988

....

The Eppich House in West Vancouver is the culmination of architect Arthur Erickson's gravity defying experiments with stepped houses, which began in the early Sixties with the Graham House (1963). Erickson famously managed to design and build landmark homes on extraordinary sites that were rich in natural beauty but also deeply challenging, given their steep and rugged topography. In the case of this home for Hugo Eppich and his wife Brigitte, Erickson was encouraged by the fact that his client was the head of a construction firm specializing in steel fabrication. Erickson's tiered building was designed to demonstrate the "plasticity" of steel-framed buildings, with its sinuous and dynamic lines. Finally completed in 1988, the house was arranged over three stacked stories stepping down the slope toward a pond sitting within the landscaped grounds. The interiors were designed in conjunction with Erickson's long-term colleague and collaborator Francisco Kripacz (1942–2000). In the living room, the curvaceous walls of glass bricks to one side are complemented by the custom fireplace and a collection of custom furniture, designed by Kripacz, which picks up on the rounded forms of the architecture. The organic tones and textures of the timber ceilings are echoed by the caramel hues of the leather upholstery used for the supersized sofa and also the matching armchairs.

Drake House

Ferris Rafauli
Toronto (CA), 2011

The epically scaled house that singer-song-writer and entrepreneur Aubrey Drake Graham has created for himself in his home-town of Toronto is known as "The Embassy." It has formed a backdrop to some of Drake's own song videos, such as "Toosie Slide," and was clearly a labor of love, encompassing—among other spaces—an NBA-sized basket-ball court, an indoor swimming pool, and an awards room. Drake, who was born and raised in Toronto, turned to Canadian archi-tectural and interior designer Ferris Rafauli to create The Embassy. For the exteriors, Rafauli opted for a neoclassical style but for interiors the aesthetic is guided by a twenty-first-century take on an Art Deco mood with an emphasis not just on grand proportions but also high craftsmanship, fine materials, and custom designs throughout. One of the most theatrical spaces is the pivotal "great room." Here, the soaring double-height ceil-ings, bronze-framed mirrored paneling, and arresting sunburst chandelier—made with Swarovski crystal and inspired by an iconic Sixties piece at New York's Metropolitan Opera House—create a sense of true drama. Within such an open volume Drake's custom Bösendorfer grand piano, by Rafauli and Japanese artist Takashi Murakami, seems almost dwarfed by the supersize windows and curtains. Dynamic and luxurious, the great room and The Embassy in its entirety certainly create a statement.

Integral House

Shim-Sutcliffe
Toronto (CA), 2009

The respected Canadian mathematician James Stewart (1941–2014) was also a musician who played the violin in the Hamilton Philharmonic Orchestra. His two passions combined in Integral House in Rosedale, Toronto, the five-story house designed by Canadian architects Brigitte Shim and Howard Sutcliffe to sit on the edge of one of the many wooded ravines of the city. The house's design took inspiration from calculus, Stewart's specialist field—the curvaceous shape of the house references the integral symbol used in mathematics, while the design works around the sloping ravine, with only the uppermost two stories visible upon approaching the house and the others set further down the hillside. Inside is the home's most unusual space: a dramatic double-height performance theater positioned at midlevel, designed for musical recitals accommodating one hundred fifty guests. The curving glass walls here are punctuated with vertical oak fins, which form an integrated brise-soleil, that also contribute to acoustic performance. Yet the green backdrop of the surrounding landscape still shines through, creating the feeling of a vast and elegant treehouse floating over the ravine below.

Yabu Pushelberg House

Yabu Pushelberg
Toronto (CA), 2011

Designers George Yabu and Glenn Pushelberg (see pp. 113 and 356) have developed an international portfolio, embracing residential, hotel, and hospitality projects around the world, including North America, Europe, and Asia. They first met at design school in Toronto where they founded their design studio, which was later joined by a second office in New York. Yet, in many respects, Toronto remains "home" and their house in the city is a personal haven for both partners. The designers bought a Toronto cottage dating from the Forties, with a modest frontage that belies the true scope and scale of the house. Yabu and Pushelberg spent eighteen months renovating and rebuilding the cottage, creating an engaging combination of old and new. The main living spaces overlook a terrace and wooded ravine to the rear of the property. Here, Yabu and Pushelberg have created a welcoming, open-plan living space with a dining area at one end, a study at the other and in between a seating zone—defined by twin armchairs by Jean-Michel Frank—arranged around a fireplace. The choice of furniture mixes custom designs with mid-century classics, including oversized glass vases in shades of blue and green and an early painting by Dutch artist Eelco Brand mounted over the dining table.

Mjölk Country House

John & Juli Daoust Baker &
Studio Junction
Stirling (CA), 2019

....

The Toronto design store and gallery, Mjölk, is known for its collections of furniture, lighting, and homeware, which draw upon the work of Scandinavian and Japanese designers, artisans, and artists in particular. Mjölk was founded in 2009, by husband-and-wife curators and tastemakers John and Juli Daoust Baker, who have applied a similar design philosophy to their homes in Toronto and the rural enclave of Stirling. Here, they have converted this derelict nineteenth-century farmhouse into a family escape, with the help of architectural designers Christine Ho Ping Kong and Peter Tan of Studio Junction. Parts of the farmhouse have an elemental rustic quality, as seen in the kitchen, with its bare stone walls and crafted kitchen units and furniture. The sitting room, or parlor, has a rather more refined feel, with limewashed walls and pale lye-treated wooden floors. There is certainly more of a Scandinavian aesthetic here, as seen in the tiled Gustavian stove, which forms a characterful centerpiece for the seating, including a Danish sofa coated in a burnt-orange velvet. Other standout pieces include a pair of high-backed Hans J. Wegner Peacock chairs, which are one of Juli Daoust Baker's favorite mid-century Modern designs.

Prairie House

Madeline Stuart & Lake|Flato Architects
Near Bozeman, Montana (US), 2011

....

The porch can play an important part in a home. Halfway between inside and out, the porch has made a very successful transition from traditional period homes to twenty-first-century living, as seen in this escapist house in southern Montana. With architecture by David Lake, of Lake|Flato Architects, and interiors by the Los Angeles–based designer Madeline Stuart the house features two porches at either end, facing east and west. The house was designed as a thoughtful response to its rural setting: the building looks across a pond to the prairies beyond. The interiors adopt a modern rustic character, with an emphasis throughout on natural finishes, textures, and tones, while mid-century pieces by Sergio Rodrigues and others blend with custom furniture designed by Madeline Stuart. Here, for the "sunrise porch," Stuart designed custom seating with greens and browns for the upholstery, as well as a low table with a rugged limestone top. Beyond the sliding wall of glass that lightly separates inside and outside, the dining area features a custom table in walnut along with a collection of vintage Hans J. Wegner chairs with leather seats and backs.

Furlotti House

Osmose Design
Portland, Oregon (US), 2019

Some of the most engaging spaces designed by Andee Hess and her Portland studio, Osmose Design, founded in 2006, have a playful retro quality. They speak in particular of the Sixties and Seventies, with their love of bold colors, dynamic lines, and disco beats. This Portland house for comedian Allie Furlotti, her artist husband Adam Kostiv, and their daughter certainly embraces the fantastical and sometimes the surreal. The five-bedroom house dates back to the Sixties with an unremarkable facade; inside, Hess was positively encouraged to push the boundaries. Within the lounge, sinuous minty-hued seating has been arranged around a semicircular fireplace, complete with a giant clamshell firewood store. Moving through to the den, Hess designed a custom DJ-and-music console, while a triptych of triffid-like floor lamps hovers over the giant mustard-yellow B&B Italia sofa. The family's two poodles, meanwhile, particularly enjoy the sink-in lamb's wool seating on the lounge chair by the Spanish collective Lievore Altherr Molina—also sourced by Hess.

Northern California Estate

Studio Shamshiri, Commune &
Mark Hampton
Northern California, California
(US), 2019

There are many layers to the design of this extraordinary palazzo in Northern California. The genesis of the house was the owner's trip to Italy back in the Nineties and the decision to recreate some of the characterful grandeur of the villas and farmhouses seen along the way. Architect Ned Forrest and designer Rory McCarthy collaborated on the initial design, while the highly respected interior designer Mark Hampton (1940–1998) concentrated on the interiors. In 2010 design studio Commune (see pp. 24 and 35) was invited to refresh certain parts of the house, while respecting Hampton's legacy. Pamela and Ramin Shamshiri, who moved on from Commune in 2016 to set up their own atelier, completed the finishing touches. One of the most engaging rooms to come out of this collaborative approach is the "great room." With its soaring ceilings painted a sky blue and walls graced with Renaissance-era portraits, this space is generous enough for both a seating area to one side and a substantial dining area to the other, where a pair of Mexican candelabra float over the table like epic cathedral thuribles. Arranged around the fireplace, an Alma Allen cocktail table mixes with a blue velvet BDDW sofa and a wingback chair flanked by a Les Lalanne sheep. Furniture, textiles, and art here fuse old and new, with each layer adding to the richness and depth of the interiors.

Wild Bird

Nathaniel Owings & Mark Mills
Big Sur, California (US), 1958

....

Architect Nathaniel Owings (1903–1984) was one of the founding partners of Skidmore, Owings & Merrill (SOM), which became one of the most successful postwar practices in the United States. Given his strained relationship with partner Louis Skidmore, Owings ran his own SOM office initially in Chicago and then in San Francisco. Soon after, he and his second wife, Margaret, found a mesmerizing site on the cliffs at Big Sur, where Owings decided to build a new home. Enlisting the help of local architect Mark Mills (1921–2007), the two designers created an organic and contextual home perched on a promontory overlooking the sea. At the heart of the house, made of concrete, redwood, and stone, was a spacious, A-framed living room. This open room was blessed with the volume of a church or barn and featured a long skylight at the apex of the roof and a glazed gable end providing a key vista of the coastline. Owings and Mills positioned a stone fireplace with a steel hood and surrounding seating to one side, and a dining table to the center. Warm and rustic, Wild Bird felt a world away from the crisp, corporate towers for which SOM became best known.

Butterfly House

Frank Wynkoop & Jamie Bush
Carmel, California (US), 1951/2018

The Butterfly House makes the most of a powerful setting. Sitting on the rocks overlooking Carmel Bay, it pushes outward to meet the ocean, as its sculptural butterfly roofline rises gently upward to create a distinctive silhouette. The house was built to serve as the family home of architect Frank Wynkoop (1902–1978), who was best known for his work designing schools and educational buildings. Wynkoop designed his dream house around a central courtyard, sheltered from the sea breeze, complete with a swimming pool and terrace. Perhaps because of the significant cost of building the house, Wynkoop sold the house after just five years. In the late 2010s, the home was sensitively restored and updated by the designer Jamie Bush, whose work respected the mid-century provenance of the house, while adding contemporary touches. One of the most glorious spaces is the living room, sitting at the prow of the house. Here, natural textures prevail within the choice of furniture—including a hanging rattan chair by Blackman Cruz and a wood cocktail table by Pedro Petry—complementing the flagstone floors and timber ceilings. A few steps down, an integrated bench faces the ocean panorama framed by wraparound windows.

Saladino Villa

John Saladino
Montecito, California (US), 2005

There is a romantic and timeless quality to John Saladino's interiors. His work fuses architecture and interiors, as well as the classical and the modern. The resulting spaces are infused with original character. One of the most clear examples of his work is his own villa in Montecito, California. The Italianate sandstone villa, arranged around a central courtyard, was originally designed and built in the Thirties by architect Wallace Frost (1892–1962) to serve as his own home. But by the time John Saladino acquired the house and garden, both were suffering from years of neglect and required a major restoration and rebuilding program that lasted four years—recorded in Saladino's 2009 book, *Villa*. Structurally, Saladino sought to preserve the original layout in many respects but combined a number of smaller spaces to create more generously sized rooms—as seen in the kitchen/breakfast room, where stone and timber contrast with stainless-steel kitchen units. With the design of the sitting room, Saladino sought to balance openness and intimacy, creating a seating area around the fireplace with self-designed sofas facing one another, complemented by select pieces of antique furniture and—on the walls—work by abstract artist Cy Twombly.

Ojai House

Commune
Ojai, California (US), 2013

Known locally as "Shangri-La," the small city of Ojai has an escapist character and a charm all of its own. One of its founding fathers was Ohio glass magnate Edward Libbey (1854–1925), who in around 1908 built a house for himself on the edge of the city, inspired by the look and feel of a Swedish hunting lodge. Just over a century later, the house caught the attention of Ramin Shamshiri, formerly of Los Angeles design collective Commune, and his wife, film-studio executive Donna Langley. Working with his sister, designer Pamela Shamshiri, Ramin decided to take the interiors back to their original hunting-lodge roots, looking to early Californian retreats, Scandinavian summer cabins, and Japanese mountain lodges. A key example is the living room, where the stone fireplace combines with warm timber ceilings, floors, and paneling. The room's chandelier is a custom piece, as is the striped sofa and the spindle-back piece opposite in the style of George Nakashima, while a custom goatskin rug anchors the seating and softens the space. In 2016, Ramin and Pamela Shamshiri left Commune in the hands of its other two principals and went on to establish Studio Shamshiri (see p. 21).

Steinman House

Craig Ellwood & Michael Boyd
Malibu, California (US), 1956/2017

Architectural designer Craig Ellwood (1922–1992) was an influential West Coast pioneer of elegant mid-century Modern pavilions. Born Jon Nelson Burke, the charismatic Ellwood reinvented himself, eventually becoming the "Cary Grant of architecture." Ellwood's work captured the attention of *Arts & Architecture* editor, John Entenza, who enlisted a number of Ellwood projects for his Case Study program. One of these, Case Study House #16 in Bel Air (1953), caught the interest of a local high-school principal Howard Steinman who asked Ellwood to design him a new family house in Malibu. Ellwood created a single-story home in steel and glass, with timber and brick elements softening the interiors. In 2017, designer Michael Boyd was commissioned by the new owners to undertake a sensitive restoration and advise on furnishings. The main living area features a monolithic double-sided fireplace, forming a partial partition between the living room and the kitchen beyond, which retains its original mahogany-veneered cabinetry. In the living room, twin Eames chairs face an Alanda coffee table by Paolo Piva for B&B Italia, while a Laverne leather-and-chrome sofa is watched over by a John McLaughlin painting. The arrangement is anchored by a Christopher Farr rug designed by Boyd himself.

Dawnridge

Tony Duquette
Beverly Hills, Los Angeles, California
(US), 1949

Theatrical, expressive, and flamboyant, the
rooms and spaces created by designer Tony
Duquette (1914–1999) were truly dreamlike. Although he worked for many celebrity clients, the master maximalist was not
an elitist, often fabricating designs in his
workshops using architectural salvage and
junk-shop treasures. Duquette's most fantastical project was Dawnridge, the Beverly
Hills house and garden he built during the
late Forties for himself and his wife Elizabeth
(known as "Beegle") with the assistance of
architect Caspar J. Ehmcke (1908–1995). The
house featured playful interiors packed with
decorative flourishes, including murals by
Elizabeth. One of the most exuberant spaces
is the living room with illusory mirrored
panels. Shades of green and mauve form
the base notes on the walls, while the ceiling
features ornate detailing and a large chandelier made with Venetian glass lilies. Hutton
Wilkinson, Duquette's former business
partner and the current owner of Dawnridge,
has curated the present choice of furniture
and art, including custom screens made with
car hubcaps and a one-off secretaire originally produced for Elsie de Wolfe. Duquette's
work could be compared with that of the
great Italian illusionist and contemporary,
Renzo Mongiardino (see pp. 281 and 303).

Fernandez House

Waldo Fernandez
Beverly Hills, Los Angeles, California
(US), 2005

Interior designer Waldo Fernandez has
always had a strong connection with
Hollywood. His first career was as a
Hollywood set designer, working alongside
the influential Walter M. Scott on films such
as *Planet of the Apes* (1968), and with clients
such as the film director John Schlesinger.
Fernandez's own Sixties hillside home in
Beverly Hills combines a touch of theatrical glamour with an intelligent curatorial
approach to contemporary art, which is one
of the designer's great passions. The spacious living room benefits from pool views,
while it draws in sunlight from the floor-to-
ceiling windows, lifting the space. The key
focal point is the fireplace and its marble
surround, while the seating arrangement—
including a pair of vintage Jacques Adnet
chairs—is anchored by the rug positioned
on the wooden floors. White walls allow
the choice art and sculpture to stand out,
which includes pieces by Lucio Fontana
and Tauba Auerbach as well as a sculpture
by Aaron Curry. This soothing and serene
room is also spacious enough for a small
herd of sheep by Les Lalanne and a grand
piano, which is positioned by the open
staircase that leads up to the primary suite.

English House

Harwell Hamilton Harris & Kay Kollar
Beverly Hills, Los Angeles, California
(US), 1950/2007

Art and color have always played an important part in the personality of the English House in Beverly Hills. The house was designed by architect Harwell Hamilton Harris (1903–1990), who worked with Richard Neutra before establishing his own practice during the Thirties. His client was a landscape artist, Harold M. English; one of the most engaging spaces is English's former painting studio, with its high ceilings and glass wall looking out over the canyons beyond. In 2007 interior designer Kay Kollar was commissioned by the building's new owner, a film-industry executive, to revive the interiors. Color formed a key element throughout, with Kollar exploring a palette of greens, in particular, alongside browns, reds, lavender, and gold tones to reflect the landscape outside. In the living room, the soft-khaki walls sit well with a large abstract painting by artist Jules Olitski—part of the owner's collection of modern art. At the same time bolder highlights, such as the red upholstery for the sofa, serve as a foil and draw the eye. Throughout, the furniture is a mix of vintage pieces by the likes of Vladimir Kagan, T. H. Robsjohn-Gibbings, Paul Frankl, and Gio Ponti, as well as comfortable pieces Kollar created in collaboration with furniture designer and craftsman David Albert.

Haenisch House

Trip Haenisch
**Beverly Hills, Los Angeles, California
(US), 2011**

Trip Haenisch's carefully curated approach to interiors has won him many West Coast celebrity clients, but is even more elegantly expressed in his own hilltop home in Beverly Hills. Haenisch, who worked with both Waldo Fernandez (see p. 25) and Martyn Lawrence Bullard (see p. 48) before establishing his own design studio, had long admired a Fifties Beverly Hills house, so jumped at the opportunity to buy when it came on the market. The bones of the house were good, but required a major update that included fresh oak floors, new bathrooms, and changes to the layout of the kitchen that helped to link it to the living spaces alongside. Walls and ceilings were painted white creating a calm backdrop, allowing Haenisch's choice of sculptural and often colorful pieces to sing out. A key example is the bedroom, used by Haenisch's son, in which the designer introduced an Eighties Masanori Umeda–designed Tawayara seating unit in the shape of a boxing ring to chiefly serve as a bed. With its vivid Memphis-style colors and stripes, the piece has the enigmatic quality of an art installation; similarly, the Archie Scott Gobber work displayed on the cabinet beyond inhabits the borderland between art and design.

Brody Residence

A. Quincy Jones & William Haines
Los Angeles, California (US), c. 1954

··

Mr. and Mrs. Sidney F. Brody were formidable patrons of the arts. Frances (1916–2009) was a key character in the founding of the UCLA Art Council and her real estate developer husband Sidney (1916–1983) was a pioneering figure in the establishment of the Los Angeles County Museum of Art. They were great collectors of works by European Modern artists—in particular, Pablo Picasso, Georges Braque, Alberto Giacometti, and Henri Matisse. The couple asked architect A. Quincy Jones (1913–1979) and interior designer William Haines (1900–1973) to design their home in Holmby Hills. Together, the designers represented something of a dream team with many Hollywood clients between them (see p. 49). For a pivotal courtyard—visible through two-story sliding glass walls—the Brodys commissioned Matisse to create *La Gerbe* (1953), a ceramic-tile mural. The inside living space of the home encompassed a range of intricate geometries created by different textures. Haines's decor was understated yet refined, employing creams and soft colors that acted as a canvas for the Brody's immaculately curated collection. Carefully deployed splashes of color were reserved for the Haines-designed furniture; pieces such as the Valentine sofa and Brentwood chair are still in production today.

Garcia House

John Lautner, Marmol Radziner &
Darren Brown
Los Angeles, California (US), 1962/2002

··

Architect John Lautner (1911–1994) combined innovative and experimental sculptural forms with interiors full of drama and delight. Much in demand on the West Coast during the Sixties, he attracted creative clients such as Russell Garcia, a Hollywood film composer and conductor who worked with many of the big studios. Garcia and his wife, Gina, secured a seductive site in the Hollywood Hills where Lautner designed a house on stilts with a soaring curvaceous, vaulted roof. One of the house's most engaging parts was the large double-height living area, featuring front-to-back glazed windows punctuated by stained glass, adding bursts of color. In 2002, entertainment business manager John McIlwee and film and theater producer Bill Damaschke became the new owners of the house—alongside their Gerald & Betty Ford House in Rancho Mirage (see p. 51)—and asked architects Marmol Radziner and interior designer Darren Brown to work on a sensitive restoration of the home. The main living area was gently warmed and softened with fresh integrated seating, shelving, and storage—like the stained-walnut cabinetry—while furnishings include an Arco lamp by Achille and Pier Giacomo Castiglioni and a coffee table by Charles Hollis Jones.

Romanek House

Brigette Romanek
Los Angeles, California (US), 2014

Interior designer Brigette Romanek and her film director husband, Mark, own a Laurel Canyon home with quite a pedigree. The house was originally built in the Twenties in a grand Mediterranean style but was rebuilt in the Fifties after a major fire. This elegant building was a former recording studio, hosting the Rolling Stones and the Beatles, with the Romaneks eventually acquiring the house from music producer Rick Rubin. One of the priorities for Romanek, who established Romanek Design Studio in 2018, was to brighten the interiors and create a family-friendly setting for her and her husband and their two children. She was careful to preserve original architectural features, and she also left the layout largely unchanged. Key spaces now include the wood-paneled den, a spacious library, and a leafy solarium that doubles as a breakfast room. The sitting room, in particular, is now a light and generously proportioned space with arched feature windows and doorways. Romanek created two distinct seating zones, framed by furry cream rugs on the dark-wood floors. One of these areas features a pair of sculptural, beige velvet Marco Zanuso chairs and a fluid Hans J. Wegner chaise longue. A coffee table laden with a collection of blue-and-white ceramics provides a whimsical stroke.

Bloom House

Greg Lynn & Jacklin Hah Bloom
Los Angeles, California (US), 2009

The dynamism seen in the work of architect and designer Greg Lynn echoes the avant-garde, shape-shifting architecture of the Sixties, which pushed back against the dominance of rectangular regularity. The design of the Bloom House in Los Angeles represents an unusual collaboration between architect and client. Film and television director Jason Bloom happens to be married to designer Jacklin Hah Bloom, who works in Lynn's office and served as project manager and a designer for the house. The Bloom's family home became a kind of "workshop," offering a degree of freedom to explore the ideal of fluid, free-flowing, and ergonomic living space. The two most striking elements within the family's living space are the semispherical custom fireplace that emerges from one wall and the fiberglass light installation that runs along the ceiling from the dining area to the rear, past the seating zone and then out of the window toward the terrace. The color palette here is predominantly one of whites and grays with periodic bursts of lipstick red, as seen on the upholstery of the custom banquette. Lynn describes the aesthetic as "integrated minimalism," yet the interiors could also be characterized as playful and expressive.

Kappe Residence

Ray Kappe
Los Angeles, California (US), 1967

For the design of his own family home in the Pacific Palisades, architect Ray Kappe (1927–2019) combined structural ingenuity with highly characterful interiors. Many regarded this steeply sloping site in Rustic Canyon as impossible to build on owing to an underground spring. But while others only saw problems, Kappe saw opportunities, choosing to work with the topography rather than fight against it. Internally, the living spaces formed a kind of ziggurat with repeated connections between the different levels and constant openings to the surrounding hill, which was treated as one expansive garden. Given the complexity of the various spatial and volumetric shifts, much of the custom furniture was integrated: steps morphed into benches and storage units doubled as partitions or screens. In contrast to the organic character of the majority of the materials—Kappe used redwood for most of the joinery and left the Douglas-fir timber frame exposed— the seating area in the living room was defined by sage-green carpeting with a playful, vivid shade of blue used for the custom armchairs and ottomans.

Eames House

Charles & Ray Eames
Los Angeles, California (US), 1949

With their shared commitment to innovation, experimentation, and communication, Charles and Ray Eames (1907–1978, 1912– 1988) played a pivotal part in shaping mid-century Modern design, working across a range of creative mediums, including architecture, furniture, graphic design, product design, and filmmaking. Many of these passions fused and combined at their own home and studio in Pacific Palisades, Los Angeles. Sitting on a hilltop meadow, the Eames' home formed part of *Arts & Architecture* magazine's Case Study program. The Eameses worked together on the interiors creating a two-story section that lead through to a double-height living room at the far end of the building. This elegant space fused the industrial and the organic, with its exposed steelwork and metal roof contrasting with a birch-paneled high rear wall. An Eames shelving system along one side formed a library wall—dressed with books and an array of keepsakes and artifacts—while rugs floating on the white-tiled floor helped define seating areas. The sofa, chairs, and tables— including the 670 Eames lounge chair and 671 ottoman—were all by Charles and Ray Eames, forming a warm, cohesive ensemble of iconic postwar designs.

Moby House

Moby
Los Angeles, California (US), 2014

....

Following the global success of albums such as *Play* and *18*, the musician Moby indulged his growing passion for real estate. While he was living on the East Coast, he owned a five-story apartment in Manhattan and a party compound upstate. Later Moby bought a West Coast twelve-bedroom mock castle known as the Wolf's Lair, complete with a gatehouse designed by John Lautner (see pp. 29, 40 and 44). Realizing that it was not so much the grandness of such residences that mattered to him but their sense of character, he was drawn instead to a relatively modest house in leafy Los Feliz dating back to the Twenties. One of the most restful living spaces in the house is the well-proportioned living room, with its wooden floors and feature fireplace. Moby opted for a calm, minimal approach to the interiors, painting the walls and ceilings white, while placing a few carefully curated pieces of mid-century furniture around the fireplace. There's space enough at the other end of the room for a Baldwin grand piano: "It's the happiest I have ever been living anywhere," Moby says. "I have realized that to be happy I don't need that much around me."

Ajioka House

Buff & Hensman & Commune
Los Angeles, California (US), 1960/2010

....

Conrad Buff (1926–1989) and Donald Hensman (1924–2002) met at the University of Southern California's School of Architecture, later forming a partnership that produced some of the most original mid-century Modern houses on the West Coast for clients such as graphic designer Saul Bass and actor Steve McQueen. The Ajioka House, a two-story building hidden away among the trees, is situated in the Hollywood Hills in Nichols Canyon, near Runyon Canyon Park. Over the years it has belonged to a number of Hollywood grandees, including producer Jerry Bruckheimer. In 2010 it was the focus of a major renovation undertaken by design studio Commune (see pp. 21 and 24), who returned the residence to its roots. One of the most dramatic spaces is the double-height living room, with its strong combination of horizontals and verticals, as seen in the exposed cross beams and the soaring fire surround coated in mirrored glass. Commune introduced recycled timber paneling and a number of custom elements, such as the fitted sofa, while other textural pieces include the patchwork cowhide rug with its sea of blues and greens, echoed by the trees outside the windows.

Henson House

Mutuus Studio
Los Angeles, California (US), 2018

When film director and puppeteer Brian Henson and his wife, actress Mia Sara, decided to build a new home in the Hollywood Hills, their priorities included maximizing the views across the city and creating a sustainable home. They turned to architect Kristen Becker, who worked for many years with the West Coast practice Olson Kundig before founding her own firm, Mutuus Studio. Becker pushed the new, two-story home into the hillside with principal spaces facing the open vista, including a choice of outdoor rooms. Another key element of the project was the creation of an open and sociable "great room" for Henson, Sara, and their children. This large living space features reclaimed oak floors, high ceilings, and large banks of glass, including a pivoting window that connects to the terrace. There's room for a kitchen toward the rear, a dining area toward the center—complete with a custom chandelier that hangs above the table—and a choice of seating areas. For the interiors, the family drew on the expertise of Sara's father, furniture dealer Jerry Sarapochiello, who helped curate a choice of mid-century pieces by Finn Juhl, Bruno Mathsson (see p. 181), Edward Wormley, Charlotte Perriand, and others, introducing warm organic colors, natural textures, and sculptural forms.

Strick House

Oscar Niemeyer & Michael Boyd
Los Angeles, California (US), 1964

The Strick House in Santa Monica is Brazilian master architect Oscar Niemeyer's (1907–2012) only completed residential project in North America. The house was commissioned by the film director Joseph Strick, who had visited Niemeyer's own home, Casa das Canoas (see p. 164), during a trip to South America. Visa restrictions meant that Niemeyer was unable to ever visit the site, but the pair pushed ahead with a long-distance design process. Two initial designs were ruled out, with the third and successful scheme adopting a more linear approach than seen at Canoas. A large, open-plan living space sits within a glass-sided pavilion that forms the dominant element of a T-shaped floor plan, while bedrooms were placed in the cross-bar. Many years later, the house was bought by designer and collector Michael Boyd (see p. 25), who has a long-standing passion for design from the mid-century period. Boyd embarked on a sensitive restoration of the house and its garden, which takes inspiration from the work of celebrated Brazilian landscape designer Roberto Burle Marx. In the main pavilion, Boyd introduced palmwood floors, as seen in the elevated platform at one end, holding the dining area and kitchen, and the principal seating area a few steps down. Boyd's collection of furniture here includes work by Charlotte Perriand, George Nelson, Jean Prouvé, and Niemeyer himself.

Sheats-Goldstein House

John Lautner
Los Angeles, California (US), 1963/1989

Over the course of more than three decades, the Sheats-Goldstein House in Beverly Crest became one of the most total expressions of John Lautner's (1911–1994, see pp. 29 and 44) original approach to architecture and interiors. The house was originally commissioned in the early Sixties by academic Paul Sheats and his artist wife Helen, for themselves and their children. The house's architecture explored the geometry of intersecting triangles, weaving the concrete building into the topography of the hillside. After just a few years the Sheats family moved on and by the time entrepreneur James F. Goldstein acquired the property in the early Seventies it was in poor condition. Goldstein reached out to Lautner and asked him "to take it to its ultimate potential." Goldstein encouraged Lautner to work again on every element of the house, including many pieces of integrated and custom furniture that echo the abstract geometrical forms explored within the architecture. The spacious living room is the ultimate example. Under Lautner's sculptural coffered ceiling he designed fitted sofas and benches, storage units and tables, taking the interiors to a fresh level of luxurious sophistication. Goldstein has promised to eventually leave the house to the Los Angeles County Museum of Art.

Stahl House

Pierre Koenig
Los Angeles, California (US), 1960

Architect Pierre Koenig (1925–2004) described the Stahl House as an "eagle's nest" positioned on a cliff edge in the Hollywood Hills looking down onto Sunset Boulevard and the city spread out below. Koenig developed an L-shaped plan for the steel-framed pavilion, meaning much of the house was open and transparent, spilling out onto a pool terrace facing the vista, protected from the sun by an overhanging roof canopy. Most dramatic of all was the portion of the house that pushed outward toward the cliff edge. This was a fluid, open space with only the double-sided central fireplace offering the lightest sense of separation between the integrated kitchen and dining area, at one end, and the lounge floating over the cityscape, at the other. Koenig's layout took open-plan living to fresh heights, while offering a defining image of mid-century style, captured so eloquently in Julius Shulman's (1910–2009) famous images of the house. Furniture in optimistic bright oranges and yellows was brought in for the shoot by designers Hendrik van Keppel and Taylor Green. In 1959, the Stahls' home was included into *Arts & Architecture* magazine's Case Study program of exemplary modern houses, becoming—arguably—the most famous and influential building within the collection.

Tarlow House

Rose Tarlow
Los Angeles, California (US), 1989

Rose Tarlow describes herself as a "collector" as much as a designer. Her first career was an antiques dealer, but she later began designing her own furniture collections. From there, Tarlow branched out into interiors. "My success in building houses comes from building furniture," she says. "You really learn to understand balance and proportion." One of Tarlow's most evocative projects is her own home in Bel Air, Los Angeles. The house feels as though it has been here for centuries, yet is actually a new building designed by Tarlow herself, taking inspiration from the work of architect Wallace Neff. Salvaged fireplaces, beams, paneling, doors, and other elements have been woven together. At the heart of the house sits a spacious living room with a high wood-beamed ceiling and a series of French doors leading out to the garden. Vines and creepers have made a home on the walls, adding to the timeless quality of the space. Seventeenth-century French stone fireplaces at each end of the room anchor a choice of seating areas comprised of comfortable, contemporary sofas and chairs. Integrated bookshelves also give the room the feel of a welcoming library, while Tarlow's collection of antique furniture mixes with twentieth-century artworks by Jean Cocteau, Richard Serra, and others.

Little Holmby

Reath Design & McKuin Design
Los Angeles, California (US), 2018

"We believe that good design ages well and avoids short-lived trends in favor of timeless decor," says designer Frances Merrill in her studio's mission statement. There is a timeless elegance to many of the roomscapes designed by Merrill over recent years, and also a romantic quality that comes from a love of color, texture, and a choice of plush materials. There is a depth to Reath's spaces, which never feel like show homes, given their multiple layers of interest and detail throughout. This is very much the case with this house in Los Angeles's Little Holmby neighborhood, an elegant Spanish Revival residence, which was acquired by architect Sherry McKuin and her family. The house has an intrinsic sense of warmth, drawn in part from its rounded forms—like the arched doorframes and curved stair railing with wrought-iron detailing. The living room features a new marble fire surround between the French doors. The fireplace is flanked by bronze sconces and twin sofas, designed by Merrill and upholstered in an earthy linen tone. McKuin curated the choice of modern art, including works by artist Barbara Probst. The space also serves as a music room, with a grand piano at one end and a set of drums at the other, within a home where every ingredient adds to the rich and original mix.

Wearstler Beach House

Kelly Wearstler
Los Angeles, California (US), 2006

Designer Kelly Wearstler is one of the best-known twenty-first-century American maximalists. The distinctive aesthetic of her residential and hotel interiors has been summed up as "Hollywood glamour" while the "mixology" seen in her work draws on influences from cinema, architecture, and graphic design while blending contemporary elements with mid-century and vintage pieces. Such an approach can be seen at the Malibu beach house that Wearstler shares with her husband Brad Korzen and their children. The designer, who grew up by the ocean, was drawn to the captivating beachside location but the original design of the Eighties house itself was undistinguished and required reinvention. The designer stripped the entire building back to its bones, while forging a much more direct sense of connection with the ocean—to the point that Wearstler now compares the beach house to the experience of living on a boat. The real star is the spacious living room, with materials and furniture adopting a suitably sandy and natural palette. There's space for a dining area at one end and a seating zone, arranged around the feature marble fireplace, at the other. A matching sofa and armchairs by Carlo Scarpa are among the standout pieces and convey Wearstler's philosophy that "everything is natural, textural, and raw."

Elrod House

John Lautner & Arthur Elrod
Palm Springs, California (US), 1968

Arthur Elrod (1924–1974) was a successful interior designer based in Palm Springs, where he secured a wave of commissions from the Fifties onward as the desert resort's status began to grow. Elrod collaborated with a number of mid-century Modern architects such as William F. Cody and John Lautner (1911–1994, see pp. 29 and 40), the latter of whom he asked to design his own landmark home high up on Smoke Tree Mountain. Lautner placed the house at the mountain's edge overlooking the valley below. Rocks and boulders entered into the interiors themselves, as seen in the extraordinary circular living room. Here, Lautner created a kind of theater in the round, sheltered by a vast circular, propeller-like, concrete canopy roof overhead, while a geometrically circular–patterned beige rug lay on the herringbone black slate floor. The kitchen was tucked away to the rear, with curved seating toward the side and center. A few steps down led to the swimming pool and terrace, revealed by a retracting curved wall of glass, which dissolved the boundary between inside and outside space. This highly theatrical room earned a starring role in the 1971 film *Diamonds Are Forever*, featuring in the memorable scene where James Bond duels with the dynamic Bambi and Thumper.

Frey House II

Albert Frey
Palm Springs, California (US), 1964

The Swiss-born émigré architect Albert Frey (1903–1998), who once worked in Le Corbusier's Parisian atelier, settled in Palm Springs during the Thirties, becoming one of the pioneers of postwar "desert Modernism." The architect's residence, Frey House II, was built in a remarkable mountainside setting, looking over the sprawling city in the valley below. This escapist retreat was tucked among the rocks, devoid of neighbors. The house consisted of a single-story pavilion that held all of the essential elements of the home, including the bedroom, in one fluid, open-plan space; only the bathroom and utility room could be described as separate spaces. Through a sliding glass wall, the living space spilled out onto the adjoining pool terrace. Most dramatic of all was the way that a mountain rock intruded into the house, sharing the space with his custom-designed and integrated furniture made from locally sourced wood, including sofas, cupboards, and a dining table. Fabrics and furnishings were chosen in colors that echoed the natural tones of the desert surroundings, its native flowers, or the vast expanse of blue sky that lay beyond the space's glass curtain walls, allowing Frey to continue exploring fresh ways of living in extreme settings.

Palevsky House

Craig Ellwood
Palm Springs, California (US), 1970

As Craig Ellwood's reputation soared during the Sixties, so too did the scale and sophistication of his projects. Among his many clients was the high-tech computer company Scientific Data Systems founded by Max Palevsky (1924–2010), who requested a newly designed production plant. The two men became good friends and so naturally Palevsky asked Ellwood to design him a new weekend house on the edge of Palm Springs. Ellwood created a walled compound comprising a guesthouse, primary pavilion, and a pool terrace with a glass balcony that faced the open vista of the desert. The primary pavilion itself was modestly scaled, but the perceived spatial generosity and openness was enhanced by the transparency of floor-to-ceiling banks of glass. In the living area, the interiors were lifted by Palevsky's extraordinary collection of modern art. Wall-mounted pieces by Donald Judd flanked the minimal, geometric fireplace and surrounding the seating zone, while an eye-catching piece by Roy Lichtenstein sat alongside the dining table. Against the pale, sandy-gray tones of the brick walls and floors, royal-blue-hued dining chairs complemented the primary color scheme, accompanied by twin Marcel Breuer Wassily armchairs.

Ridge Mountain House

Steven Ehrlich
Palm Springs, California (US), 2019

Situated on the raw and rugged edges of
Palm Springs, where the city gives way to
the open desert, Ridge Mountain House
is a considered response to a remarkable
setting. The two-story, three-bedroom
house sits among the mountains and gullies,
accompanied by terraces, a pool, and a
standalone casita, which serves as both
a pool house and guest lodge. For the interiors, architect Steven Ehrlich—founding
partner of EYRC Architects—created a vivid
sense of connection with the surroundings.
A "great room" on the ground floor, with a
vast wall of floor-to-ceiling glass, not only
offers a wide view of the mountainous landscape, but slides away allowing the living
area to flow freely out to the pool terrace.
The room's prevailing tones and textures,
seen in the floors, walls, and ceilings, are
neutral, yet the choice of furniture (selected
by Ehrlich's clients) adds gentle notes of
color, as seen in the dark-purple sofa framed
by a geometric rug covering the polished
concrete floor, or the quartet of tan Gerrit
Rietveld Utrecht armchairs seen in the secondary seating area. The overall impression
is one of space, volume, and openness, with
the epic landscape a constant presence.

Kaufmann Desert House

Richard Neutra & Marmol Radziner
Palm Springs, California (US), 1947
....

The Kaufmann Desert House was designed
and built, primarily, for the month of January.
This was when the Pittsburgh-based depart-
ment-store magnate Edgar J. Kaufmann
(1885–1955) and his family wanted to enjoy
their winter retreat, when the days in Palm
Springs are warm, even if the evenings have
a chill to them. Kaufmann had commissioned
Frank Lloyd Wright (1935–1939) to design
Fallingwater in rural Pennsylvania just a few
years earlier, but for the Palm Springs escape,
he wanted something completely different
and commissioned the Viennese architect
Richard Neutra (1892–1970), who had worked
briefly with Wright before founding his own
practice in Los Angeles. Neutra's design
balanced mass and transparency, with banks
of glass spilling out to the pool terrace and
gardens. A key element within the design as
a whole was the provision of outdoor rooms
and fresh-air retreats, including the "glori-
ette" that sat on the upper level of the building. Local planning restrictions ruled out a
dedicated second story, but Neutra worked
around this with a semienclosed roof terrace,
offering views across the desert to the
mountains. Complete with a fireplace, fitted
seating, and a partial brise-soleil, this escapist open-sided living room floated above
the landscape.

Villa Grigio

James H. McNaughton & Martyn
Lawrence Bullard
Palm Springs, California (US), 1963/2016
....

Television set designer–turned-architect
James H. McNaughton (1912–1979) designed
a sequence of houses in and around Palm
Springs after settling there in the late
Fifties. One of his most enticing projects was
undoubtedly Villa Grigio (1963). The villa
characteristically fused "desert Modernism"
with Italianate neoclassicism—expressed
by the arched colonnades that threaded
through the house and flowed out onto the
pool terrace. Built for the business couple
the Kramers, who lived there until 1971, one
of the villa's most glamorous later occupants
was rumoured to be the James Bond actor
Roger Moore. In 2014, interior designer
Martyn Lawrence Bullard, who has lived in
Los Angeles since the early Nineties, knew
he had to have the property as his weekend
retreat. Bullard embarked on a restoration
that maximized the house's dramatic architecture. The spacious living room features
a predominantly white color palette punctuated with bursts of hot-fuchsia pink, as
seen in the Kravet upholstery for the semicircular sunken sofa that looks out over the
secret courtyard garden. Other standout
pieces include a pair of curvaceous Vladimir
Kagan sofas arranged around an Angelo
Mangiarotti cocktail table, referencing the
engaging mid-century heritage of the house.

Sunnylands

A. Quincy Jones & William Haines
Palm Springs, California (US), 1966

The scale of Sunnylands is almost palatial. Over the years the house has hosted world leaders, politicians, and celebrities in its role as the center of The Annenberg Foundation Trust. Yet it was originally designed as a family home, commissioned by publishing magnate and diplomat Walter Annenberg (1908–2002) and his wife Leonore, who were great patrons of the arts, architecture, and educational institutions. The couple enjoyed spending the winter months in Palm Springs; they were good friends with Frances and Sidney Brody, who had commissioned architect A. Quincy Jones (1913–1979) and interior designer William Haines (1900–1973) to design their house in Los Angeles (see p. 29). The same team were asked to work on Sunnylands, and as the Annenbergs were fond of Mexico they suggested a Mayan theme. From the exterior this was expressed in a vast pyramid roof dominating much of the house. Inside, the roof and coffered ceilings stood out as key elements, seen most vividly in the central atrium, which served as the central circulation point but also doubled as a generous reception room and art gallery. With its marble floors and indoor garden arranged under the apex of the pyramid, the dramatic mid-century space has transitioned easily into its twenty-first century charitable function.

Kenaston House

E. Stewart Williams
Rancho Mirage, California (US), 1957

....

Architect E. Stewart Williams (1909–2005) was one of the key pioneers of Desert Modernism in Palm Springs during the postwar period. Following Williams's university years, he toured Europe and Scandinavia, where he was influenced by designers such as Alvar Aalto, taking note of their use of warm, natural materials. In 1946 he joined his family's architectural firm in Palm Springs where one of his first and most famous projects was the 1947 Twin Palms house for Frank Sinatra. During the Fifties, Williams designed a series of houses in and around the Thunderbird Country Club in Rancho Mirage, including a residence for Roderick W. Kenaston. As one of the best-preserved exemplars of his work, the house encapsulated many of the key characteristics of Williams's design philosophy: splicing natural and industrial materials, while forging a vivid indoor-outdoor relationship. The spacious living room offered contrasting textures, with one wall coated in corrugated aluminum and another built in stone featuring a floating fireplace. A vivid line of greenery came from indoor planters as well as a view outside. Following a sensitive restoration, in 2005 the house took a starring role in a celebrated *W* magazine photo shoot with Brad Pitt and Angelina Jolie to promote their film, *Mr. & Mrs. Smith*.

Firestone Estate

William Pereira & Sam Cardella
Rancho Mirage, California (US),
1957/2015

....

Architect William Pereira (1909–1985) is well known for futuristic landmark buildings such as the Geisel Library (1970) at the University of California San Diego and the Transamerica Pyramid (1972) in San Francisco. But there was also a quieter side to his work, as seen in the calm and contemplative Rancho Mirage home built for the entrepreneur, philanthropist, and diplomat, Leonard Firestone (1907–1996) in 1957. Overlooking the Thunderbird Country Club, the house was built with slump-block walls and banks of glass opening out to the pool court, gardens, and golf course. A restoration by interior designer Sam Cardella and landscape designer Marcello Villano for new owners has seen the house brought back to life. Original features have been retained and restored, while Cardella added fresh furnishings in keeping with the period of the house. The spacious living room, for example, which overlooks the terrace and grounds, features a choice of seating areas anchored by two rugs and served by a custom double-sided sofa. Twin Pierre Paulin Ribbon chairs in a vivid blue catch the eye, while the Jumbo marble coffee table is by Gae Aulenti; both designs date back to the mid-century period.

Ford Estate

Darren Brown & Welton Becket & Associates
Rancho Mirage, California (US), 1977

Following Jimmy Carter's victory in the 1976 presidential election, former president Gerald Ford (1913–2006) and his wife Betty (1918–2011) retreated from Washington, D.C. to California. In Rancho Mirage, Welton Becket & Associates had designed them a spacious seven-bedroom home looking over the green fairways of the Thunderbird Country Club. Planned to ensure privacy, the villa made the most of the mountain views, while being positioned around the pool court. The original interiors were a wealth of texture and color, including playful elements, such as a bucolic dining-room wall mural by artist Garth Benton. When the current owners acquired the house in 2012 after Betty Ford's passing, many original pieces of furniture were still in place. These have largely been restored with the help of architects Marmol Radziner (see p. 29) and interior designer Darren Brown, who updated the house while preserving the characterful and texture-heavy Seventies aesthetic of the key living spaces and bedrooms. Deep shag-pile carpets soften the primary bedroom with its wraparound curtains and Larsen Fabrics striped wallpaper. The bed itself floats on a raised stage next to matching vintage twin armchairs, illuminated by an original ceiling-light installation.

High Desert House

Kendrick Bangs Kellogg & John Vugrin
Joshua Tree, California (US), 1993

There is a fantastical, otherworldly quality to High Desert House. It has the biomorphic look and feel of something that has grown out of the rugged landscape itself, or has arrived from a different universe entirely. Commissioned by artist Bev Doolittle and her husband, this escapist residence is perhaps the most ambitious project of architect Kendrick Bangs Kellogg and designer John Vugrin. Kellogg designed the super-organic home using a collection of overlapping concrete canopies, which shelter the spaces below. Inside, rocks push into the house itself, meeting the pebblestone floors. Vurgin—a frequent collaborator of Kellogg's and used to working with the unique structures of his buildings—worked for a decade on the house's interiors, custom designing and making the furniture, fixtures, and fittings. Vugrin's tables, consoles, and Sputnik-like lighting installations emerge from the walls and ceilings in materials like copper, bronze, mahogany, and marble. A hand-mosaiced tub offers views of the desert landscape. With every detail woven into the design concept the house is a Gesamtkunstwerk—a total work of art.

Rocky Mountain Ski Retreat

Peter Marino
Rocky Mountains, Colorado (US), 2015

The architect and designer Peter Marino has been collecting art for many years. There are many strands to Marino's extensive collection, which rapidly expanded from the Eighties onward, including Pop art and German abstract art, particularly many pieces by artist and sculptor Anselm Kiefer. "I find postwar German art particularly moving and meaningful," Marino has said, referencing Kiefer and Georg Baselitz. Kiefer's paintings are especially well suited to an alpine setting. Their gray-and-white compositions often include mountain scenes, while incorporating natural materials and pigments. They offer, as the designer put it, a "dialogue" with the rugged landscape around Marino's winter home and played an important part in the evolution of his ideas for the ski house. Marino's three-story residence forges a vivid sense of connection with the surroundings, echoed by his choice of natural materials such as swaths of cedar wood and slate. A number of Kiefer's paintings, along with one of his sculptures, inhabit the double-height entrance hall, where a wall of glass frames the snow-capped peaks. In the primary bedroom a Frank Thiel photograph hangs over a custom cedar bed, which is adorned at its head with twin steel lamps by Marino, while a work by Gregor Hildebrandt commands attention above a black leather Poul Kjærholm daybed.

Aspen Ski House

Shawn Henderson & Scott Lindenau
Aspen, Colorado (US), 2015

Modern mountain living involves a balancing act between seeking refuge and enjoying the natural beauty of the surroundings. This was very much the case with the design of the Aspen Ski House in Colorado, with its views of Elk Mountain. A modest log cabin on the site was recycled and replaced with a new two-story house and guest cottage designed by Scott Lindenau of the Colorado-based practice Studio B. For the interiors of this mountain retreat, which includes a meditation room and library, the owners turned to New York–based interior designer Shawn Henderson. One of the spaces to achieve both refuge and natural beauty is the spacious living room with walls of floor-to-ceiling glass looking out over the mountain panorama. Recognizing that the vista would always be the dominant element, Henderson opted for a neutral palette and natural textures. One of the two distinct seating areas is focused on the fireplace, which is inset into one wall below a pale-blue, jewellike mirror by Sam Orlando Miller acting as a gentle focal point. Much of the furniture was custom designed by Henderson, with the exception of the high-backed Peacock chair by Hans J. Wegner.

Aspen Chalet

Pauline Pitt
Aspen, Colorado (US), c. 2005

The romantic ideal of log-cabin living
remains strong in the United States, particularly in the Rocky Mountains. There is
a bucolic charm to the notion of a house
so intimately tied to the natural world, using
timber and stone to ground such a building
in the landscape. Interior designer Pauline
Pitt's Aspen chalet offers a gentle reinterpretation or revival of the log house, fusing
an innate sense of warmth and character
with modern comforts. The Palm Beach,
Florida–based designer began spending time
in Colorado just after 2000 and eventually
came across the house, designed by Aspen
architect Theodore K. Guy, surrounded by
trees and looking out toward Pyramid Peak.
An extensive renovation process followed,
with Pitt making her mark on the interiors
in particular. The most sociable space in the
house is, naturally, the "great room" with its
stone fireplace and exposed timber walls,
ceilings, and beams. Comfortable twin sofas
from Ralph Lauren Home flank the fire,
layered with soft cushions and throws, while
the antler chandelier and mirrors provide
organic, sculptural elements. The colorful oil
painting above the fireplace, by Crow Nation
artist Earl Biss, captures a compelling image
of Plains Indian horsemen, serving as a
reminder of the history of the site.

RRL Ranch

Ralph Lauren
San Juan Mountains, Colorado (US), 1982

Ralph and Ricky Lauren's ranch in Colorado
encompasses around 16,000 acres (6,500
hectares) and a choice of guest cabins,
a cookhouse, and other buildings, as well
as the couple's personal retreat. Lauren
was consciously searching for an alternative to his urban base in Manhattan when he
first came across the ranch. RRL is a place
where Lauren and his wife can slow down
and immerse themselves in nature—through
horse riding, hiking, and exploring—while
enjoying time with family and friends. At
the same time, the ranch has a life of its
own as a working farmstead. The cattle
ranch's interiors sum up Lauren's unique
take on American style. The log cottages
and the ranch house, with their verandas
and porches, embody an authentic and
organic take on the evocative Western rustic
style perfected by Lauren over the years,
expressed in both his fashion and homeware
collections. The references that inform both
RRL's interiors and outdoor rooms include
cowboy culture, settler cabins, Navajo blankets, and textiles from New Mexico. The
common threads are North American craftsmanship and natural materials, rooted in the
landscape. "I have other houses and I love
them," Lauren has said, "but the ranch makes
me aware of the natural world; it puts everything into perspective."

Las Vegas House

Atelier AM & William Hablinski
Architecture
Las Vegas, Nevada (US), 2011

....

The city of Las Vegas is home to countless illusions. In many respects, it is the ideal setting in which to realize grand dreams, as was the case with the family that commissioned this extraordinary house founded on their deep-rooted love of neoclassical Italian architecture and design. Architect William Hablinski designed the house fusing Palladian references with more contemporary touches, using Roman travertine as his material of choice. For the interiors, the family turned to Alexandra and Michael Misczynski of the Los Angeles–based Atelier AM, much respected for the textural richness and layered elegance of their projects. Key spaces include the generously scaled living room, with its central skylight and a combination of plaster walls, herringbone-tiled floors, and fine antiques, as well as a reflective copper-disc sculpture over the fireplace by Anish Kapoor. The loggia, in particular, has the dreamlike feel of Italy, providing a halfway point between house and garden. Custom seating by Atelier AM helps to create an enticing vantage point for enjoying the gardens, framed by a triptych of soaring stone arches. The house feels refined and authentic, while standing a world away from the stereotypical image of Las Vegas glamour.

Zorkendorfer House

McLean Quinlan & Joanne Zorkendorfer
Jackson Hole, Wyoming (US), 2016

....

Joanne and Rico Zorkendorfer share a love of the mountains. Joanne, a furniture and homeware designer, grew up in New Zealand while her husband, Rico, who works for Apple, grew up in Germany. When they first encountered Jackson Hole in Wyoming, the couple felt instantly at home: "The place is spectacular, but it also pulls on our heartstrings," said Joanne. The couple came across a Fifties cabin for sale and, although the house itself was in poor condition, they saw the potential of the extraordinary site with its open views of the valleys and mountains. UK-based practice McLean Quinlan, led by mother and daughter principals Fiona McLean and Kate Quinlan, designed a new house of timber and stone in reference to the vernacular tradition of settlers' cabins. The interiors are a collaboration between the practice and the Zorkendorfers themselves. In the open-plan living area at the heart of the house natural textures and finishes prevail, suggesting the aesthetic of a sophisticated twenty-first-century cabin with a double-sided fireplace also serves the room beyond. The comfortable sofas are from Restoration Hardware while gentle touches of color come from ottomans and cushions, which are from Joanne Zorkendorfer's atelier, Olli.

Easton & Steinmeyer House

David Easton
Tulsa, Oklahoma (US), 2011

Having studied at the Pratt Institute, David Easton (1937–2020) joined Parish-Hadley, the New York firm of Sister Parish (see pp. 85 and 123) and Albert Hadley (see pp. 85 and 98). At Parish-Hadley he became one of the most prominent designers to perfect his craft: "It taught me a certain awareness about comfort, the placement of furniture and its relationship to people using a room," said Easton. Establishing his own studio in 1972, he began securing key commissions, such as the restoration of a Virginia estate known as Albemarle for John and Patricia Kluge, cementing his reputation during the Eighties. In 2007 Easton and his partner, artist James Steinmeyer, bought a house in Tulsa, Oklahoma, where the latter grew up. The couple settled on a modern redbrick house—a radical departure for Easton, who suggested that he had grown less interested over time in "traditional environments." The living room featured a custom fireplace set between a pair of French doors leading to the garden, while Easton placed arm-chairs of his own design around the fireside; crimson notes for the upholstery of the ottoman and antique French slipper chairs stand out against the pale walls and floors, while a focus on comfort and composition is still very much present.

Houston House

Fern Santini & Paul Lamb
Houston, Texas (US), 2013

The home that interior designer Fern Santini created for her sister in Houston, Texas, could be described as a twenty-first-century Arts and Crafts house. Designed in conjunction with architect Paul Lamb, the house references the English masters of the movement, such as Edwin Lutyens and C. F. A. Voysey; but there is also a contemporary quality throughout, particularly in the fluid floorplan, with its free-flowing connections to the adjoining terraces and rear garden. The new two-story house was designed within the central loop of Houston to serve as a principal residence for Santini's sister, along with her husband and their four teenage children. One of the most timeless spaces in the house is the inviting living room. Here, sitting between two large windows, the Terra Verde limestone fireplace forms a key focal point. Above a circular mirror by Christian Astuguevieille—crafted from gold-painted rope—hangs over the mantelpiece. The color palette is soothing; the neutral tones of the plastered walls are complemented by the gentle pattern of the rug and the soft grays of the sofa by Holly Hunt (see p. 65) placed under the arched window. In this context, darker pieces such as the coffee table and two black chairs stand out, their sculptural silhouettes enhanced and enriched.

Houston House

Miles Redd
Houston, Texas (US), 2013

....

While the exuberant colors of this Houston living room inevitably catch the eye, it is the giant mosquito on the ceiling that intrigues it. The piece is a giant-sized French scientific model, which dates back to the Forties, that Miles Redd sourced from a Christie's auction. Characteristically for a designer known for his love of playful touches, the fly captured his imagination in a home packed full—of course—of a rainbow collection of colors and patterns. The house itself dates from the Nineties and was designed with a neoclassical aesthetic that suggests the look of a French chateau. Redd's clients encouraged his imaginative maximalist approach, which has brought Redd to Texas on many occasions and is also in evidence at his own New York townhouse (see p. 108) and an exuberant vacation home in the Bahamas (see p. 147). For the theatrical Houston sitting room, Redd opted for walls in a sky blue satin, which host a focal point painting by Agustin Hurtado. A crisp white sofa sits beneath this artwork, flanked by twin armchairs in a red and white candy stripe fabric by C&C Milano, with these ruby red notes repeated periodically throughout the space. The yellow curtains, meanwhile, take the color palette in a different direction, offering—along with the mosquito—one of a multitude of surprizes seen throughout every room in the house.

Blake Residence
Joseph Minton
Dallas, Texas (US), 2009

Having studied history and law, Joseph Minton went on to work as a City Attorney in Forth Worth. During the Fifties, while serving with the U.S. Air Force, he was stationed in England where he became fascinated by period architecture and antiques while touring the country's grand country houses, such as Woburn Abbey. Returning to Texas, Minton began a long and successful career in design, with his work widely published from the Seventies onward. One of his loyal long-term clients and collaborators was Betty Blake (1916–2016), known to her friends as "Boop." A collector and curator, Blake opened the first Modern art gallery in Texas during the Fifties and was an active patron of the arts until her death. In the Forties, Blake acquired a distinguished set of furniture designed by the influential tastemaker Syrie Maugham (1879–1955), which she took with her from home to home. For the interiors of her final Dallas residence, the Maugham designs naturally became the lynchpin of the living room. Minton had the sofa and two matching armchairs re-covered in Egyptian cotton, punctuated by tufts and rosettes, while artworks from Blake's collection also played an important part. Here, the focal piece is an oil painting by the Guatemalan-American artist Alfred Jensen entitled *The Ten Thousand Things*, while the piece on the plinth by the window is by the American sculptor José de Rivera.

Douglas House

Richard Meier
Harbor Springs, Michigan (US), 1973

Combining a mesmerizing natural setting and original design can create a home that is not just engaging but also iconic. Such is the case with Richard Meier's Douglas House, positioned on a steep wooden shoreline overlooking the northern tip of landlocked Lake Michigan. The house was one of the most important and influential early commissions for Meier, who worked with Marcel Breuer before founding his own architectural office in 1963. It is an ambitious and complex house, full of light, exploring multiple internal shifts in volume, height, and scale. Like Eileen Gray's famous residence E-1027 (1929) on the French Riviera, the house holds echoes of a ship, with a series of decks and terraces facing the water. These include the roof, which is an integral part of the house, serving as the main point of entry (via a bridge from the uppermost point of the hill), as well as holding a substantial skylight and leading to an enticing sun deck. The funnel-like flues reaching up from the fireplace in the living room below, along with Meier's trademark use of crisp-white finishes, reinforce the maritime feel of the interiors.

Farnsworth House

Ludwig Mies van der Rohe
Plano, Illinois (US), 1950

The country escape that Ludwig Mies van der Rohe (1886–1969) designed for his client and friend, the Chicago kidney specialist Dr. Edith Farnsworth, was radical in terms of both its architecture and its interiors. The pavilion by the Fox River was, famously, a glass house with a steel frame, curtain walls, and integrated terraces, all floating a few feet above the meadow in the hope of avoiding flood risk. There were echoes of the Bauhaus master's Barcelona Pavilion (1929) in its purity and elegance, yet with the Farnsworth House Mies also applied his ideal of a universal space. The architect was able to preserve a vital sense of openness and transparency by introducing a "service core": an installation that holds a fireplace on one side, a galley kitchen on the other, and compact bathrooms at each end. Barely touching the ceiling, the timber-faced core reads like a piece of furniture, while the spaces around it—used for relaxation, dining, working, and sleeping—are largely defined by the position of the Mies-designed furniture on the travertine floors. Farnsworth suggested that she was shocked by the uncompromising character of the space and declared it unliveable—however, despite this, she kept hold of her pioneering home until 1972.

Hunt Apartment

Holly Hunt
Chicago, Illinois (US), 2015

As well as designing her own line of furniture and taking on select interior design commissions, Holly Hunt has always been an entrepreneur. Starting with her first showroom in Chicago in the mid-Eighties, Hunt has gradually developed her company into a global concern. Having initially collaborated with designers including Christian Liaigre (see p. 152) and Rose Tarlow (see p. 41), Hunt now works with a portfolio of designers that include Christian Astuguevieille, Paul Mathieu, and others. Hunt's own apartment in Chicago plays host to furniture by many of these names, as well as pieces of her own design. Hunt bought the apartment, which sits within a 1914 Beaux Arts building overlooking the waters of Lake Michigan, in 1997, although it has since evolved a number of times over the years. A collection of Abstract Expressionist art plays an important role throughout, with focal point pieces by Robert Rauschenberg and others. In the sitting room, there is work—for example— by Louis Nevelson and Helen Frankenthaler, as well as Robert Motherwell. There's space enough here for a choice of seating areas, with a custom Vladimir Kagan sofa by the bay window and then, framed by an Astuguevielle rug, a central zone with chairs by Mathieu and standing lamps by Liaigre either side of a Holly Hunt-designed sofa.

Miller House

Eero Saarinen & Alexander Girard
Columbus, Indiana (US), 1953

....

The Miller House on the green edges of
Columbus, Indiana, represents an extraordinary collaboration between architect Eero
Saarinen (1910–1961), interior and textile
designer Alexander Girard (1907–1993),
and two progressive clients: J. Irwin Miller,
head of the Cummins engine company,
and his wife, Xenia—both of whom were
philanthropists and patrons of architecture and the arts. Saarinen designed the
single-story house in the form of a spacious square pavilion, overlooking gardens
designed by Dan Kiley (1912–2004). The
centerpiece of Girard's interior scheme was
the free-flowing communal living area, lifted
by the use of white marble for the internal
walls and travertine for the floors. A conversation pit offered an escapist space, layered
with Girard's colorful textiles—different
sets of which were rotated in tune with
the seasons—and then another living area
arranged around a circular fireplace with
a floating flue drum that morphed into the
ceiling. A dining area to one side of these
seating zones and a den to the other could
be lightly separated using curtains on ceiling
tracks. Girard's folk-tradition rug added a
further layer of color, pattern, and character; he even designed the family's custom
dinnerware and napkins—just one of an
abundant playful details.

Collector's House

Peter Pennoyer
Rowdy Meadow, Ohio (US), 2019

....

Architect Peter Pennoyer is best known for
his work in a neoclassical or Greek Revival
style, offering a contemporary take on traditional forms and ideas, as seen in his own
country house in the Hudson Valley, New
York State (see p. 75). Here, on an estate in
rural Ohio, Pennoyer's client wanted to take
a very different direction, inspired by twenty-first-century Czech Cubism on a visit to
the Czech Republic. The movement, which
occurred just before World War I, was short
lived but full of original ideas and expressive
forms. Pennoyer's client asked him to design
a modern Czech Cubist house in rural
Ohio, within a 70-acre (28 hectare) holding
known as Rowdy Meadow. The estate holds
not just the new house, but also a private
sculpture park hosting pieces by artists
including Richard Serra, Andy Goldsworthy,
and Anish Kapoor. Art plays a dynamic role
within the new house, too, which includes
a dedicated gallery displaying work by Luc
Tuymans, Damien Hirst, and Ai Weiwei (see
p. 75). The Cubist inspiration can be seen
in the wood-paneled library with its angular,
geometrical ceiling and sculptural stone
fireplace. As well as the white ceilings and
the natural tones of the joinery, indigo blue
is seen in the velvet sofas and echoed by the
colors of the geometric-patterned rug and
the console by Ingrid Donat; the portrait
over the fireplace is by the Belgian painter
Michaël Borremans.

Schafer House

Gil Schafer
Brooklin, Maine (US), 2015

....

Gil Schafer has fond memories of spending
the summers in Maine as a child. More
recently, the New York–based architect
began renting houses around Blue Hill Bay
until, eventually, he came across a house by
the sea that he decided to buy. The original
design was a substantial A-framed cabin,
with a large open room at one end leading
onto a deck facing the water. Schafer, who
comes from a family of architects, saw the
potential to radically reinvent the building,
introducing dormer windows, for example,
which allowed him to bring the partial attic
level back into use. For the "great room,"
Schafer sought "a balance between modernity and tradition." Floors, walls, and ceilings
are all in white, creating a crisp beach-house
feel, while Schafer zoned the lounge in two
parts with back-to-back sofas grounded
on jute rugs; one of the sofas faces the deck
and the water while the other looks back
to a fireplace. "My hope is that the house
belongs unmistakably to the present yet
retains a connection to traditional Maine
architecture that is neither old-fashioned
nor gimmicky," writes Schafer in his recent
book, *A Place to Call Home* (2017).

Skylands

Martha Stewart
Mount Desert Island, Maine (US), 1997

During the Eighties and Nineties, Martha Stewart was America's greatest homemaker. Through her books, magazines, and television shows, Stewart became a design brand in her own right. Her empire was founded on the look and style of her own homes; the most extraordinary of which is Stewart's country house on Mount Desert Island, along the coast of Maine. The house was built in 1925 for Edsel Ford—the president of Ford, the Detroit car giant founded by his father, Henry—and his wife Eleanor and their family, to a design by architect Duncan Candler (1874–1949). Remarkably, the house came with not only its architectural integrity intact but also with much of its original furniture and furnishings, including the Fords' dinnerware. Stewart has carefully balanced her guardianship of the house with the need to tailor the interiors in a more contemporary style, documenting and storing pieces where necessary to make space for her own curated choices. In the "great hall," for example, custom sofas flank the original stone fireplace while a faux bois table and benches by Studio Cortes form a characterful modern centerpiece. As only the third owner of Skylands and its estate, which features gardens by Jens Jensen (1860–1951), Stewart sees herself as "the caretaker of an American treasure."

Windy Gates Farm

Keith McNally & Ian McPheely
Martha's Vineyard, Massachusetts (US), 1991

Floating off the Cape Cod peninsula, the Massachusetts islands of Martha's Vineyard and neighboring Nantucket feel wonderfully removed from the daily trials and tribulations of the mainland. The English restaurateur Keith McNally first discovered the Vineyard during the Seventies, not long after settling in New York, taking his bike over on the ferry to explore at a gentle pace. Windy Gates Farm in Chilmark, to the west of the island, offered a place where McNally could cook, entertain, and explore a degree of self-sufficient living, with a vegetable garden, orchard, and some livestock. As with the design of his other homes (see p. 196) and restaurants, McNally took a thoughtful and considered approach to every detail of the farmhouse interiors. Original elements were combined with choice pieces of architectural salvage and flea-market finds to create a timeless but rustic, modern style. As with his landmark Manhattan eatery Balthazar, there is a touch of France in the dining area overlooking the garden with its choice of banquettes and bistro chairs, sitting on broad wooden floorboards. "I didn't want the place to look too designed or polished," McNally said of the house, "but of course that always takes a lot more work."

Hagan House

Victoria Hagan & Ray Pohl
Nantucket, Massachusetts (US), 2010

....

The soothing palette favored by designer
Victoria Hagan is well suited to island
living. In many respects her family home on
Nantucket represents the perfect fusion
of her distinctive aesthetic with a particular sense of place. The architecture and
interiors of Hagan's house are fully in tune
with their unique and characterful setting.
Having enjoyed spending time on the island
for many years, as well as designing a
number of Nantucket residences for clients,
Hagan had long nurtured the idea of building a summer retreat here. Eventually,
in 2010, she managed to purchase 3 acres
(1 hectare) within sight of the sea. With
both house and garden, Hagan, assisted
by architect Ray Pohl, managed to create
a timeless quality in keeping with the
genius loci. Naturals and neutrals dominate
throughout, but with gentle maritime notes.
In the living room, for example, white walls
and linens combine with wooden floors and
Scandinavian touches, such as a pair of
Hans J. Wegner chairs facing the fireplace.
The Barbara Zucker artwork over the fireplace also speaks of restraint, while seaside
hues come from the cushions on the white
sofas and the pale gray-blue linen armchairs, which help make up the secondary
seating area.

Robshaw House

John Robshaw
Litchfield County, Connecticut (US), 2016

....

"When you look at my textiles, it's as if you've
been on the world tour alongside me," says
interior designer John Robshaw of his many
travels. After studying fine art at the Pratt
Institute in New York, Robshaw traveled to
India, Thailand, and Indonesia researching
traditional block-printing techniques
and learning from local artisans. Back in
the United States, he built an ambitious
textiles business based on these collaborations. His own country home, a traditional
nineteenth-century farmhouse in a bucolic
rural setting in Litchfield County, offers a
masterclass in Asian-inspired maximalism.
Robshaw layered the house with vivid hues
and patterns, as well as countless treasures
gathered on his many journeys, such as
his collection of Dutch plates purchased in
Sri Lanka, which now hang on a wall in the
kitchen. The walls here are painted in Rose
Quartz and the cabinetry in Starry Night
by Benjamin Moore Paints, providing a bold
backdrop for the light marble countertops
and a pale-gray Richard Wrightman Chatwin
settee. In the living room, Robshaw has
run riot with the fabrics, from the custom
candy-hued dhurrie on the floor to the
striped custom armchair by the fireplace.
As Robshaw's interiors suggests, his designs
offer an epic journey contained only by the
room's four walls.

Connecticut House

India Mahdavi
Litchfield County, Connecticut (US), 2010

....

"I think there's something quite sensual about the way that I work with color and shapes," says interior and furniture designer India Mahdavi. Mahdavi's sophisticated design philosophy is infused with influences from her peripatetic early years following her family's move from Iran to the United States to Europe, as well as her university years in Paris and New York. She went on to work in France with Christian Liaigre (see p. 152) for many years, before founding her own Parisian atelier in 1999. The Connecticut House was designed for clients who had relocated from England to New England, acquiring a substantial rural estate with a farmhouse, barn, and outbuildings. The family's collection of contemporary art makes its presence felt throughout, with Sol LeWitt wall murals in the play barn, a James Turrell light installation, and land art by Richard Long. One of the warmest and most welcoming spaces inside the farmhouse is the spacious living room, where a soft, soothing backdrop of neutrals allows sculptural elements to shine, including Mahdavi-designed twin yellow sofas by the window and a pair of André Arbus chairs by the fireplace; the mirrored screens and coffee tables are also by Mahdavi.

Round Hill

Tommy Hilfiger & Martyn Lawrence Bullard
Greenwich, Connecticut (US), 2016

....

The "restless" fashion designer Tommy
Hilfiger rarely stays still for long. Hilfiger
and his wife Dee's complex calendar involves
time spent in homes in Mustique, Florida,
and the Hamptons, as well as an apartment in New York City at the Plaza Hotel
and Round Hill, their Connecticut retreat.
Round Hill was built in the Thirties by architect Greville Rickard (1889–1956) and was
originally known as Chateau Paterno, after
its original owner. By the time the Hilfigers
acquired the mansion, it was in need of
restoration, duly undertaken by architect
Andre Tchelistcheff and interior designer
Martyn Lawrence Bullard (see p. 48), who
also worked on the Hilfigers' Florida home.
The Hilfigers wanted to "preserve the feeling
of being in a European country house" and
Bullard duly obliged, combining English and
French period grandeur with more contemporary elements. One of the most playful
spaces is, fittingly, the family's games room
and lounge, now situated in the "great hall,"
where a billiards table with a vivid-red baize
stands out, matched by the choice of red-
patterned armchairs flanking the stone fireplace. The former billiards room, meanwhile,
now serves as Hilfiger's study.

Glass House

Philip Johnson
New Canaan, Connecticut (US), 1949

....

One of American architect Philip Johnson's
(1906–2005) earliest and most important
architectural projects was his own house:
the Glass House, on the green edges of New
Canaan, Connecticut. The design of the
house owes much to the work of Johnson's
mentor, Ludwig Mies van der Rohe, and
has many elements in common with Mies's
Farnsworth House (see p. 65)—including the
steel frame, flat roof, and glass curtain walls.
The setting was certainly sublime, with the
house positioned on the crest of a hill in
Johnson's private estate, looking across the
valley. Inside the house, Johnson took the
notion of a universal living space to a fresh
extreme. Essentially, the home was a single
room with various zones within it defined
largely by the arrangement of the furniture;
the only fully self-contained element was
the "bathroom" sitting in a brick drum. The
main seating area was defined by a rug floating on the brick herringbone floor and furniture by Mies, including Mies and Lilly Reich's
Barcelona chairs and a daybed he designed
for Johnson. Behind this arrangement hangs
one of three versions of Nicolas Poussin's
c. 1648 painting *Burial of Phocion*. Its verdant
greenery matches that of New Canaan's
landscape, which Johnson once famously
alluded to as the "very expensive wallpaper."

Risom Summer House

Jens Risom
Block Island, Rhode Island (US), 1967

The furniture designer Jens Risom (1916–2016) grew up in Denmark, immigrating to the United States in 1939. There, he designed some early pieces for Hans Knoll's new furniture company, including the iconic 600 Series chairs, before establishing his own firm, which went from strength to strength during the mid-century period. In the late Sixties, at the height of its success, he decided to build a family summer house in the north of Block Island, an escapist retreat off the southern coast of Rhode Island. Risom chose a prefabricated A-frame kit house produced by a company called Stanmar, Inc. in Massachusetts. The open-plan living-and-dining area faces a wall of glass that connects with the north-facing terrace to allow as much light in as possible. The furniture here is, naturally, by Risom himself—upholstered largely in shades of orange, turquoise, and cream—with its mid-century character perfectly in tune with the interiors and the distinctive aesthetic of the A-frame. A Risom Rocker sits next to a RAIS wood-burning stove; while the sofa is a prototype that never went into production. Risom has said about the house: "It's a place to be taken seriously. On the other hand, it's full of charm."

Hudson House

David Mann & Fritz Karch
Hudson, New York (US), 2008

....

Architect David Mann is known for his crisp and contemporary minimalistic buildings and interiors. His partner, antique dealer and stylist Fritz Karch, describes himself as a maximalist. When it comes to their own home in the historic town of Hudson, the two have managed to find a harmonious understanding within a process of "complex collaboration." The redbrick house itself dates back to 1785 and was built for a prosperous local lawyer. Over the years, many changes had been made, including a substantial makeover during the 1830s in the Greek Revival style, which added layers of grandeur. Mann began the restoration process by paring down. This included stripping away the intense colors chosen by the previous owners and painting the spaces white, allowing the sense of proportion and scale, as well as any original detailing, to be better understood. This was true of the living room, for example, where Mann and Karch opted for white walls, bare wooden floors, and unadorned windows. In this context, a pair of bold-blue sofas custom designed by Mann shine out, as well as art pieces such as the Björn Abelin photograph on the mantelpiece.

Pennoyer & Ridder House

Peter Pennoyer & Katie Ridder
Hudson Valley, New York (US), 2014

Situated in the gentle green landscape of the Hudson Valley and carefully positioned overlooking a pond and a bucolic vista, this "contemporary classical" house encapsulates a marriage between an architect and an interior designer. Architect and writer Peter Pennoyer (see p. 67) is known for his twenty-first century take on neoclassicism and his imaginative reinterpretations of traditional ideas and compositions. His wife, Katie Ridder, is an interior designer known as an "intrepid colorist," who is "as fond of peacock blue and emerald green as she is of tangerine and lemon yellow." The main living spaces of their family home, near Millbrook, revolve around a large entrance hall with a mosaic floor of shiny purple, hexagonal tiles, illuminated by a top-lit atrium. For the living room, Ridder selected a rose-pink wallpaper from de Gournay (see p. 203) with green linen for the curtains and pelmets. Around the fireplace, she opted for a blue-and-white-striped sofa and a fuchsia-pink easy chair. One's eye is also drawn to the crimson-red sofa by the window. The house and garden are fully documented in Pennoyer and Ridder's book, *A House in the Country* (2016).

Tsai Residence

Ai Weiwei & HHF Architects
Near Ancram, New York (US), 2009

The Chinese artist Ai Weiwei has nurtured a strong interest in architecture and design for many years. There were a number of projects in China, including the Beijing National Stadium, designed in conjunction with Herzog & de Meuron for the 2008 Olympics. Shortly afterward, Weiwei completed work on this house in the Hudson Valley, designed in conjunction with the Swiss practice HHF Architects. The house, near Ancram, was a project for an investment manager and a fashion designer, who shared a love of contemporary Chinese art. Weiwei served both as the "conceptual designer" and the "inspiration behind the house," which was his first and only residential project in America. Inside, the thoughtful manipulation of natural light was a key concern within the design of the main living spaces on the ground floor, which sit within a fluid plan and revolve around a brick fireplace. The dining area features a dining table by Clodagh Design, with custom benches, and a top-lit artwork on the white walls by Xie Nanxing, while in the lounge a large gunpowder painting by Cai Guo-Qiang hovers above a gray B&B Italia sofa. Art, architecture, and interiors fuse comfortably throughout, with a number of Ai Weiwei's own pieces also featuring prominently.

Cloudline
Toshiko Mori
Hudson Valley, New York (US), 2012

Cloudline offers a delightful confluence between the worlds of architecture, interiors, and art, assisted by a sublime setting in the Hudson Valley. Designed by architect Toshiko Mori, the house was commissioned by a New York–based art dealer and gallerist for himself and his family, as well as their collection of pieces by contemporary artists such as Antony Gormley, Richard Long, and Peter Liversidge. Mori positioned the house on a plateau at a high point in the topography of the Hudson Valley, with a green backdrop of trees and open views to the front, where the land falls away steeply. This gives the two-story house the feeling of a belvedere, with the interiors framing open views that stretch all the way to Albany with the Catskill Mountains in the far distance. The main ground-floor living spaces are arranged as a triptych of interconnected rooms facing the vista. The morning room hosts furniture by Marc Newson and Poul Kjærholm and looking out across the open landscape a Gormley figure can be glimpsed through the window. The main living room houses artworks by Callum Innes, Marina Abramović, and Los Carpinteros, while the arrangement of the welcoming L-shaped Minotti sofas creates a room within a room.

Dragon Rock

Russel Wright & David Leavitt
Garrison, New York (US), 1961

In the Algonquin language, Manitoga translates as "place of the great spirit." Here, in
1942, designer Russel Wright (1904–1976)
and his wife Mary bought 70 acres (28 hectares) of former logging country, including
a small cabin, seeking to "demonstrate and
enhance its natural beauty and charm," as
Wright put it. When Mary Wright—who had
played an important part in the evolution
of Wright's growing atelier—died in 1952,
her husband continued with their plans for
Manitoga. He built a new retreat, Dragon
Rock, for himself and his young daughter,
along with a small studio, in conjunction
with architect David L. Leavitt (1918–2013).
The main house sits on a slope overlooking
a quarry pond below and is bordered by
trees. Dragon Rock is arranged over eleven
interconnected levels, with the granite
periodically pushing into the spaces within.
The dining area, for example, features an
Eero Saarinen–designed table positioned at
the bottom of a stone staircase and next
to the base of a cedar-tree trunk that helps
to support the roof; the ceramics displayed
form part of Wright's best-selling American
Modern dinnerware collection. Sliding glass
doors connect the space to a terrace, while
a semi-open kitchen is crowned with a
custom panel, called *White Clouds*, installed
by Wright as a subtle reference to the sky.

Station House

Federico de Vera
Dutchess County, New York (US), 2012

Federico de Vera's home in Dutchess County began its life back in 1905 as a railway station. It was a stop on the old Harlem Line, which took both passengers and freight from upstate New York down to Manhattan. The passenger trains stopped service in the Seventies and then the line closed completely in the Eighties; the former track now serves as a hiking trail. The old station house was originally converted into a home during the early Nineties but caught the attention of gallery owner, designer, and curator de Vera, who—after many years of searching—decided that it would make the perfect rural escape. The most spacious part of the house is the former waiting area, which is now an airy living room. A series of white-painted, glass-fronted cabinets hold part of the gallerist's library and the contents of his "diary": a visual record of his travels, including crystals and shells, glass and ceramics, and carvings and cake stands. The gray sofa is by Thomas O'Brien while the eye-catching daybed, with its emerald upholstery, is nineteenth-century Italian. Other pieces here also mix the antique and the modern, including a T. H. Robsjohn-Gibbings armchair and a Gae Aulenti coffee table.

Rhinebeck Cottage

Zack McKown & Calvin Tsao
Near Rhinebeck, New York (US), 2011

For designers Calvin Tsao and Zack McKown, one of the greatest delights of their Hudson Valley escape, near Rhinebeck, has been the luxury of time. The cottage and surrounds—85 acres (34 hectares) of woods, orchards, and pasture—offer an idyllic alternative to the busy pace of their working life in Manhattan. By the time Tsao and McKown came across the cottage, dating back to the 1850s, it had almost been reclaimed by the forest and required an extensive renovation, although the designers took great care to preserve the distinctive character of the building. As well as restoring the ground-floor kitchen, living room, and dining room, Tsao and McKown added a screened porch to serve as a halfway point between inside and outside. Upstairs, there were originally three bedrooms, but one of these was converted into a bathroom. The primary bedroom has the feel of an attic escape, with its sloping roof and a central window framing a view of the trees. Walls and ceilings are painted a crisp white, while the low bed at the center of the room is custom. The designers added shelves within the low wall niches to either side of the space, displaying part of their eclectic collection of curios, including small artworks and a Fifties orrery found in a flea-market.

Sills House

Stephen Sills & James Huniford
Bedford, New York (US), 1991

The Bedford retreat owned by designer
Stephen Sills was originally known as
High Low Farm, owned by the gardener
and author, Helen Morgenthau Fox, who
published a book about the farm back in
1965 entitled *Adventure in My Garden*.
By the time Sills discovered the property,
the garden was overgrown, and the house
largely dilapidated. Sills, who originally collaborated on the project with his former
partner James Huniford (see p. 116), remodeled the two-story residence extensively,
introducing French doors and limestone
floors, with Egyptian marble columns
framing doorways between one space and
the next. In the living room Sills introduced
sculpted and fluted plaster walls, painted
a soft white, which form a gentle but textural backdrop. A dark stone fireplace to
one side also added a degree of contrast.
Each piece of furniture here has a story
to it, including eighteenth-century daybeds
by Georges Jacob and a globe that once
belonged to ballet dancer Rudolf Nureyev,
while the painting over the sofa is by the U.S.
artist Harold Stevenson. The interiors of
the home have continued to evolve over time:
"You have to edit your life, move forward,
and understand the times that you are living
in," says Sills.

Witthoefft House

Arthur Witthoefft
Armonk, New York (US), 1957

Architect Arthur Witthoefft studied at the University of Illinois and the Cranbrook Academy of Art before joining Skidmore Owings & Merrill (SOM). The firm was best known for its mid-century skyscrapers, such as Lever House (1952) in New York and Sears Tower (1973) in Chicago. But the house that Witthoefft designed for himself and his interior designer wife Eleanor, could be described as a "landscraper," tucked into a semirural setting in Armonk in Westchester County. The steel-framed house sits on a gently sloping site, with a backdrop of woodland behind it. The Witthoeffts' house is essentially single story, with banks of floor-to-ceiling glass, connecting the house to the landscape. Arthur and Eleanor worked together on the interiors, creating an open-plan living and dining area, with a custom fireplace in steel and travertine forming a focal point but also lightly separating the two zones. More recently the house has been restored by creative director Andrew Mandolene and real-estate specialist, Todd Goddard, who introduced their own collection of mid-century furniture, including a Paul McCobb sectional sofa in the living room and blue vintage slipper chairs; these form part of a series of subtle blue notes that stand out against a predominantly white-and-neutral palette.

Cindy Sherman Penthouse

Billy Cotton & Cindy Sherman
New York City, New York (US), 2018

The designer Billy Cotton has worked on
a number of artists' and photographers'
homes. Most prominent among these is
Cindy Sherman, who Cotton got to know
after the artist saw a house that he had
worked on for a friend. "Billy's work struck
a balance between practicality, funkiness,
and chic," said Sherman. For the main living
spaces of Sherman's Manhattan penthouse,
Cotton coated the walls in "popcorn stucco"
plasterwork, creating a textured white
surface. In the main living room this combines with a generously sized custom sofa
designed by Cotton, vintage Paul Evans
armchairs, and part of Sherman's extensive art collection. For Sherman's bedroom,
Cotton took inspiration from the Viennese
personal retreat that Adolf Loos designed
for himself and his first wife Lina in 1903,
which featured white walls, curtains, fabrics,
and furniture, all floating on a deep-blue
carpet. For Sherman, Cotton designed a
custom bed and bedside tables, while softening the walls with wraparound linen
curtains. Instead of the Loos-like blue, color
comes from Sherman's choice of artworks,
including a painting over the bed by Esther
Pearl Watson.

Mindel Apartment

Lee Mindel
New York City, New York (US), c. 1994

Architect Lee Mindel began collecting furniture by twentieth-century masters of architecture and design during the Eighties, starting with pieces such as a Piero Fornasetti screen that he brought back on the plane from a trip to Europe. "If you value a designer's architecture, their objects and furniture are usually interesting too— a capsule of their voice," says Mindel, who in 1978 cofounded SheltonMindel with the late Peter L. Shelton (1945–2012). Mindel's Manhattan apartment, in the Flatiron District, sat on the top floor of a former hat factory, offering views out across the cityscape toward both the East River and the Hudson. Mindel drew inspiration from the water towers that punctuate the Manhattan skyline, creating a central rotunda that served both as an entry hallway and lightwell. The living room, with its ribbon of windows to one side, as well as a focal point fireplace designed by Mindel, offered a sense of welcome and warmth, while hosting many key pieces from the architect's collection. These included furniture from Scandinavian masters such as a Poul Kjærholm daybed in black leather and a Poul Henningsen lamp, as well as a round table at the center of the space by Jean Prouvé anchored by natural linen mats covered in latex and presided over by a Günther Förg painting.

Vreeland Apartment

Billy Baldwin
New York City, New York (US), 1957

....

The modestly sized Manhattan apartment
owned by Diana Vreeland (1903–1989)—one
of the most influential fashion magazine
editors of the twentieth century—and her
husband was among the most famous spaces
in the United States during the late Fifties.
Vreeland later complained that she was
never particularly well paid by her publishers and the budget for the interiors of her
apartment was limited. She was, however,
extremely well connected and asked her
friend Billy Baldwin (1903–1983, see p. 278)
to assist, famously requesting a home that
looked like a garden: "Not just any garden,
but a garden in hell." On a trip to Madrid,
Baldwin found an exuberant red floral fabric
by Gastón y Daniela, which became the foundation of Vreeland's "garden," applied not
just to the walls but also used to upholster
sofas and armchairs in the living room, in
combination with a vivid-crimson carpet.
Baldwin created a dining alcove to one side,
using a bright stripe on the walls and for
the fitted banquette seating. The apartment
became a hot focal point for the extensive
social circle that gathered around Vreeland,
who moved on from *Harper's Bazaar* to
Vogue in 1963.

Astor Apartment

Sister Parish & Albert Hadley
New York City, New York (US), c. 1960

....

During the Forties, the writer, tastemaker,
and socialite Brooke Astor (née Russell,
1902–2007) became the features editor
of American *House & Garden*. She stayed
with the magazine for eight years and then
worked briefly with interior designer Ruby
Ross Wood, who counted Billy Baldwin
(above) among her staff. Following the death
of her second husband and her marriage,
in 1953, to William Vincent Astor everything
changed. She became part of the wealthy
Astor family, assisting her husband with his
real estate and hotel empire, including the
redesign of the Hotel St. Regis. When William
Astor died in 1959, his partner inherited
much of his some one hundred twenty million
dollar fortune and devoted herself largely
to writing and philanthropy, while moving
into a Park Avenue penthouse in a Rosario
Candela–designed building. The penthouse
marked a fresh beginning. She turned to
interior designer Sister Parish (1910–1994,
see p. 123), who joined forces with Albert
Hadley (1920–2012, see p. 98) just a few
years later. In the vast dining room, the duo
opted for emerald-green walls that play
host to a collection of antique tapestries. The
vivid use of color gives the space a modern
edge while the furniture is more traditional,
suggesting the nature of the Parish-Hadley
aesthetic approach.

Upper East Side Apartment

Virginia Tupker
New York City, New York (US), 2017

....

Interior designer Virginia Tupker learned
her craft as a homes editor and stylist at
magazines such as the U.S. editions of *House
& Garden* and *Vogue*, where she worked for
six years. This home on Manhattan's Upper
East Side marked a collaboration between
Tupker and the art and fashion writer/
journalist Derek Blasberg, who acquired
an apartment in a Twenties building close
to Central Park. Blasberg enlisted Tupker
to work on the renovation and remodel,
along with architectural designers Yaiza
Armbruster and Marina Dayton. Changes
to the floorplan included combining two
small rooms to create the "gossip room":
a den with walls and curtains in a print from
Ralph Lauren Home. In the living room, a
Vladimir Kagan–style sinuous, emerald-hued
sofa is a linchpin of the design, along with
a Willy Rizzo cocktail table and two chairs
by Olivier Mourgue. The dining room also
exhibits playful touches. The dominant
colors are black and white, visible in the
shining lacquered table and chairs, which
stand out against the white walls and pale
rug. Yet yellow and orange highlights also
sing out from the curtains and other pieces,
including the palatial wicker fern stand,
while the pair of Instagram prints are by
Richard Prince.

West Chelsea Apartment

Deborah Berke Partners
New York City, New York (US), 2016

....

The relationship between the art world
and the architectural practice founded in
1982 by Deborah Berke—dean of the Yale
School of Architecture—has been strong and
consistent for many years. The firm's cultural projects include a new addition to the
Rockefeller Arts Center at New York's SUNY
Fredonia and a fresh arts incubator, known
as NXTHVN, in New Haven, Connecticut.
Residential projects have also, at times,
overlapped with the art world. This was
very much the case with this apartment for
gallerist Marianne Boesky in West Chelsea,
New York. The three-bedroom apartment
was reworked with a softer and paler color
palette throughout, providing a fresh
context for the curation of both furniture
and art. Grass cloth was used on the walls
to add texture and as a backdrop for pieces
by artists including Damien Hirst, Adam
Helm, and Yoshitomo Nara, whose *Cosmic
Girl: Eyes Closed* (2008) forms a focal point
above the fireplace in the living room. This
key space features an Yves Klein table, filled
with a magenta pigment, rather than the
more familiar blue, a zigzag sofa in a gentle
lavender tone, and a pair of armchairs by
Holly Hunt (see p. 65).

Manhattan Townhouse

Sheila Bridges & David Hottenroth
New York City, New York (US), 2011

Interior designer Sheila Bridges—well known for her bold and playful use of pattern and color—is now based in New York's Harlem, which was the inspiration for her Harlem Toile de Jouy wallpaper, which is held in the collection of the Cooper Hewitt Smithsonian Design Museum. For the redesign of this Gramercy Park townhouse, dating from the 1850s, Bridges's clients wanted to create a family-friendly home that would be "beautiful but also liveable and comfortable." Architect David Hottenroth helped reconfigure the key living spaces on the ground floor, in particular, to create an easier and more informal sense of connection between them. Many original period features, including the ornate marble fireplaces, were retained. The main living room was painted a vibrant yellow—Farrow & Ball's Yellow Ground—echoed by the tones of the geometric Florence Broadhurst textile chosen to upholster the Art Deco sofa and armchairs. The dining room, which is now open to the kitchen, benefits from a pair of floor-to-ceiling French doors, dressed with striped silk curtains. Importantly, for a family with children, the space is relaxed and friendly yet still encourages the display of art—as well as glass, ceramics, and other treasures.

Park Avenue Apartment

Kelly Behun
New York City, New York (US), 2015

With its combination of seductive Russian Blue lacquered walls and a dazzling gold leaf ceiling, the library forms one of designer Kelly Behun's favorite spaces in this characterful Park Avenue apartment. Behun—who worked with hotelier Ian Schrager's design team, as well as Andrée Putman (see p. 257) and Philippe Starck, before founding her own New York studio—started the project with a blank canvas. Her client—a globe trotting art collector with a large, extended family of children and grandchildren—had bought two and a half apartments within a prestige Forties building on Park Avenue with the aim of creating a single new home to suit the needs of three different generations. There were no period details left at all, leaving Behun and her client to collaborate on adding interest through layers of color and pattern, as well as an engaging collection of artworks and furniture. In the library, for example, armchairs by Josef Hoffmann pair with a velvet banquette; the geometric carpet is by Stark and the photograph is by Bert Stern. Behun experimented with a range of blues here until she found a tone that reminded her client of the color she had loved in her previous home. "I really wanted to do the gold leaf ceiling, which is something that the client had not tried before," says Behun. "She brought the blue and I brought the gold and together they help make the space really special."

Greenwich Village Residence

Rafael de Cárdenas
New York City, New York (US), 2013

....

New York–based Rafael de Cárdenas is known for his adventurous approach to interior design, favoring bold colors and expressive forms, and a curated approach to furniture and modern art. This penthouse apartment in Manhattan's Greenwich Village suggests a degree of restraint in terms of color, with a gentle and neutral palette dominating many of the key spaces, yet in other respects the de Cárdenas hallmarks are much in evidence. The penthouse—a fusion of two earlier apartments—is situated in an elegant Art Deco building, with the sitting room being the most generously pro-portioned space in the home. De Cárdenas opted for a pale parquet floor here, while the ceiling becomes the key canvas for pattern: a custom mural of malachite swirls but in subtle whites and earthy browns. There is space enough for three distinct seating zones, with one arranged around an alcove facing the fireplace and two at each end of the room. Here, by the entrance to the kitchen, a pale-gray rug helps frame the seating arrangement, including a sofa by de Cárdenas and a sculptural chair with a golden frame by Mattia Bonetti; the abstract artwork over the sofa is by Isabelle Cornaro. The stairway, at the rear, offers a surprise burst of brilliant-blue carpeting.

100 UN Plaza

Leyden Lewis
New York City, New York (US), 2020

....

Brooklyn-based architect and designer Leyden Lewis runs his own practice, teaches at Parsons School of Design, and also exhib-its as a fine artist—which was an advantage on a recent New York project. Lewis was asked to redesign his clients' apartment in the UN Plaza, a Midtown highrise, which had last been refreshed during the Eighties. Despite its well-placed location and sublime cityscape views—including the Chrysler Building—the pied-a-tèrre's dated interiors required radical reinvention. During the redesign, the homeowners' own collection of art played a prominent role in the division of the interior space. Lewis set the kitchen inside a sculptural cube within the main living area. Here, a dining area and study sit at one end, where a framed photograph by Thomas Ruff forms a focal point. Flowing through into the central seating zone, art becomes more crucial with a series of pieces—including the eye-catching water-melon diptych—by artist Ana Mercedes Hoyos. The sequence of wooden stools alongside the white sofa also acts as tables and plinths for sculpture, while the darker monolith to one side—hosting a piece by artist William Kentridge—serves as a partial partition to the bedroom beyond.

Van de Weghe Townhouse

Annabelle Selldorf & D'Apostrophe Design
New York City, New York (US), 2014

Architect and designer Annabelle Selldorf founded her practice in New York in 1988 and has since exhibited extraordinary dexterity when it comes to shifts in scale. Her work encompasses major cultural projects—the firm came to prominence with renovation and opening of the Neue Galerie New York in 2001—and highly respected residential work. These projects include a number of commissions in Manhattan itself, where Selldorf was asked to reinvent this 1880s townhouse on the Upper East Side for art dealer Christophe Van de Weghe, his wife Anne-Gaëlle de Weghe, and their family. A radical rebuild behind the historic facade created the opportunity to increase ceiling heights throughout and introduce banks of glass to the rear of the five-story house, which overlooks a courtyard. Respectful references to the provenance of the building can be seen in the oval skylight over the stairway, with its crafted balustrade. The living spaces—with interiors by Francis D'Haene of D'Apostrophe Design—are contemporary and characterful. The formal living room features a seating area anchored by the fresh fireplace, and two vintage Paul Evans sofas with golden casings. Other mid-century references include a Forties armchair by Jean Prouvé (see p. 268) and an Alexander Calder mobile, while the white walls host works by Jean-Michel Basquiat.

River House

Studio Sofield
New York City, New York (US), 2016

Interior decorator William Sofield describes himself as a "Modernist by temperament and a historicist by training." He studied architecture and urban planning at Princeton University before founding his Manhattan-based Studio Sofield in 1996. Working with Irish-born architect Emma O'Neill, the atelier's portfolio spans architecture and interiors with clients including fashion designer and director Tom Ford, and artists Brice and Helen Marden. This extraordinary New York triplex overlooks the East River from a landmark, period apartment building. The residence benefits from an intrinsic sense of grandeur owing to the scale and proportions of the rooms, which have been likened to those of a Venetian palazzo. The living room is spacious enough for a series of seating zones, in the manner of a grand salon, and features floor-to-ceiling windows offering river views. In this lyrical space a large baroque-style mirror from antiques specialist Gabrielle Laroche reflects Lucian Freud's etching *Pluto Aged Twelve* (2000). Below is a Jansen sofa upholstered in powder-blue lambskin, while a pair of rope stools placed on a custom silk rug further enliven this richly layered space.

Belnord Residence

Anna Karlin
New York City, New York (US), 2021

London-born designer Anna Karlin and her New York–based atelier embrace a broad spectrum of mediums and disciplines, including furniture and lighting, textiles and glassware, graphics and set design, as well as interiors. Such cross-pollination is evident at the four-bedroom residence Karlin designed at the Belnord, an iconic 1908 apartment building on the Upper West Side, which inhabits an entire Manhattan block. Originally designed in an Italianate neoclassical style by architects Hiss and Weekes, the thirteen-story building was renovated and refreshed under the guidance of architect Robert A.M. Stern, while Rafael de Cárdenas (see p. 90) worked on many of the communal spaces. Karlin's model apartment draws on the original history and character of the building. A largely gentle color palette prevails with a few surprises. The living room, which has spaces for both seating and dining, characteristically mixes custom elements, antiques, and vintage pieces. Among the mix are dining chairs by Afra and Tobia Scarpa and a curvaceous mid-century sofa; but there are also pieces by Karlin herself, such as the sculptural Face Light in one corner, while the burnt-orange chair alongside provides a sunburst of standout color.

Blass Apartment

Bill Blass & MAC II
New York City, New York (US), 1985

The American fashion designer Bill Blass (1922–2002) established his own atelier in 1970, yet was also an influential tastemaker when it came to interiors. This Midtown penthouse at the top of an elegant building was designed by Sicilian American architect Rosario Candela (1890–1953). Blass was a tenant in the building for many years but after purchasing the penthouse in 1985 he enlisted the help of Mica Ertegun and Chessy Rayner (1931–1998) of MAC II to help remodel the apartment, which Blass continued to refine and edit during the Nineties. In the living room and the adjoining library, Blass introduced window shutters to avoid the need for curtains, while contrasting dark, polished timber floors with pale walls and simple, pared-down stone fire surrounds. These elegant, masculine spaces became a stage for Blass's collections of art and antiques, assembled with a discerning eye from dealers in the United States and Europe. In the living room, a pair of Regency daybeds flanked the fireplace, along with twin classical busts, highlighting the designer's love of symmetry. Yet there was also a generously sized white sofa at the center of the room, adding a more contemporary note and an emphasis on comfort as well as style.

Sui Apartment

Anna Sui
New York City, New York (US), 2017

The fashion designer Anna Sui has lived in Greenwich Village since the late Nineties, when she first took up residence in her late nineteenth-century apartment building. Sui grew up in Detroit, within a Chinese-American family, but moved to New York to study at the Parsons School of Design and has lived here ever since, while also launching her own label in 1980. The designer's original apartment was much photographed and praised around the turn of the millennium but eventually the golden opportunity arose to buy the apartment next door as well. Sui embarked on a three-year project to fuse the two apartments into one, while reinventing the interiors throughout and introducing a secret doorway in the library that connects them both together. Sui is famously obsessive about detail and craft. Color, pattern, and ornate decoration shine through in many of the spaces, with each room possessing a distinctive character of its own, while drawing on a myriad of references. Her love of chinoiserie wallpaper, for example, as seen in the living room, was partly inspired by pioneering postwar interiors created by interior designer Rose Cumming, featuring a similar combination of bucolic scenes floating on a shimmering metallic backdrop. Here, the mauve tones of the sinuous sofa and the upholstered chairs ties in with the florals, while the introduction of darker pieces of furniture creates a vibrant sense of tonal and textural contrast.

Calvin Klein Residence

Joe D'Urso
New York City, New York (US), 1975

....

After studying design at the Pratt Institute in New York and Manchester School of Art in England, Joe D'Urso went to work with designer Ward Bennett (see p. 116). Like his mentor, D'Urso became a polymath after opening his own studio in New York, in 1967, embracing interiors, furniture, and other design disciplines. He became famous for a High-Tech Seventies aesthetic style, using fresh and semi-industrial materials within pared-down spaces. His furniture is still in production today, including a collection for Knoll. One of his first residential commissions was a glamorous studio apartment that featured on the cover of *Interior Design* magazine. The home caught the eye of fashion designer Calvin Klein, who commissioned D'Urso in the mid-Seventies, when Klein's company was growing rapidly. Situated on Manhattan's 58th Street, the apartment featured lacquered white walls and ceilings that helped throw light through the interiors. D'Urso contrasted this shimmering backdrop with a dark tonal palette for the floors and much of the furniture, as seen here in the living room. The supersized black leather sofa anchors the space, complemented by a collection of pieces made with gleaming tubular steel frames. The designer's choice of track lighting, more commonly seen in stores and offices at the time, adds to the uncompromisingly inventive character of the space.

Hadley Apartment

Albert Hadley
New York City, New York (US), 1978

Parish-Hadley was an unlikely but highly successful partnership (see p. 85). On the one hand there was Sister Parish (1910–1994), an instinctive interior designer and well-connected socialite, whose work has been described as "American country" with a strong English influence, featuring a wealth of prints and chintz. Albert Hadley (1920–2012), on the other hand, studied architecture and then design at the Parsons School of Design. He joined forces with Sister Parish in 1964, just after her success on Jacqueline and John F. Kennedy's private quarters at the White House (see p. 123). "We complemented each other," said Hadley. "But I was a bit more adventurous." From

the late Seventies onward Hadley lived in this apartment on the Upper East Side. Hadley's generously scaled home office had a surprisingly contemporary character. There were custom bookcases to either side of a fireplace, with a sunburst mirror over the mantelpiece, while Hadley placed his Twenties desk on wooden floors, bare apart from a cowskin rug. An abstract painting sat between the unadorned windows, alongside a sculpture by Cornelia Kavanagh. Composed, and restrained, the space feels a world away from Sister Parish's more traditional aesthetic.

Palazzo Chupi

Julian Schnabel
New York City, New York (US), 2007

The artist, film director, and designer Julian Schnabel was first introduced to his home in Greenwich Village during the late Eighties by the artist Roy Lichtenstein. His relationship with the former perfume factory began by renting a loftlike space to serve as his painting studio, but this was just the beginning. In 1997 Schnabel managed to buy the three-story building and ten years later he completed its transformation into Palazzo Chupi—adding another nine floors, and drawing on a legion of design influences, including the Scrovegni Chapel in Padua with its Giotto frescoes, Venetian and Moorish architecture, and the work of United States architects Addison Mizner

and Stanford White. The palazzo is painted a distinctive "Pompeiian Red" and encompasses Schnabel's studio, a swimming pool, and five separate residences. In the artist's own duplex, the Italianate references shine through in combination with a blend of antique and contemporary furniture, as well as Schnabel's art collection, including work by Francis Picabia, Man Ray, Luigi Ontani and, of course, the artist himself. The primary bedroom, in particular, feels like a room in Venice, with its high ceilings, rose-pink walls, and ornate furniture, as well as the artworks, which has included Picasso's *Femme au chapeau* (1971).

Beekman Place Townhouse

Paul Rudolph
New York City, New York (US), 1978

Following his early years of practice in Florida and then his Connecticut years, combining major commissions on a monumental scale with teaching at Yale University, Paul Rudolph (1918–1997) moved on to New York. He established a new office in Manhattan, while living in a rented apartment within a period brownstone at 23 Beekman Place on the East Side. One of Rudolph's most original and inventive residential commissions was his own penthouse, built on top of the Beekman Place townhouse, which he bought in 1976. The steel-framed penthouse was arranged over four levels, with various shifts in height and volume. The complexity of the floor plan was enhanced by the layers of illusion created by the repeated use of reflective surfaces, including mirrored finishes on supporting columns and beams, as well as transparent materials such as Plexiglass, which Rudolph even used on the bottom of his bathtub, looking down into the kitchen below. The most theatrical spaces within this dream-like "quadriplex" included the living room, where the seating area, with its wraparound sofa flanked by walls of books, looked upward through an open atrium to the floors above. There have been a number of renovation projects at Beekman Place since Rudolph's death, while the house now has New York City Landmark status.

Berkus-Brent Duplex

Nate Berkus & Jeremiah Brent
New York City, New York (US), 2014

When it comes to the design of their own personal space, interior designers Nate Berkus and Jeremiah Brent are uniquely positioned: both run their own successful design practice, while they share a television show and, as a married couple, a home in New York. Their own home represents a rare opportunity for Berkus and Brent to collaborate and experiment freely with new ideas: "Our rule is that if it's really important to one of us, then we will try it," says Berkus. "Maybe it won't work every time, but if you just shoot down ideas, then it won't foster creativity." In around 2014, "home" for Berkus and Brent was a penthouse in Greenwich Village. The couple managed to combine two existing apartments to create a duplex, creating three bedrooms on the lower level, plus a family den, while the key living spaces were arranged on the floor above within a major process of renovation and renewal. Brent and Berkus adopted a gentle black-and-white palette for many of the key rooms, as seen in the living room, with its white walls, plasterwork ceilings, and linen curtains, which contrast with the stone fireplace and other darker notes. The gray rug on the pale parquet neatly frames the seating ensemble, with a Cassina sofa by Afra and Tobia Scarpa, also in white, alongside a pair of Fifties French armchairs.

Hendifar-Anderson Apartment

Apparatus
New York City, New York (US), 2018

The highly crafted lighting, furniture, and design objects by Jeremy Anderson and Gabriel Hendifar—founders of Apparatus—have tended to explore characterful, textural materials like marble, Carpathian elm wood, eel skin, leather, and horsehair. Anderson and Hendifar's own home, in the Flatiron District of Manhattan, adopts similarly rich narratives focused on artisanal craftsmanship and fine materials, which contrast with the semi-industrial character of this period apartment building. The tour de force is the loftlike "great room," where Anderson and Hendifar created a curving timber wall to help lightly delineate spaces, such as the dining area and kitchen from the entry hallway; a bucolic Thirties mural by artist Albert Emiel placed on the wall, creates a theatrical backdrop in the manner of a stage set. Custom timber shutters have been punctured with round peepholes, while the floors are in polished wood. An oval rug helps define the dining area at one end, with a marble dining table and Seventies chairs, while the seating area at the other is anchored by mid-century Milo Baughman sofas combined with a number of Anderson-Hendifar designs, including the cocktail tables and the Interlude cabinet.

Karan Apartment

**Donna Karan & Bonetti/Kozerski
Architecture
New York City, New York (US), 2004**

For fashion designer Donna Karan, texture
and materiality are key elements within
any space: "To me, texture is a way to add
an almost sculptural dimension to a room,
whether with a tactile fabric, like cashmere
or linen, or via a wall or floor surface,"
the designer has suggested. Karan's calm,
ordered, and pared-down New York residence, at the top of an Art Deco building
overlooking Central Park, was designed in
conjunction with architect Dominic Kozerski
of Bonetti/Kozerski Architecture. Part of the
design process involved mock-up walls and
prototype models, so that Karan could touch
and test every surface. An open and fluid
sense of connectivity ties the living spaces
of this spacious apartment together, while
also flowing out to a roof terrace alongside.
In the main living area, Karan chose travertine for the floors and Italian plaster for
the walls. A long plinth or platform, also
in travertine, runs alongside one side of
the space serving variously as a bench, a
display surface, and as a step to the terrace.
A choice of natural materials for cushions
and seating, including moleskin and linen,
softens the space throughout.

Stilin Loft

Robert Stilin
New York City, New York (US), 2010

Interior designer Robert Stilin divides his time between his home in the Hamptons and this apartment in SoHo, New York, which sits in a modern building designed by Gwathmey Siegel Associates Architects (see p. 114). Contextually, the town and country settings are radically different yet the interiors feel as though they are from the same hand. Modern art and photography play an important part in both of Stilin's residences, along with a blend of custom furniture and twentieth-century classics by designers such as Charlotte Perriand, Jean-Claude Duboys, and Poul Kjærholm. The apartment explores the contrast between white walls, which offer a suitable backdrop for Stilin's extensive art collection, and darker tones expressed in the wooden floors, rush matting, and the earthy colors of pieces such as the custom sofa in the living room and the accompanying armchairs. The dining room has the feel of a study, or library, with books stacked on every surface. The focal point is the dining table by Guillerme et Chambron, bordered by vintage chairs, and the graphic, supersized, twin prints by Wade Guyton on the wall behind it. The arresting pairing lends the room additional depth and drama.

Redd House

Miles Redd
New York City, New York (US), 2000

Interior designer Miles Redd's exuberant approach to color and pattern is evidenced by commissions ranging from a vacation retreat in the Bahamas (see p. 147), to a family mansion in Houston, Texas (see p. 61), described by Redd's clients as "a world's fair of decorating." Unsurprisingly then, the maximalist's own home—an 1820s townhouse in the NoHo neighborhood of Manhattan—is packed full of imagination and theater, referencing many of his favorite design masters, including Madeleine Castaing (see pp. 269 and 277) and Nancy Lancaster (see p. 213), as well as Bunny Williams (see p. 151), who Redd worked with for five years before setting up his own firm in 1998. The living room is a sumptuous salon, with satin-pink walls, a banquette in red velvet, and multiple artworks and treasures. But Redd's own personal Versailles, as he puts it, is his bathroom. This extraordinary, mirror-paneled room was originally designed in the Thirties by architect David Adler for an Illinois mansion. When the bathroom was torn out during a renovation, it was rescued by a salvage dealer and then by Redd, who shipped the room to Manhattan and reassembled it like a jigsaw puzzle. With its marble bathtub and sparkling walls, the room speaks of Art Deco–infused glamour.

Wolf Loft

Vicente Wolf
New York City, New York (US), 1993

....

The Cuban-born interior designer and photographer Vicente Wolf began living and working in New York during the Seventies. On his home in the Garment District of Manhattan he has said: "The first time I entered the space it just felt so New York with the right light and the right views." Wolf's home, on the eleventh floor of a semi-industrial building dating back to the Twenties, benefits from a sense of openness, which Wolf preserved as far as possible. Partitions have been minimized, while window treatments are simple to encourage the flow of light. Wolf, who is known for his relaxed interiors and the use of "mercurial" colors, painted the walls, floors, and ceilings white creating a soothing foundation. The neutral colors also allow Wolf's choice of art, photography, and furniture to be fully appreciated in a gallery-like setting. The corners of the loft, in particular, help to frame key spaces such as the main lounge, with its mix of contemporary, vintage, Asian, and custom furniture, while fitted shelves are used to display art; houseplants add a layer of greenery. The choice of pieces continues to change over time, with the canvas of the loft allowing for easy evolution.

Derian Residence

John Derian
New York City, New York (US), 2012

During his early twenties John Derian became fascinated by antiques and decorative paint techniques while living and working in Boston. When he moved to New York in the late Eighties and established his own design studio, Derian and a small team of artisans began by concentrating on decoupage, drawing inspiration from eighteenth and nineteenth century prints. Their work included glass plates, bowls, and other homewares, with Derian's collection expanding to embrace furniture, textiles, and lighting. Derian's Manhattan home for many years was this former artist's studio in an 1850s building, which provided a compelling collage of Derian's many passions. The pale walls possess a degree of characterful patina, but also form a backdrop for a curated choice of art and antique mirrors. The choice of furniture includes a daybed and a sofa by Derian, in combination with an ottoman coated in vintage Caucasian textiles, while cushions introduce additional pattern and texture throughout. "The way all the pieces interact in a home is important," Derian has said. "And you want to make sure the objects have space to breathe."

Geller House II

Marcel Breuer
Lawrence, New York (US), 1969

During the Sixties, architect and designer Marcel Breuer (1902–1981) began to move beyond the conventions of the International Style, replacing its rigid focus on linear geometry with more expressive and experimental designs exemplified by Geller House II. Breuer first met Bertram and Phyllis Geller back in the Forties, when he designed Geller House I (1946) in Lawrence, which sits just to the north of Atlantic Beach. The house was designed as a family home for the couple and their three young children but over twenty years later, the Gellers asked Breuer for a very different kind of home in the same neighborhood. Geller House II was designed with a parabolic shell structure, creating an overarching canopy that sheltered the spaces beneath. The front portion of the house was devoted to an open-plan "great room" facing the garden and an ocean view. The kitchen and dining area sat at one end, while at the other Breuer designed a conversation pit next to the fireplace. The upholstered red cushions for the integrated pit seating sang out against the gray flagstone floors, the exposed concrete roof, and the dark tones of the kitchen, creating a vivid contrast, while a collection of Flos Taraxacum Cocoon lights by Achille and Pier Giacomo Castiglioni floated from the ceiling like hovering satellites.

Amagansett House

Yabu Pushelberg
Long Island, New York (US), 2009

The Canadian designers George Yabu and Glenn Pushelberg split their work commitments between twin studios in Toronto and New York. Over recent years this has meant a collection of multiple homes, including a townhouse in Toronto (see p. 19), an apartment in Manhattan, and this ocean-side escape near Amagansett, Long Island. The designers, who share a long-standing love of the water, were tempted by the idea of a weekend and vacation retreat when they spotted an advertisement for a parcel of land among the dunes of the South Fork. They took some time to get to know the site and its weather patterns, before designing a two-story home that offers views out across the Atlantic. Guest bedrooms and a semisheltered veranda were positioned at ground level. In the key living spaces, timber walls and floors lend the interiors a relaxed and organic character suited to beachside living. The main seating area features a large L-shaped sofa by Frigerio Salotti facing both a custom fireplace and the ocean vista. Maritime notes come through in the choice of cushions and the large artwork by Hiroshi Senju, entitled *Waterfall*. Vintage pieces, such as the twin Joaquim Tenreiro armchairs and the leather campaign chair, complement the natural finishes and textures seen throughout.

Gwathmey House

Charles Gwathmey
Long Island, New York (US), 1966

The first house designed by architect Charles Gwathmey (1938–2009)—a commission from his parents—was, arguably, his most influential. Long before the Hamptons became a fashionable resort, painter Robert Gwathmey and his wife Rosalie, a textile designer, bought an acre (0.5 hectares) of land near Amagansett. They asked their son to design the new house, but their budget was limited to thirty-five thousand dollars. Charles realized that the only way to complete the project was to serve as lead contractor himself. The initial plan to build the house in concrete was shelved and Gwathmey turned to timber instead. For a relatively small house, Gwathmey introduced a wealth of ideas, creating a sculptural gray building floating on a green lawn, complemented later by an additional structure holding his father's studio. The main living area was largely double height, spilling out onto the adjoining terrace; a mezzanine gallery above held the primary bedroom. The combination of cedar and white walls was offset by the red, yellow, and black accents of the window frames. When Gwathmey eventually inherited the building himself, his choice of furniture included a pair of black Grand Confort armchairs by Le Corbusier and twin Wassily chairs by another Modernist master, Marcel Breuer (see p. 112), complemented by a large light-gray L-shaped sofa.

Huniford House

James Huniford
Long Island, New York (US), 2008

Having rented a house in the Hamptons for many years, interior and furniture designer James Huniford (see p. 80) eventually decided that he would like a place here of his own, eventually securing a beach house in a quiet Bridgehampton backwater. The house dates back to the 1860s, but much of its original character had been lost under later additions. Huniford began by stripping away these superfluous layers: "The greatest challenge for me was to keep it simple, authentic, and pure," said Huniford. "There is a bit of ruggedness to it and I love the country feel." In the living room, Huniford uncovered the original floorboards, ceiling beams, and a steel joist. He opted for a custom wall color that the designer calls "foggy summer squall," creating a pale celadon-blue backdrop. The mix of furniture includes self-designed pieces, such as the sofa, blended with rustic antiques, including the eighteenth-century English settle. Among the more playful touches is the giant pencil on the wall by the window, a piece of vintage Americana. Huniford also created a series of sculptural installations using repurposed pieces of agricultural salvage, as seen with the four metal discs hung in a line over the fireplace.

Springs House

Ward Bennett
Long Island, New York (US), 1968

One of the great American polymaths of the postwar period, Ward Bennett (1917–2003) trained as a sculptor under Constantin Brâncuşi in Paris and Louise Nevelson in New York, before embracing product and furniture design, creating more than a hundred pieces for Brickel Associates alone. There were also textiles, ceramics, jewelry, and interiors, including a Sixties apartment in Rome for Gianni and Marella Agnelli (see pp. 282 and 334), his own apartment in Manhattan's Dakota Building, and this Long Island retreat in East Hampton. Bennett's home was often compared to his furniture, with a pared-down aesthetic that spliced an innovative approach to structure with characterful, crafted materials. The main living space was topped by a square skylight, while retractable redwood walls to one side opened up to frame an open view out across the dunescape toward Accabonac Harbor. The main seating zone was partly defined by a set of floor runners reminiscent of Japanese *tatami* mats; the low coffee table and side table also hold echoes of Japan. The choice of furniture includes a pair of Ward Bennett model 1226 lounge chairs, produced by Brickel in ash and suede. The designer also opted for a simple hammock alongside them, offering a magical spot from which to enjoy the coastal panorama.

Adler-Doonan House

Jonathan Adler & Gray Organschi
Shelter Island, New York (US), 2010

Designer Jonathan Adler is America's leading advocate of joyful interiors, creating spaces infused with color, pattern, and texture. He began his career as a potter, selling his first collection to Barneys department store in the mid-Nineties. One of the most rounded and personal expressions of the distinctive Adler aesthetic is his own home on Shelter Island, shared with his husband, the English author Simon Doonan. The couple have owned a retreat here for many years, beginning with a Sixties A-frame cabin, but eventually decided to build a home of their own by the water's edge. Adler and Doonan worked with architects Gray Organschi, who designed a single-story, four-bedroomed house facing the water. The interiors offered Adler the opportunity to experiment with his own designs, as exemplified by the main living area where he designed a number of special pieces, including a concrete screen Adler made in his pottery studio that helps lightly separate the space from the entrance hall. Here, the embroidered cushions are also Adler designs; the wall hanging is by Andy Harman and the eye-catching firepit and hood are custom. Twin hanging wicker chairs add a characteristically playful touch. Doonan has described the overall look as "a blend of Big Sur bohemian and rich Ibiza hippie."

Water Island House

Jed Johnson & Alan Wanzenberg
Fire Island, New York (US), 1988

This enticing retreat on Fire Island is a collaboration between architect Alan Wanzenberg and his partner Jed Johnson (1948–1996), who began working together in the early Eighties. Johnson was famously a key member of Andy Warhol's Factory in New York before devoting himself to interior commissions, but his career was cruelly cut short in 1996 by the TWA Flight 800 plane crash off Long Island. It was left to Wanzenberg to continue work on their vacation escape situated on this picturesque barrier island, with Great South Bay on one side and the open Atlantic on the other. The beach house adopted a restrained and pared-down aesthetic, with a focus on texture, natural materials, and simple pleasures. The living room, for example, features oak floors, as well as bare wooden walls and ceilings, with pale, diaphanous curtains at the windows. A pair of timber-framed chairs by Charlotte Perriand, with rattan seats and backs, reinforce the organic palette, with soft-blue notes seen on the Swedish sofa, the cushions, and the doorframe as well as the ceramics displayed in the "blue alcove" to one side. Natural tones in combination with the setting itself create a deeply soothing environment.

Frank House

Andrew Geller
Fire Island Pines, New York (US), 1958

....

During the Fifties and Sixties architect Andrew Geller (1924–2011) designed a series of modest but imaginative beach cabins and vacation retreats on Long Island—with nicknames like Box Kite, the Cat, and the Milk Carton. In the mid-Fifties Rudolph Frank, the owner of an ice-cream enterprise, and his wife Trudy, an artist and illustrator, asked Geller to design a home for them at Fire Island Pines, a hamlet situated off the southern coast of Long Island. The Franks had recently been to Mexico where they had admired the Mayan temples. Geller took this as a point of inspiration, creating a mid-century temple of wood and glass that peers out over the trees. The house has recently been restored by a new owner, artist Philip Monaghan, and architects Larson Paul. In the light-filled living area, the seating area flows through to the dining area, with its Eero Saarinen table and Charles and Ray Eames dining chairs, illuminated by a George Nelson pendant lamp overhead. The new kitchen alongside can be lightly partitioned from the rest of the space by drawing across a sliding timber screen. The natural tones and textures of the joinery, walls, and floors combine with the greenery viewed from the large windows all around the house to create a restful, organic escape.

Oldham Residence

Todd Oldham
Milford, Pennsylvania (US), 2015

Following on from his first career as a fashion designer, Todd Oldham began to explore fresh opportunities in the wider world of design. Through his own atelier, Todd Oldham Studio, he began stepping into photography, television, publishing, furniture design, and interiors, with his own characterful retreat in Pennsylvania encapsulating many of these interests. The house was distinctive even before Oldham purchased the property during the late Nineties. The gardens had been used as a three-hole golf course and required extensive landscaping and planting, while the two-story, timber-clad house is tucked into the gently sloping topography, bordered by trees to the rear. Inside, there are multiple shifts in proportion and volume but also a strong sense of connectivity between the key living spaces, including the double-height living room. As evident elsewhere in the house, Oldham made the most of bolds colors and patterns here, with geometric carpet tiles and a wall mural painted above the focal point fireplace. The large L-shaped sofa to one side and the matching ottoman are Oldham designs for La-Z-Boy, while the sequence of framed bird prints on the wall are by mid-century artist Charley Harper, who is also the subject of a richly illustrated monograph edited by Oldham.

Nakashima Guesthouse

George Nakashima
New Hope, Pennsylvania (US), 1975

The master craftsman and woodworker George Nakashima (1905–1990) sought to give his materials, born of nature, a second life: "In order to produce a fine piece of furniture the spirit of a tree lives on," he said. Nakashima's workshops and family home on a farmstead located at New Hope, Pennsylvania, offered a rural setting in keeping with the designer's deep-rooted love of the natural world. Nakashima was also a talented architect, working with the pioneering organic Modernists Antonin and Noémi Raymond in Japan during the Thirties. The farmstead at New Hope was not only a bucolic atelier, but also a kind of laboratory where Nakashima was able to explore his ideas related to architecture, interiors, and design. The guesthouse, in particular, explored a fusion of Japanese and American influences, while drawing on natural materials throughout, particularly stone and wood. The "great room" featured a seating area around the fireplace and a dining area alongside, populated with pieces by Nakashima. The sliding *shoji* screens to one side disguise the galley kitchen, while a *tatami* room can be glimpsed through the open doorway by the fireplace. The space also features a substantial Nakashima-designed plank-backed daybed, which can be used either as a sofa or as a bed.

Esherick House

Louis Kahn
Philadelphia, Pennsylvania (US), 1961

Louis Kahn's (1901–1974) Esherick House, in the genteel Philadelphia neighborhood of Chestnut Hill, manages to combine a sense of Modernist monumentality—which Kahn is commonly associated with—and a particular sense of character and warmth. The house was commissioned by Margaret Esherick, who ran a bookstore nearby. In many ways, the program was modest, requiring a home for a single person. Yet Kahn, characteristically, managed to incorporate of wealth of ideas, and there are surprises throughout. These delightful subversions began at the front door, which was placed off center on the entry porch. Stepping inside, the entrance hall leads through to a spacious dining room, or to the double-height living room. Here, the craftsmanship of the interiors could be fully appreciated, seen in the joinery of the boxed central staircase and the balcony of the mezzanine gallery above. Other integrated elements included a library wall and a beautifully crafted custom kitchen, created by the original owner's uncle, wood craftsman Wharton Esherick (1887–1970). The current owners of the house have fully respected the provenance and character of the building, while introducing gentle updates and their own collection of vintage and mid-century furniture, combined with a number of more contemporary pieces.

Short Hills

Fawn Galli
Short Hills, New Jersey (US), 2017

The Manhattan-based interior designer
Fawn Galli grew up in California before
moving to Paris, where she eventually joined
the furniture department of the auction
house, Christie's. Settling in New York, Galli
then worked with Robert A.M. Stern and
Peter Marino (see p. 54) before establishing
her own studio in 2007, with emphasis on
characterful residential projects lifted by a
passion for pattern, texture, and—naturally—
carefully curated assemblies of furniture,
drawn from the Sixties and Seventies especially. The exterior architecture of this
new two-story house was designed by Douglas
Wright, referencing period shingle-coated
houses although with twenty-first century
touches, including an enticing cabana by
the swimming pool. Inside, a run of interconnected family spaces suggest Galli's love
of both color and pattern, with a lounge
arranged around a monolithic fireplace featuring a vivid double-sided sofa in purple
floating on a geometric carpet. A bar to
one side points the way through to a games
room and den, where an ethereal Florence
Broadhurst floral wallpaper lines the walls.
The gradated curtains and Berber style rug
here add to the varied layers of texture,
while the assortment of sculptural seating
includes twin armchairs by Marco Zanuso.

Kennedy Private Quarters

Sister Parish & Stéphane Boudin
Washington, D.C. (US), 1962

The White House was designed by Irish architect James Hoban (1755–1831) and was completed in 1800, becoming over time the most famous home in the world. In 1961 the new President Kennedy and his wife Jackie Kennedy moved in and renovated with style. The cost of the redecoration of their family quarters has been estimated at an extraordinary two million dollars; Jackie famously employed not just one interior designer but two. As a great Francophile, she turned to Stéphane Boudin (1888–1967), who designed the Duke and Duchess of Windsor's Paris residence in the early Fifties (see p. 252), for the State Rooms. Boudin was known for his vivid use of color and choice of French antique furniture—advised by collector Henry Francis du Pont. The Kennedys also wanted to recreate some of the look and feel of their former home in Georgetown, designed by the celebrated decorator Sister Parish (1910–1994), and asked her to focus on the private quarters—including the West Sitting Hall. Perhaps inevitably, tensions developed. After a dramatic falling out between Jackie and Parish, Boudin was invited back to rework a number of additional personal spaces. In February 1962, Jackie proudly unveiled the interiors via a televised tour broadcast by CBS.

Darryl Carter's Townhouse

Darryl Carter
Washington, D.C. (US), 1997

The former attorney Darryl Carter opened his eponymous design studio in Washington D.C. during the late Nineties. Around the same time, Carter bought a townhouse within the city's old diplomatic quarter. Dating back to 1910, the elegant Beaux Arts house was once home to the chancery of the sultanate of Oman yet played a vital part in the evolution of Carter's design philosophy. Throughout the house he adopted a calm base palette, which became the background for a thoughtful fusion of period pieces and modern art and design, creating sophisticated and timeless spaces. The living room, for example, validates Carter's belief that "white is generally the most sublime backdrop for beautiful objects." White walls and ceilings, as well as a pale carpet, provide a crisp canvas. A Twenties sofa sits alongside the windows, where Carter introduced shutters for simplicity, while the round table in front of the fireplace is a Regency piece. The polished concrete coffee tables are contemporary designs by artist Margaret Boozer, who also created a wall relief for one side of the room. Over the years the curation of these pieces has changed, allowing the purposeful evolution and the refinement of Carter's ideas.

Indian Bean

Rodman Primack
Louisville, Kentucky (US), 1998

....

The characterful interiors created by designer Rodman Primack, founder of New York–based design firm RP Miller, encompass homes in London, Mexico City, Guatemala, and Hawaii. Common threads include a thoughtful use of pattern and texture, as well as furniture with a history and provenance. In this respect, Primack was a perfect match for his clients in Kentucky with their own passion for twentieth-century Italian furniture and design. The estate of Indian Bean, which is named after the native catalpa tree common to this part of the United States, is owned by entrepreneur and museum director Stephen Reily and his partner, historian and writer Emily Bingham. Two of the most engaging spaces at the farmhouse are the dining room and the adjoining study/library. The dining area features a vivid floral wallpaper by Marthe Armitage and a round table by Jonathan Muecke teamed with Marcel Breuer cantilevered chairs. The study, meanwhile, features a collage of African wax-print wallpapers that run around the room and make their way behind the bookcases. Comfortable armchairs with vibrant Josef Frank upholstery add another playful note, standing on a custom Primack rug in recycled rope. The result is an enticingly escapist library that combines both personality and purpose.

Aldridge & Followill House

Pierce & Ward
Nashville, Tennessee (US), 2018

....

Having joined forces in New York back in 2012, interior designers Louisa Pierce and Emily Ward founded their own design atelier and moved to Nashville. With their focus on glamorous but comfortable eclecticism, Pierce & Ward have won an equally glamorous clientele, including the model Lily Aldridge and her husband, Kings of Leon frontman Caleb Followill, who was born in Tennessee. The designers and their clients met when Aldridge and Followill first settled down in Nashville, collaborating on the design of the couple's shared apartment. Characteristically, the design inspiration for this project—a Thirties house in a Tudor Revival style—were myriad, including mid-century notes, Moroccan influences, English-country style, and a touch of Arts and Crafts. The living room encapsulates the idea of sophisticated comfort, with its multiple layers of character and interest bonded by color, shape, and texture. Twin arches, either side of the window, frame bookcases and display surfaces, backed in a teal blue that stands out against the predominantly white walls. The teal highlights continue with the curtains and the sink-in twin armchairs, while more playful touches include the rattan hanging chair to one side and the zodiac pendant light by Visual Comfort.

Curtis House

Lee Ledbetter & Nathaniel Curtis
New Orleans, Louisiana (US), 1963/2013

From its modest beginnings in Louisiana in 1947, the architectural firm Curtis & Davis, founded by Nathaniel C. Curtis (1917–1997) and Arthur Q. Davis (1920–2011), grew into a major enterprise; the practice famously designed the New Orleans Louisiana Superdome in 1975. The Curtis House was designed in the Sixties by Curtis for himself, his wife Frances, and their seven children in the Uptown neighborhood of New Orleans. He designed a triptych of mid-century-style, steel-and-glass pavilions arranged around courtyard gardens and patios. In 2013 the Curtis family sold the house to another architect and designer, Lee Ledbetter, who undertook a gentle restoration process. The main living spaces are lifted by the connections to the courtyard and the rich quality of natural light, while the white brickwork of the boundary walls provides a neutral but textural backdrop for Ledbetter's thoughtful choice of furniture and art—including a vintage Florence Knoll sofa and a pair of brass armchairs by Harvey Probber. In this context even modest bursts of color stand out, from the cushions on the sofa to the artwork on the wall by Robert Helmer.

Rogers House

Peter Rogers & Chuck Palasota
New Orleans, Louisiana (US), 2012

During his childhood, growing up in Mississippi, creative director Peter Rogers would take regular trips to New Orleans with his family. Formerly based in New York, he eventually decided to relocate there, settling on a characterful French Quarter period house, complete with a spacious courtyard garden. One of Rogers's key ambitions, supported by interior designer Carl Palasota and restoration advisor Chuck Ransdell, was to turn the former dining room at the front of the house into a "treillage"—a French-style garden room, with walls decorated in trelliswork. For the wall color, Rogers opted for a soothing pea-green combined with a black-and-white chequerboard floor. A custom sofa was placed to face the French windows, while a mesmerizing painting of a heron in flight by artist Simon Gunning floated on the trellis. On the stairway, Rogers assembled a collection of black-and-white photography by Richard Avedon and others, drawn from ad campaigns that he was involved in as a creative director. The combination of soft greens and a black-and-white palette creates a quasi-opulent atmosphere that is in keeping with the context of the French Quarter.

Trammell Shutze House

Tammy Connor
Atlanta, Georgia (US), 2016

In the city of Atlanta, neoclassical houses designed by architect Philip Trammell Shutze (1890–1982) are much in demand. They have a unique Beaux Arts sensibility, reflecting the architect's years studying architecture in Europe before eventually settling in Atlanta. Interior designer Tammy Connor has worked on the restoration of a number of Trammell Shutze houses, including this elegant example, set in a generous garden. When Connor's client and her family decided to relocate from London to Atlanta they viewed five of the architect's houses from the Twenties and Thirties before setting their hearts on this one. The key challenge was to make the house more family friendly, adding more playful touches that would help to balance out the formality of the original architecture. The welcoming atmosphere is established in the entrance hall, where Connor restored the gracious, winding stairway and introduced a marble floor that she discovered on the architect's original drawings but had been left unrealized. A collection of seventeenth- and eighteenth-century Italian artworks, inherited by Connor's client, grace the walls of the stairway while the mid-century bronze Sputnik chandelier adds an unexpected but delightful element, which speaks to the thoughtful marriage of tradition and modernity.

Hable Smith House

Susan Hable Smith
Athens, Georgia (US), 2009

Textile designer Susan Hable Smith and her family fell for the charms of this early twentieth-century cottage in Athens while they were still based in New York City—the project ultimately proved to be such a success that the family decided to move to Georgia full time. Given Hable Smith's particular love of color and pattern, both play a strong role in her home. The theatrical dining room, for example, adopts a pink palette seen in the graphic wallpaper and rug, while elsewhere, including the kitchen, pale blues and soft lilac-purple tones put in an appearance. One of the most dynamic spaces in the house is the family living room, dominated by blues and greens. The walls are in Oval Room Blue by Farrow & Ball, while the sofa is coated in a sea-blue pattern designed by Hable Smith. The swirling pattern of the curtains, also by the designer, adds a kinetic quality to the space, echoed by the wave sculpture by the window, which was originally created as a stage prop for an opera. The green Belgian armchairs add just a subtle sense of contrast, enhanced by the greenery of the garden, which is framed by the three generously sized windows.

Klein Residence

David Piscuskas
Palm Beach, Florida (US), 2012

Over recent years architect David Piscuskas
and his firm, 1100 Architect, have created—
among many other projects—a standout
sequence of waterside houses. They include
homes on Long Island, the Japanese island
of Ikema and this engaging inner-coast
retreat in Palm Beach, Florida. Here, photographer and author Kelly Klein secured a
parcel of land and asked Piscuskas to design
a fresh family home. The new, single-story
residence opens up to the rear garden
and the Intercoastal Waterway with a fluid
sequence of living spaces at the center and
bedrooms in the wings to either side. The
interiors of the house combine a natural
sense of warmth with a sophisticated beach
house feel. Timber ceilings and joinery in
the main living and dining area contrast with
white stucco walls, while a coir rug helps
define the seating zone. The choice of furniture includes a custom oak dining table
by Lars Bolander and seating from Donna
Karan's Urban Zen collection (see p. 104),
while the choice of photography on the walls
is drawn from Klein's extensive collection.
The wall of glass to the adjoining veranda
retracts, allowing free-flowing connection between inside and outside, with the
veranda itself serving as an extension of the
living space, including a fresh-air seating
zone arranged around an outdoor fireplace.

Weishaupt House

Martin L. Hampton & Stephan Weishaupt
Miami, Florida (US), 1932/2013

Along with designers George Yabu and Glenn Pushelberg (see pp. 19, 113 and 356), Stephan Weishaupt is the cofounder of Avenue Road, the furniture company largely based in Toronto, Vancouver, and New York. But as Miami became an important port of call for the business, Weishaupt was keen to establish a satellite there. The opportunity arose from a 1932 Art Deco villa, designed by architect Martin L. Hampton (1890–1950), which serves both as Weishaupt's home from home and an occasional showcase for Avenue Road furniture. Weishaupt embarked on a gentle restoration, or "freshening up," of the two-story house and its garden; the floor plan and original features were fully respected. One of the most stylish spaces is the living room, with its supersized porthole window looking out onto the verdant gardens, echoed by the green terrazzo floors and skirting. The rug by Kelly Wearstler (see p. 42) softens the space, while the choice furniture around the fireplace includes an Unam armchair with a woven back and marble-topped coffee tables by Sebastian Herkner, along with a standout burnt-orange Serpentine sofa by Vladimir Kagan.

Baratta Duplex

Anthony Baratta
Miami, Florida (US), 1982

Southampton, Long Island–based interior designer Anthony Baratta is known for his bold and uncompromising use of color. His own duplex apartment in Miami, which he uses as a weekend retreat, offered the perfect setting to realize a design full of vivid, sunshine colors. The primary bedroom, for instance, features a custom bed by Baratta with a marshmallow headboard of white-padded disks set against hot-red walls and flanked by a pair of Damien Hirst spot paintings. The dining room houses a wall mural with geometric flashes of white and yellow, inspired by the work of mid-century designer Alexander Girard. The spacious living room offers a masterclass in maximalism, while realizing Baratta's maxim: "Color is everything." Here, the walls are coated in a red-orange vinyl coating while a collection of abstract ink-drop paintings by artist Ceal Floyer hang over a custom Baratta Bolster Arm sofa in bright orange. Other highlights include the target rug, a pair of sculptural Jan Bočan armchairs, along with a Seventies Boomerang desk by Maurice Calka and a Milo Baughman chaise longue, both in bright yellow. Such playful pieces add rich mid-century notes to a space with a big personality.

Versace Mansion

Gianni Versace
Miami, Florida (US), 1994

The unique style developed by the Italian fashion designer Gianni Versace (1946–1997) encapsulated the hedonism of the Eighties. Purposefully overstated, excessive, and explicit, he combined inspiration from Greco-Roman classicism, Pop art, and the worlds of film and theater. In 1992 Versace bought a Miami Beach, Spanish Revival–style mansion—built in 1930 in for Alden Freeman, the heir to an oil-industry fortune. The extraordinary home comprised three living rooms and eight bedrooms, and required a team, including Palm Beach–based designer Terry Scott, to complete the project. Versace's final interiors were suitably opulent and expressive. The centerpiece was the Moroccan-style courtyard, with its tiled floors and central fountain, which became a vast outdoor room overlooked by the observatory that topped the house. Elsewhere, murals graced the walls and ceilings of the primary bedroom, while Versace fabrics layered the bed and choice seating. The ornate character of the original architecture fused with Versace's flamboyant aesthetic approach throughout, creating a famous hymn to maximalism. Following Versace's assassination at home in 1997, the house became a hotel and readopted its original name, Casa Casuarina.

Aparicio House

Carlos Aparicio
Miami, Florida (US), 2013

Architect, designer, and gallerist Carlos Aparicio bought his home in Miami without viewing it. The decision came after glimpsing some pictures of the Thirties house with its charming Palladian facade flanked by towering palm trees. Largely based in New York, Aparicio was looking for a second residence close to the beach and, with a love of sea and sun, was deeply tempted by the Surfside setting. His new residence offered an opportunity for a fresh winter escape, but only after a major renovation. Aparicio stripped back the interiors of the U-shaped house with the aim of creating a central open-plan living area, while forging a renewed sense of connection with the private gardens to the rear, including a new swimming pool and terraces. A series of small rooms was amalgamated to create the sweeping living room, fitted with pale-coral limestone floors and uplifting, neutral tones for the walls and curtains. Aparicio introduced a number of twentieth-century French and Scandinavian pieces of furniture, including a Jean-Michel Frank blue silk-coated armchair and cocktail table by the custom sofa, as well as a pair of chaise longues. Scandinavian influences come from the Swedish rugs and a piece by Danish sculptor Jens Jakob Bregnø.

Court House

Terence Riley & John Keenen
Miami, Florida (US), 2005

For many years architect, educator, and writer Terence Riley (1954–2021) was based in New York, where he was chief curator of the architecture and design department at the Museum of Modern Art. He was initially tempted to Miami as a getaway from Manhattan, but when offered the directorship of the Pérez Miami Art Museum in 2006, he made the fulltime relocation. By then, Riley had already designed and built his own house in Miami Design District. Assisted by John Keenen, coprincipal at their joint practice K/R (Keenen/Riley), Riley took inspiration from a series of unbuilt houses by Ludwig Mies van der Rohe (see p. 65) created around the idea of internal courtyards. The twin, single-story pavilions that make up the Court House are separated by a central courtyard. A primary seating area arranged to one side of the largely open-plan living space looks into this secret court. Here, as elsewhere in the home, contemporary furniture coexists with striking pieces of modern art. A Campana Brothers armchair, made of recycled toys, is positioned alongside a Zanotta sofa and a colorful array of circular tables and stools by Maya Lin for Knoll. The artwork by painter Tim Bavington, titled *Unicorn*, provides a vivid strip of color that stands out against the muted tones of the rug here.

Central America

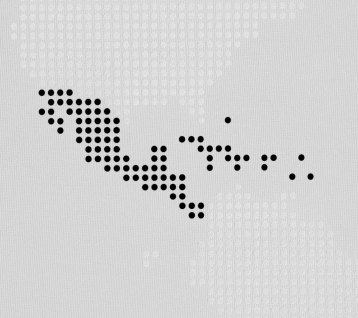

Casa Grande

Ken Fulk & Victor Legorreta
Baja California (MX), 2018

....

An original collaboration between Mexican architect Víctor Legorreta and the American interior designer Ken Fulk resulted in this extraordinary, breezy new home on the Baja California peninsula. The family that commissioned the waterside vacation home desired a retreat that would be well suited to hosting celebrations. They wanted the design to be "unlike any they had seen," taking inspiration from the setting and its sea views. Having long admired the work of the influential Mexican architect Ricardo Legorreta (1931–2011) the family asked his son Víctor, who now heads up the practice, to design Casa Grande. The heart of the building is a generously scaled courtyard, the surrounding walls painted hot pink, with a shimmering pool of water at its center flanked by palms. Walls of glass slide back to connect this outdoor room to the double-height sitting room, which features pale stone floors and creamy plaster walls. Here bursts of color and pattern mingle with natural textures, as seen in the macramé-like chandeliers by Alex Randall. In the living room, Fulk covered built-in banquette seating with an array of character-filled Mexican textiles; he introduced the mismatched freestanding chairs as if they were pieces of jewelry adorning the space. This room flows freely onto the pool terrace, and offers a tantalizing vista through sliding glass doors of the azure ocean beyond.

Casa Luna

Manolo Mestre
Costa Careyes (MX), 2001

....

Situated on the Pacific coast, Casa Luna is a vibrant modern take on the *palapa*, a vernacular Mexican shelter that is often open sided and topped with a canopy of palm leaves. "One of the unique things about a *palapa* is that it creates this cathedral-like structure that allows the home to breathe," says architect Manolo Mestre. He designed this vacation home for a Los Angeles–based family that wanted a retreat in these tranquil, picturesque surroundings. The house combines natural, organic textures, such as palm fronds and timber, with more robust materials, like the concrete used for the walls and floors. Yet even these more modern surfaces have a rounded quality and a neutral patina, creating a tactile canvas for introducing color and pattern. The *palapa* forms a vast umbrella over the main sitting room, which flows out onto the terraces facing the ocean. Mexican arts and crafts are incorporated within and without— for example, in the vivid blue painting by artist Sergio Hernández, which forms a focal point in the sitting room; and an Aztec-inspired bird of paradise inlaid into the terrace floor.

Guadalajara House

Alejandra Redo
Guadalajara (MX), 2015

....

This dynamic family home on the green edge of the Mexican city of Guadalajara makes the most of its verdant hilltop setting. The two-story house is anchored to the steep side of the hill, with views down to the gardens and tennis court in the valley, as well as out over the treetops. This vivid green backdrop gives the principal living spaces the feel of a tree house. The family asked Mexico City–based interior designer Alejandra Redo to introduce a sense of warmth and character that would help soften the distinctly modern outline of the home's architecture and fit in well with the natural drama of the surroundings. One of the most engaging spaces in the house is the glass-sided living/dining room. Here Redo created two distinct zones with the placement of Persian rugs on the polished concrete floors. One zone is the main seating area, where the deep hues of the Maxalto sofas are offset by two crimson chairs that offer a more playful note. At the opposite end of the spacious room is a dining zone, where a sculptural contemporary chandelier hovers over the Eero Saarinen dining table. This part of the house offers access to a glass elevator, used to reach the tennis court and gardens below.

Casa Arcadia

Alix Goldsmith Marcaccini
Cuixmala (MX), c. 1985

....

In the early Eighties the financier Sir James
Goldsmith (1933–1997) and his family bought
Cuixmala, a sprawling estate in a large
nature reserve alongside the Pacific coast.
With the help of architect Robert Couturier,
Goldsmith built a waterside palace known
as La Loma, or Casa Cuixmala, as well as a
series of guest lodges and villas within this
tropical dreamland with its own private
beaches, wild zebras, and a rich array of
birdlife. Today Goldsmith's daughter, Alix
Goldsmith Marcaccini, and her husband,
Goffredo, manage Cuixmala, with many parts
of it open to visiting guests. The Marcaccinis'
own private villa, Casa Arcadia, was one
of just a few existing buildings, which Alix
remodeled, along with its many terraces
and outdoor rooms. The character of the
interiors is partly defined by the sequence
of vaulted terra-cotta-hued brick ceilings
in Catalan style, which contrast with the
white polished cement floors. The spacious
living room features built-in sofas combined
with traditional Mexican *equipale* armchairs.
The space is rich in textiles gathered
by the Marcaccinis on their many travels,
including Indonesian blankets draped on
the chairs and lengths of Fijian tapa cloth
mounted on the far wall.

Casa Senosiain

Javier Senosiain
Naucalpan de Juárez (MX), 1984

....

In the city of Naucalpan de Juárez,
slightly northwest of Mexico City, Javier
Senosiain—a key figure in the organic
architecture movement—has constructed
a unique biomorphic home. Tucked into
the hillside like a sleeping creature or
a partially submerged sea monster, the
sinuous, molded concrete house twists and
turns. Senosiain folded the house into the
contours of the site like a piece of Land Art.
Vast curving windows and apertures, which
have the look of open mouths or eyes, serve
to introduce light and air deep into the
winding body of the beast. Internally, there
is hardly a straight wall or a right angle
to be found. The rounded shapes of every
room led Senosiain, inevitably, to create
custom furniture and integrated designs,
such as bookshelves, wardrobes, and seating
that have been woven into the structure
of the walls. A prime example is the main
living room, where a long, fitted sofa runs
along one wall and under the vast window
looking out onto the garden. The few
freestanding pieces here include a handcrafted timber coffee table, a wicker chair
suspended from the ceiling, and a chair
in the shape of a hand by the Mexican sculptor Pedro Friedeberg.

Casa Legorreta

Ricardo Legorreta
Mexico City (MX), 1997

The masterful Mexican Modern architect Ricardo Legorreta (1931–2011) described himself as a "romantic." Like Luis Barragán (see pp. 144 and 145), with whom he is often compared, Legorreta combined respect for Modernism with a love of Mexican culture and vernacular architecture, both indigenous and Hispanic. This was expressed in his approach to proportion, scale, landscape, light, and color. His own home in Mexico City communicates Legorreta's design philosophy on a much more intimate scale than many of his other major commissions, which included hotels, cathedrals, and museums. Situated in the leafy Las Lomas district of Mexico City, Casa Legorreta is a Cubist architectural composition designed with just a handful of key spatial elements. The architect created a fluid and informal set of interconnecting volumes for living, eating, and working. These spaces are full of books, art, and color, particularly reds, ochres, and other organic, earthy tones. In Legorreta's study, square shutters made of a tropical hardwood from southern Mexico have been used against the windows. This room looks across another important and integral part of the house: the courtyard. A wall of steel-framed glass helps to frame this hidden space created in conjunction with the artist Francisco Toledo (1940–2019).

Casa Barragán

Luis Barragán
Mexico City (MX), 1947

....

The godfather of modern Mexican architecture, Luis Barragán (1902–1988), nurtured a deep-rooted love of color. An artist as much as an architect, he understood how it could transform both architecture and interiors. There was a sculptural minimalism to much of his work, yet it was never cold or severe, because of his ability to infuse depth and delight through planes of intense color—particularly the vivid pinks and earthy reds that we tend to associate with Mexico, going back to its *haciendas* and *pueblos*. Barragán's houses were, arguably, the most important expression of many of his key ideas about space, light, color, and form. From the street, Barragán's own home felt largely closed and hidden away, although hints and promises were provided by the planes of color on the exterior walls. The house only unfolded and revealed itself beyond the entrance hall, with its mixture of single- and double-height spaces, connections to the secret courtyard garden—complemented by a roof terrace at the top of the house—and the rich use of planes of different hues, as seen in the stairway. Here a wall of soft pink invigorated the space while a gold-leaf painting by painter, sculptor, and friend Mathias Goeritz (1915–1990) added a shimmering, enigmatic focal point at the turn of the staircase.

Cuadra San Cristóbal

Luis Barragán
Mexico City (MX), 1968

Along with color, another of Luis Barragán's greatest passions was the garden. A love of outdoor spaces was triggered during the architect's childhood when he noted not only the beauty of Mexico's villages and churches but its fountains, ponds, and patios. His respect for the natural world helped to set him apart from contemporaries working in the International Style, who were not always so sensitive to context. Gardens, courtyards, and outdoor rooms played an important part in all of Barragán's residential designs, including his own house (opposite). But one of the most rounded and uplifting exemplars of the fusion of architecture and landscape is surely Cuadra San Cristóbal on the north-western edge of Mexico City. Here, Barragán was commissioned by Folke Egerström to design not just a house but also a compound with stables for the family's thoroughbred horses. Horses can be added to the list of Barragán's greatest loves, earning San Cristóbal a special place in the architect's affections. The compound is a village in miniature where the family home is a white, Cubist family home—dressed with custom pieces, like Barragán-designed benches and his Miguelito chairs (1951)—in contrast to the bold pink and red forms that delineated the various courtyards outside.

Casa Reyes

Pedro Reyes
Mexico City (MX), 1980/2015

Before establishing himself as an artist, Pedro Reyes trained as an architect at the Ibero-American University in Mexico City. He designed this house for himself and his wife, fashion designer Carla Fernández—whose fashion house is focused on pre-serving and revitalizing indigenous textile traditions in Mexico—together with an adjacent studio and workshop. The Eighties building is in the neighborhood of Coyoacán, south of central Mexico City. Reyes decided to radically remodel the building in a neo-Brutalist style over time, making the most of the textural character of concrete and stone—installed by local artisans—while exploring multiple shifts in the height and volume of the main living spaces. At the heart of Reyes and Fernández's home is a multifunctional double-height zone with a vast library wall to one side, which spans two levels; a stairway leads up to a mez-zanine walkway that is used to access the uppermost shelves. Within this huge open room, Reyes designed a raised platform that serves as both a sitting room and a kind of gallery for displaying art, such as a sculp-ture of a supersized head of Vladimir Lenin. Much of the furniture here was also designed by Reyes, while Fernández introduced color through her choices of indigenous Mexican textiles.

Highlowe

Alessandra Branca
Harbour Island (BS), 2013

....

One of the smallest but most tempting islands
in the Bahamas, Harbour Island, which is
solely accessible by boat from neighboring
Eleuthera, is much loved for its long beaches,
colorful houses, and escapist quality. The
Italian-born, Chicago-based interior designer
Alessandra Branca was so taken with the
island's charms that she decided to build a
vacation home here for herself and her family.
The residence is on a secluded high point
that offers views across the palm trees to
the sea beyond. Branca designed a house of
two parts, with the primary residence overlooking the garden, terraces, and swimming
pool. Known for her love of color, Branca
chose a gentle red-and-white theme for many
of the key spaces, such as the double-height
living room, which features campaign chairs
upholstered in a Schumacher stripe of
Branca's design. The color scheme continues
in cheerful outdoor spaces, such as the elevated veranda with an open vista of the lush
surroundings. Here the red-and-white theme
echoes the color of the woodwork on the
Chinese Chippendale–style railings. Textiles
with coral red accents combine with a vintage
French rattan chair and an RH sofa, adding
natural textures to the mix.

Great Abaco House

Tom Scheerer
Great Abaco Island (BS), 2015

....

Tom Scheerer describes his Bahamian
escape as a "barefoot" kind of house. The
New York–based interior designer has been
spending time in the Bahamas for many
years and previously had a beach house
on Harbour Island to the south. Then he
discovered a sublime setting on Great
Abaco, within a stone's throw of the beach
but bordered by palm trees and other greenery. He designed the home as a collection
of modest pavilions with hipped tiled roofs
and whitewashed walls. Like a village in miniature, these pavilions are punctuated by
terraces, courtyards, and outdoor rooms.
For the low-maintenance interiors, Scheerer
opted for a beach-house aesthetic that
blends practicality, restraint, and elegance.
The floors throughout are made of concrete
mixed with sand, while the walls are painted
a soft, creamy white. Within these soothing surroundings, even modest touches of
texture and color shine out, with an emphasis on natural materials and finishes. One
of the most delightful spaces is the dining
room, with its high ceilings and a gracefully
spiraling pair of antique kudu horns
above the fireplace. A set of vintage chairs
surrounds an Eero Saarinen Tulip table,
and the ensemble is subtly grounded with
a hemp rug.

Pineapple Hill

Miles Redd
Lyford Cay (BS), 2012

The American designer Miles Redd is well known for his exuberant approach to pattern and color. He is one of the great contemporary maximalists, never afraid to say less is a bore. This sumptuous vacation home in the Bahamas offered a liberating context in which he could express himself to the full. The owners offered Redd carte blanche following the successful outcome of an earlier commission to design the interiors of their principal residence in Texas. Redd's clients bought Pineapple Hill, which was scarcely ten years old, in 2011. In Redd's glamorous design, almost every space in the house is a hymn to playful patterns and uplifting ideas. A blue-and-white palette is repeated in many of the principal rooms, including the dining room with a tentlike ceiling. This space is riotously clad with an Oscar de la Renta for Lee Jofa fabric and features a chandelier by Stephen Antonson and two crisp white plaster columns topped with urns. In the media room, a blue-and-white wall pattern by decorative artist Chris Pearson contrasts with a fuchsia sofa, echoed by items such as lampshades and throws, while the art picks up on the twin themes of nautical adventures and natural wonders.

Terrenia

Lulu de Kwiatkowski
Lyford Cay (BS), 2016

Artist and textile designer Lulu de Kwiatkowski grew to love Lyford Cay on New Providence island in the Bahamas as a child. Her late father, Henryk, bought a house here in the Seventies after making his fortune in the aviation industry, and he asked the celebrated New York interior decorator Sister Parish (1910–1994) to design the interiors. When de Kwiatkowski was drawn back to Lyford Cay in 2016, she and her husband happened to visit another house nearby that was for sale and fell for its charms. Terrenia was originally designed by architect Henry Melich around 1970, with interiors by Alain Demachy and gardens by Russell Page (1906–1985). The house had been rather neglected and was in poor condition, but de Kwiatkowski saw its potential. She opened up the house, redesigning the interiors and making the most of outdoor rooms, such as the veranda overlooking the back garden. Ceilings were raised where possible, and walls in many of the communal spaces were painted a crisp white that creates the perfect back-drop for de Kwiatkowski's own artworks and a number of other treasured pieces. The breezy family room, in particular, is an exuberant space where a large blue-and-white screen designed by the artist is joined by a colorful collection of her framed prints. Overhead, the Aerin for Visual Comfort chandelier is a playful ensemble of white glass spheres.

Round Hill Residence

Ralph Lauren
Montego Bay (JM), 1987/1996
....

Ralph Lauren's own homes have always
played an important role in conveying the
idea of a dream lifestyle encapsulated by
the designer's fashion and homeware
collections. They include multiple residences
in the United States, such as his ranch
in Colorado (see p. 57), and this serene
Jamaican hideaway. Ralph and his wife,
Ricky, designed their Caribbean retreat in
two distinct phases. During the late Eighties
they bought their first property, overlooking
Montego Bay, within the Round Hill resort,
which includes a range of villas and a small
hotel. This first house, known as High Rock,
dated back to the Fifties and required
a major redesign, which the Laurens set in
motion while building a new swimming pool
and a spacious screening room. Then in
1996 the Laurens bought a second house
closer to the beach known as White Orchid
and, once again, embarked on a redesign.
Here they opted for an aesthetic that Lauren
has described as "clean, barefoot, and luxurious," dominated by a palette of uplifting
whites and neutrals, along with occasional
blue notes echoed by the adjacent pool and
the sea views. The residence is open, light,
and spacious, with sun decks and terraces
facing the ocean; the Laurens have compared their enjoyment of White Orchid to
the experience of living on a deluxe boat.

Casa Guava

Celerie Kemble
Playa Grande (DO), 2015
....

Designer Celerie Kemble has described
designing the Playa Grande Beach Club,
including her own family retreat here, as
her once-in-a-lifetime "fantasy project."
The setting is certainly picture-postcard
perfect, with Playa Grande sitting between
a turquoise sea and acres of verdant jungle
on the northern coast of the Dominican
Republic. For Kemble, who runs the New
York office of the family interior design firm,
the project encompassed the Beach Club
itself as well as a collection of bungalows
and her own two-story vacation home, Casa
Guava. For her design of the architecture
and interiors, she drew inspiration from
the local vernacular, along with Palm Beach
design, particularly the home designed by
her mother, Mimi Maddock McMakin, who
founded Kemble Interiors in Florida during
the early Eighties. Casa Guava adheres to
the romantic tropical aesthetic that Kemble
developed for the Beach Club as a whole,
but with a more personal touch. She chose
a pale-green-and-white theme for the living
room, where white walls and floors combine
with locally made verdigris-copper lights
shaped like pineapple tops. Artworks and
textiles, including the upholstery of the
Kemble-designed twin chairs facing the
French doors, add summery splashes of
pattern and color.

La Colina

Bunny Williams & John Rosselli
Punta Cana (DO), c. 1997

Interior designer Bunny Williams and her husband, antiques dealer John Rosselli, are widely revered as two of the most influential American tastemakers. After spending just over twenty years with the legendary New York firm Parish-Hadley, Williams launched her own eponymous design studio in 1988. Williams and Rosselli were first shown the Punta Cana spot where they decided to build La Colina by their friend, fashion designer Oscar de la Renta, who owned a beachside home nearby. Seduced by the setting, the couple enlisted architect Ernesto Buch to help realize their ideas for the house, which fuses the scale of a grand Palladian villa with a profusion of garden rooms. Williams designed each of the house's six bedrooms with a dedicated color palette in mind, from sunshine yellows to minty greens. Some of Rosselli's antiques from his former farmhouse in New Jersey add to the character-filled layers of art and furniture. But it's the calming spaces along the loggia, including a fresh-air sitting and dining room, that really come into their own in this beachside setting. The furniture here includes a Punta Cana sofa of Bunny Williams' design, cloaked in a soft-blue Duralee cotton slipcover, while a carved wood mirror by Harrison & Gil draws the eye. "When we're here," Williams has said, "we live outside."

Casamota

Carlos Mota & Weetu
El Limón (DO), 2014

The interiors stylist and editor Carlos Mota describes himself as "Latin at heart." He grew up in Venezuela before settling in New York during the late Eighties. Various subsequent visits to the Dominican Republic reminded Mota of his homeland, and he eventually decided to build a vacation house for himself here at El Limón on the Samaná Peninsula in the north of the country. He found a quiet beachside setting and commissioned Kevin Estrada of Weetu to design the architecture of the new house, while Mota devoted himself to the interiors and gardens. The single-story villa opens up around an internal courtyard and even more so as it spills out onto a veranda and pool terrace facing the sea, decorated with Mota-designed geometric tilework. The interiors explore the contrast between the pale, neutral tones of the concrete walls and floors and vibrant splashes of color and more natural textures. In the living room, for example, sofas in a vivid papal purple capture the eye at once, along with a vintage American wall mirror featuring a graphic series of concentric circles. The more organic notes come from the rattan and wicker chairs, the rug, and wool stools by designer Hernan Arriaga, complemented by an array of house plants.

Liaigre House

Christian Liaigre
Marigot (BL), 2003

The French designer Christian Liaigre
(1943–2020) had a love of the sea. He was
born at La Rochelle, on the west coast of
France, and kept a residence on the Île de
Ré nearby. He also designed and built this
modest but charming beachside home for
himself and his family on the Caribbean
island of St. Barts.Liaigre first started visiting the island during the Eighties and, later,
designed a hotel here called Le Sereno, as
well as a number of private residences for
clients. Then in 2003 he decided to build a
house in a quiet setting overlooking Marigot
Bay, within a protected nature reserve. This
suited Liaigre, who designed a three-bedroom timber cabin, drawing inspiration from
the local vernacular and the setting, while
working around the trees that help shade
the beachfront terraces. Inside, he used
timber floors and painted the walls and ceilings white, creating a soothing backdrop.
In the combined kitchen and dining area,
the furniture is either custom designed or
from Liaigre's own collections, made of only
natural materials. The wicker light shade
hanging over the wood surface of the table
adds another organic touch. The overall aesthetic is simultaneously refined and relaxed.

Ludes House

Wolfgang Ludes
(BL), 2009

....

The German-born, New York–based
Wolfgang Ludes has spent most of his
professional life as a photographer,
but embarked upon a second, parallel career
as a designer. The spur for this new adventure was the redesign of his own home
in the Hamptons, New York, followed by
a vacation house for himself and his wife
on the island of St. Barts. Here Ludes found
a mesmerizing site up in the hills overlooking St. Jean Bay. Drawing inspiration from
the setting and views, Ludes designed the
house as a sequence of pavilions with interconnected adjoining terraces that lead
to an infinity pool. For the crisp interiors
Ludes used a contrasting palette of pale
travertine floors, which flow from inside to
out, and dark wenge timber for the ceilings
and joinery, in an aesthetic that could be
described as tropical minimalism. The contrast between pale and dark tones can be
seen in the sitting room—featuring white
B&B Italia sofas and armchairs standing out
against the woodwork—which flows gently
to the elegant kitchen/dining area. Here,
a triptych of semispherical white ceiling
lights seems to float over the long dining
table by Antonio Citterio (see p. 292) flanked
by Hans J. Wegner chairs.

Les Jolies Eaux

Oliver Messel
Mustique (VC), 1978

....

For Princess Margaret (1930–2002), Les
Jolies Eaux was one of her most precious
possessions but also a safe haven, a world
away from her life and royal duties back
in England. She described it as "my house,"
the only property that she owned fully and
in her own right. Located on the southern
tip of Mustique, overlooking the sea, the land
was a wedding gift from her friend Colin
Tennant, who bought the island in the late
Fifties. The princess and her new husband,
Lord Snowdon (1930–2017), first visited
the site during their honeymoon in 1960,
but she always regarded the creation of
Les Jolies Eaux as a very personal project.
For the architectural design of the house,
she turned to Lord Snowdon's uncle, the
celebrated stage set designer Oliver Messel
(1904–1978), who is credited with creating
the Mustique style, fusing theatrical neoclassicism with a contextually sensitive approach
to the island's vibrant coastal setting.
Princess Margaret's villa became a stage
where, arguably, she could truly be herself,
decorating the interiors in her own style,
fusing English comforts and florals with the
light touches and pale palette of island
living. Presenting the house in *Architectural
Digest* in 1979, the princess clearly took
pride and pleasure in what she had achieved.

Rossferry

Kit Kemp
St. James (BB), 2015

....

"I don't like my designs ever to get too serious," designer Kit Kemp once said. "They need to make you smile." Her own family retreat in the Caribbean is a house that could bring a smile to anyone, with its idyllic beachside setting and its exuberant interiors. Kit and her husband, Tim, cofounders of Firmdale Hotels, bought the house around 2005 to create a welcoming retreat from their busy work life. About ten years later they decided a major rebuild and renovation were needed, given the years of wear and tear. It was also an opportunity for Kit to instill the house's new incarnation with her own distinctive aesthetic. The bedrooms were designed as a collection of cabanas, offering the family and their guests their own private pods. The main house contains inviting communal spaces for gathering and entertaining, including this vibrant veranda overlooking the garden, pool, and beach. A joyful indoor-outdoor room for relaxation and dining, the space is lifted by the sky-blue ceilings and a joyful assembly of rugs that softens the setting. The sofas and armchairs are upholstered in colorful textiles, adding fresh layers of pattern, while lighting and furniture feature natural textures, such as shells, tree branches, and beads.

South America

Casa Cartagena

Richard Mishaan
Cartagena (CO), 2010

The New York–based designer Richard
Mishaan was born in Columbia and grew up
in Bogotá. He studied in the United States,
including time at the architecture school
at Columbia University, before serving an
apprenticeship in the office of Philip Johnson
(see p. 72). Following a foray into the world
of fashion during the Eighties, Mishaan
devoted himself to interiors, establishing
his own practice and designing collections
of furniture and lighting. While on a work
trip back to his homeland, Mishaan revisited
the coastal city of Cartagena, overlooking
the Caribbean Sea. After coming across a
characterful building in the Old Town with
rooftop ocean views, Mishaan was persuaded
to create a family retreat. The reinvented
main living area sits within the oldest,
single-story section of the original residence.
Here Mishaan uncovered the original ceilings, placing the dining area at one end and
the seating zone at the other, framed by
a striped woolen rug. The sofas and armchairs are by Mishaan, while the custom
bookcase takes up the end wall forming
a key focal point and hosting a curated
collection of treasures; a painting of a
sailing scene can be seen in a mirror hung
directly on the bookcase.

Casa Anderson

Wilbert Das
Trancoso (BR), 2015

During Wilbert Das's first visit to Bahia in
2004, the Dutch designer fell in love with
picturesque town of Trancoso. Stepping
away from his post as creative director of
the Italian fashion giant Diesel, Das opened
UXUA Casa Hotel & Spa there with business
partner Bob Shevlin. Named after the local
Pataxó word for "wonderful," the hotel benefits from a magical setting on the edge of
the *quadrado*—a town square, graced with
a series of colorful houses once owned by
local fishing families, and a picture-postcard, sixteenth-century missionary church.
Seduced by the many charms of the hotel
and its setting, CNN anchorman Anderson
Cooper asked Das to design a home for him
on one of the last vacant parcels of land
around the *quadrado*. Das designed a compound house in four parts, including two
guest lodges and a main pavilion, which
looks over the pool zone and surrounding
jungle greenery. The choice of furniture
in the primary living spaces consists of
custom pieces by Das, vintage finds, and
antiques, including a collection of Brazilian
shrines mounted on shelves set against a
turquoise wall. A choice of subtle-blue tones
echoes throughout the pavilion, standing
out against the neutral hues and textures
of the walls, floors, and ceilings.

Sand House

Studio MK27 & Serge Cajfinger
Trancoso (BR), 2019

The French fashion designer Serge Cajfinger spent part of his childhood in Brazil, returning to Europe in his teens. In 1987, he founded the Paule Ka ready-to-wear label in Paris and launched the first of its stores, building the brand over time into a global enterprise. But Cajfinger always remained fond of Brazil. Eventually, he managed to buy a sublime beachside parcel of land near Trancoso in Bahia, commissioning the Brazilian architect Marcio Kogan and his practice, Studio MK27, to help him realize his dreams. Kogan wove the house into this extraordinary setting, creating a series of pavilions placed under a continuous eucalyptus timber canopy. These include the "capsules" devoted to the living room, dining room, kitchen, the primary suite, and guest rooms but also the spaces between, which offer partially shaded terraces and seating zones. The interiors, overseen by Diana Radomysler, feature rustic, textural pieces of furniture, some of it made locally— like a bench in bench in braúna wood by Studio MK27—while the fashion designer introduced a number of mid-century pieces from his own collection, including a Jangada chair by Jean Gillon paired with a tiled side table by Roger Capron, to help furnish the pavilions.

Bergamin House

Sig Bergamin
Trancoso (BR), 2010

....

Interior designer Sig Bergamin is the great Brazilian maximalist. His fearless approach to color, pattern, and texture has helped to earn him a following not just in South America, but also in the United States and Europe. A case in point is Bergamin's own characterful beach house in the relaxed Bahian coastal resort of Trancoso. This is a town of great charm, drawn from its pictur-esque colonial architecture, inviting beaches, and a vibrant creative community. Here Bergamin and his partner, architect Murilo Lomas, have fashioned a welcoming escape from their day-to-day life in São Paulo, where Bergamin's office is based. The house is suitably calm and inviting, with free-flowing connections to the lush tropical gardens. For the interiors, there is an unusual touch of restraint—for Bergamin—in the choice of crisp white and neutral base colors, but this is simply a canvas for a typically eclectic mix of art and furniture from the four corners of the world. The living room, for example, features sofas and ottomans by Bergamin himself coated in vibrantly patterned fabrics, mixed with an African armchair, Kenyan masks, plus a pair of Barcelona stools by Mies van der Rohe. The focal point paint-ing between the windows was a Hamptons flea-market find.

Casa Wilbert

Wilbert Das
Trancoso (BR), 2017

....

Following on from the success of Wilbert Das's Trancoso-based UXUA Casa Hotel & Spa, and local residential projects for clients such as Anderson Cooper (see p. 160) and the British art dealer Ivor Braka, the designer began to think about creating a house for himself. Das built his home next door to the hotel, even constructing a secret tunnel between the two. He sought to create a timeless feel using architectural salvage, gathered from former *fazendas* (colonial plantations) across the region; these characterful elements, with their own texture and patina, include beams, doors, and window frames, many of them still carrying their original paintwork. One of the most important spaces is the open-sided living room, overlooking the lushly planted garden. Given the warm climate, this is a retreat that can be used all year round, with the open walls inviting a gentle, cooling breeze to pass through. The canopy roof was made with wooden shingles, known locally as *taubilha*, while the terra-cotta-tiled floor is both warm in color and highly practical. Much of the furniture, including the sofas and chairs, was designed by Das and made locally, while the cushions were made with vintage Italian, Bulgarian, and Romanian textiles dating back to the Fifties.

Casa das Canoas

Oscar Niemeyer
Rio de Janeiro (BR), 1951

....

Many of the houses designed by the Brazilian Modernist master architect Oscar Niemeyer (1907–2012) over the course of his long career helped to inform his larger and more ambitious projects, acting as important agents of invention. This was very much the case with his own home, Casa das Canoas, built on a hillside in the leafy edges of Rio de Janeiro. The interiors of the glass-sided pavilion explore vivid contrasts between dark and light. The principal level is largely open plan, with the exception of a kitchen tucked away behind a curvaceous timber screen. Dining occurs on a circular table on a circular rug, which floats on a black-tiled floor intercepted by a large raw stone that intrudes into the house from the garden and swimming pool. The rock, along with a sculpture by Alfredo Ceschiatti, points the way to a stairway to the lower story—a cavelike semisubterranean zone embedded in the hillside itself. While helping Niemeyer develop his ideas about architectural "plasticity," with its famous focus on "free-flowing, sensual curves," the house also hosted a crucial visit from Brazil's new president Juscelino Kubitschek, who invited Niemeyer to help him realize his dreams for a new capital, Brasília.

Cabana Penaguião

Mónica Penaguião
Paraty (BR), 2015

The rural escape that interior and furniture designer Mónica Penaguião created for herself and her family has evolved gradually over time. The Portuguese-born Penaguião first began coming to Paraty and the Costa Verde around 2003, eventually purchasing a parcel of land up in the hills, with views toward the coast. Within this tropical farmstead, Penaguião began to create a house of many parts—a small pavilion used by her children or guests, a sleeping pavilion, and a primary pavilion holding the main living spaces—placed thoughtfully together on the hillside. A thatched cabana spills out onto the pool terrace. Largely open to three sides it allows an intimate sense of connection with the verdant surroundings, as well as drawing in a cooling breeze during the warmer times of the year. The wooden floors are coated in white deck paint, while the main seating area is arranged around the wood-burning stove, used for colder evenings. The white sofa is by Cappellini, while the two blue sofas are by Penaguião herself, together creating a pleasing blue-and-white theme. Blinds can be dropped down around the edges of the cabana whenever shade or shelter might be needed.

Paraty House

Alberto Pinto
Paraty (BR), 2012

The Moroccan-born designer Alberto Pinto (1943–2012) nurtured a particular fascination with Brazil. He studied, lived, and worked in Paris for much of his life, but regularly visited South America as his parents were originally from Argentina. With commissions in Brazil, Pinto eventually acquired a duplex apartment in Rio de Janeiro to serve as an Ipanema beachside retreat. One of these commissions was a project in the picturesque coastal town of Paraty, to the southwest of Rio de Janeiro. Here, a long-standing client came across a former hotel and asked Pinto to convert it into a welcoming private escape. The characterful exteriors of Paraty's Portuguese colonial-period houses typically feature whitewashed walls with brightly colored doors, window frames, and shutters. Pinto adopted a similar approach for the house's interiors, creating gentle standout bursts of color. The spacious living room features repeated pulses of red, as seen in the repurposed textiles used to cover the comfortable sofas and armchairs. A pair of seventeenth-century paintings sit between the windows, while a collection of sculpted silver fish decorates the walls to either side, providing an elegant reminder of Paraty's coastal heritage and the fishing boats that still line the harbor.

Residência BV

Jacobsen Arquitetura
Near Porto Feliz (BR), 2011

....

Residência BV, near Porto Feliz, was one of
the first completed residential projects by
Jacobsen Arquitetura, headed by architects
Paulo and Bernardo Jacobsen. Designed
as a triptych of interconnected pavilions,
the primary volume is sheltered by a high
canopy roof, which protects both the key
communal spaces, including the living room
and dining area. The glass walls lightly
divide the inside and outside space, sliding
away to allow these realms to blur into one
another, while the open vista is a constant
presence. The aesthetic of the interiors,
designed in conjunction with associates
Jaime Cunha and Eza Viegas, is distinctly
modern but warmed by the extensive use
of natural materials, such as timber and
stone. The seating zone is defined by the
fireplace—which is set within a white monolith wall that stands out against the stonework of the spinal hallway beyond—as well
as the rug flanked by two white sofas.
The pair of sculptural Diz armchairs are
by the celebrated Brazilian furniture
designer Sergio Rodrigues, while the
abstract artwork is by Elizabeth Jobim.

Motta Farmhouse

Carlos Motta
Monteiro Lobato (BR), 2005

The journey from the epic urban sprawl of São Paulo to furniture designer Carlos Motta's farmhouse is something of an adventure. The three-hour drive northeastward of the city takes you through picturesque towns and villages, before climbing up into the mountains of Serra da Mantiqueira. Eventually, after some time on dirt roads and tracks, a wooden gate marked with a star, Motta's symbol of choice, leads the way toward his self-designed farmhouse, constructed with the help of local craftspeople. Motta built the house and interiors with wood: aroeira for the pillars that hold the house on the hill, itaúba for the structural frame, cumaru for the floors, and angelim for the interior wall panels and ceilings. Naturally this gives the interiors a sense of organic warmth, but there is also a refreshing sense of openness to the main living spaces, which spill out onto a large terrace, and a treehouse feel that comes from the elevated position. The main seating area is arranged around a stone fireplace, with the dining area alongside; the furniture is largely by Motta himself, including his famous Astúrias rocking chair and matching stool.

Casa Tomie Ohtake

Ruy Ohtake
São Paulo (BR), 1968

Two of architect Ruy Ohtake's most famous commissions connect with the life and work of his mother, the artist Tomie Ohtake. Tomie was born in Japan but later settled in Brazil; she began showing her work—paintings and monumental abstract and geometric sculptures—from the Fifties onward. Ruy designed both the Instituto Tomie Ohtake in São Paulo, which opened in 2001, and his mother's house and studio in the Vila Mariana neighborhood of the city. The house reveals itself by degrees, with the single-story building arranged around a secret courtyard garden, which hosts a swimming pool, fresh-air living spaces, terraces, and a number of Tomie's sculptures. Inside, the main living room is fluid, offering an easy sense of connection with neighboring spaces and the courtyard. The seating revolves around a fireplace where the open hearth (often pictured full of pot plants) morphs into a coffee table and the flue is a floating concrete cube held aloft by the coffered ceiling. The seating here includes an LC4 recliner by Le Corbusier, Pierre Jeanneret, and Charlotte Perriand; Diamond chairs by Harry Bertoia, and a pair of Mole armchairs by the Brazilian furniture designer Sergio Rodrigues; the tubular, twirling sculpture suspended from the ceiling is by Tomie Ohtake.

Casa Grecia

Isay Weinfeld
São Paulo (BR), 2010

With Casa Grecia, architect Isay Weinfeld has created a true urban escape evoking a tranquil oasis where the metropolis of São Paulo beyond the outline of the walled garden can almost be forgotten. Weinfeld purchased a generous parcel of land in the Jardins district of the city, bordered by mature trees, which help to form a green screen around the gardens. Much of the house is arranged on one level, but a dip to one side provided the perfect spot for a swimming pool and a lower ground floor that holds spaces such as a gym and playroom. The living room benefits from its central position in the house, connecting with an adjoining veranda via a sliding wall of glass, which also frames views of a secret garden. A custom U-shaped sofa, designed by Weinfeld, faces this vista, while wrapping around a vintage tree-trunk coffee table sourced in New York. Other custom elements include the integrated library wall to the rear. Curated pieces include a table by Sergio Rodrigues and a pair of Boalum lights by Livio Castiglioni and Gianfranco Frattini, while out on the veranda the table and chairs are by George Nakashima (see p. 119).

Casa Torres

Guilherme Torres
São Paulo (BR), 2011

The Brazilian designer Guilherme Torres describes himself as a "romantic Modernist." The architect within him is something of a purist, but the decorator inside is decidedly expressive and experimental. Both these aspects of Torres's design philosophy are evident at his own home in São Paulo. Torres first launched his own architectural design practice in the northern city of Londrina, but eventually decided to relocate to São Paulo. He began searching for a home in the central district of Jardins, until he eventually found a two-story house dating back to the Forties that was ripe for reinvention and modernization. The entrance leads directly into an open-plan study and living area, which, in turn, leads into a dining area and kitchen that Torres created in the former backyard, complete with a top-lit indoor garden. Teal blues feature repeatedly in the living area, used on the wall around the entrance and for the stairway alongside, but are also echoed in the sofa—designed by Torres—and the patchwork rug that it sits on. The choice of eclectic artworks includes a piece by Pinky Wainer, who created an illuminated lightbox that hangs to one side of the sofa.

Casa Millán

Paulo Mendes da Rocha
São Paulo (BR), 1970

Paulo Mendes da Rocha's (1928–2021) Casa Millán represents a fusion of the world of art and architecture. The house was one of a number of original Brutalist concrete residences designed by da Rocha during the Sixties and Seventies—which also included his own home and Casa Masetti (see p. 174)— and was originally designed for art dealer Fernando Millán, a friend of the architect. Seen from the streetscape, this avant-garde building is enigmatic and mysterious. It resembles an extraordinary urban bunker, with few outward signs of domesticity beyond the swimming pool and courtyard garden. Inside, the house begins to reveal itself in dramatic fashion with a vast double-height living room serving as the heart and hub of the building. This top-lit space has the pure and pared-down feel of a gallery, with raw concrete walls forming a surface for art and photography, while the curva-ceous lines of the spiral staircase lend it a sculptural quality. The house was eventually sold to another art dealer, Eduardo Leme, who worked with the architect on a renova-tion and modest update, while introducing his own choice of art, furniture, and lighting.

Casa Milan

Marcos Acayaba
São Paulo (BR), 1975

....

This experimental house in São Paulo began
life as a commission for one of architect
Marcos Acayaba's clients, psychoanalyst
Betty Milan, sister of his wife, Marlene
Acayaba, a writer and critic. When Milan
relocated to Paris before the project was
finished, the Acayabas decided to make the
house their home. The site itself is urban,
but surrounded by verdant greenery,
creating an escapist setting even in the
heart of the metropolis. The soaring roof
canopy works around the sloping topography of the lush site, sheltering all of
the living spaces within. Inside, Acayaba
created three distinct but interconnected
platforms, with the kitchen to one side,
the bedrooms on a mezzanine level to the
other, and the main living spaces right at
the center. These benefit from a dramatic
sense of height, scale, and openness, while
spilling out to the gardens at either end via
walls of glass. Terra-cotta tiles help warm
the space, contrasting with the raw concrete
and the ever-present garden greenery.
The terra-cotta notes are echoed by the
raspberry-hued cushions of the built-in sofa
that forms part of the main seating area,
which is lightly delineated by the placement
of a rug and two dark Chesterfield sofas.

Casa de Vidro

Lina Bo Bardi
São Paulo (BR), 1951

The Italian architect and designer Lina Bo Bardi (1914–1992) began her career in Milan, where she worked in the office of architect Gio Ponti (see pp. 296 and 323). Just after World War II, in 1946, she immigrated to Brazil with her new husband, the art curator and writer Pietro Maria Bardi. Recognized in due course for her landmark new building for the São Paulo Museum of Art (1968), Bo Bardi had first begun exploring ideas of lightness and elevation with her own home in Morumbi, which became her first completed project in Brazil in 1951. At the time, Morumbi was a verdant neighborhood on the edge of São Paulo. Bo Bardi had found a lush site, aiming to build a kind of observatory for appreciating the beauty of the natural surroundings. She elevated the main part of Casa de Vidro (Glass House) above the ground on slim *piloti*, wrapping the walls in floor-to-ceiling glass. In the primary living space, Bo Bardi covered the floors in pale-blue mosaic tiles and blended her own furniture designs—including her Chair with Brass Balls (1950) and her famous Bowl chair (1951)—with other mid-century pieces, as well as antiques and statuary. The surrounding vegetation, which had grown and grown over the years, provided a vivid background to her sophisticated domestic melange.

Casa Masetti

Paulo Mendes da Rocha
São Paulo (BR), 1969

The Brazilian architect Paulo Mendes da Rocha (1928–2021) first captured attention in 1957 with his dynamic design of the São Paulo Athletic Club. He became known for his original "Paulist Brutalist" style, using raw concrete but in imaginative and sometimes highly expressive buildings. These included an influential sequence of urban houses completed during the Sixties and early Seventies, such as the Casa Millán (see p. 170) for art dealer Fernando Millán, his own home in the neighborhood of Butantã (1964), and the 1969 São Paulo house, Casa Masetti. The house was designed for the civil engineer Mario Masetti, who embraced the idea of raising the home up on vast concrete pillars. Elevating the house lends drama, of course, but it also helps make the most of the natural light, opening the house to the vista. Inside, swaths of concrete are softened and balanced by the use of colorful Portuguese floor tiles. The main living area circulates around an integrated fireplace, which is also made of shuttered concrete. The current owners, who have carefully restored the house, have introduced additional touches of color and texture by thoughtful choices of furniture, including a number of mid-century and vintage pieces that bring their own patina.

Casa Iporanga

Arthur Casas
Near Guarujá (BR), 2009

....

Since establishing his own practice in 1999 in São Paulo, Brazilian architect Arthur Casas has built a broad portfolio of projects ranging from interior design to furniture. Whenever Casas wants to escape the busy pace of city life, he heads to a rainforest retreat of his own design near the coastal town of Guarujá. "I always wanted a place in the middle of the forest, a place where I could recharge," said Casas, who shares the house with his wife, architect Maraí Valente, and their daughter. The house itself invites the landscape inside via vast sliding banks of glass to either side of a double-height living space at the center of the house. Natural textures prevail in the interiors, including the cumaru wooden floors and a rug that anchors the seating area, crisp white sofas, and a supersized coffee table by Casas himself. The suspended fireplace by Dominique Imbert creates a gentle focal point, while the mid-century leather chair and footstool by Martin Eisler once belonged to the architect's grandmother. The floating bridge that connects the upper level of the two wings is protected by a glass balcony, alluding to the house's theme of transparency.

White O

Toyo Ito
Marbella (CL), 2009

....

Having established his own practice in Tokyo in 1971, one of architect Toyo Ito's most influential early projects was the U House (1976), built in the same city for his sister. The fluid home wrapped its way around an internal courtyard that provided a "garden of light," as Ito put it. The U House was unfortunately demolished in 1997, but Ito was given a fresh chance to explore similar ideas in his design for White O in Chile. The house forms part of a residential development project, launched by Chilean entrepreneur Eduardo Godoy, known as Ocho al Cubo, in the coastal resort town of Marbella. Like the U House, the White O is a structure without a clear beginning or end, with the building forming a ring around a central courtyard garden. The main living space is an inviting open-plan zone that looks across the courtyard through swaths of glazing to an elevated bedroom wing, accessed by twin ramps—one internal and one external. The furnishings in the living area sit well with the sinuous character of the architecture, with an oval table anchoring the dining area at one end and sofas and chairs—including a collection of rockers—at the other.

Europe
North

Ekensberg

Lars Sjöberg
Lake Mälaren (SE), 1976–ongoing

The designer, historian, and writer Lars Sjöberg spent thirty-six years working as a curator at the National Museum of Sweden, specialising in eighteenth and nineteenth-century Scandinavian furniture. He went on to design his own furniture range for IKEA and published a number of books on Swedish architecture and interiors. Since the Sixties, Sjöberg has undertaken a sequence of restoration projects, including a number of Swedish manor houses. The most ambitious challenge of Sjöberg's career in this field is undoubtedly the revival of this villa in Ekensberg, his home on the shores of Lake Mälaren, to the west of Stockholm. Sjöberg acquired the Italianate villa, which dates from the late eighteenth century, in 1976. The three-story neoclassical building dates from a period when Italianate architecture and interiors were highly popular, following an extended Grand Tour undertaken by King Gustav III. Part of the charm of the residence lies in the combination of such original period detailing with a degree of simplicity, as seen in this dining room. The blue-and-white tiled fireplace forms a foundation for a palette of soft whites and pale gray-blues, seen in the curated choice of furniture and ceramics. Texture and patina play a key part throughout, evident upon the walls, faded floors, and the sideboards.

Erskine House

Ralph Erskine
Drottningholm (SE), 1963

England was architect Ralph Erskine's (1914–2005) home country, he grew up in London and trained as an architect there. During the late Thirties he settled in Sweden with his wife, opening his own practice just a few years later. After a few years living in a country house of his own design to the south of Stockholm, Erskine and his family were drawn closer toward the city itself. They rented a house in Drottningholm, which translates as "the Queen's islet," and is where the Swedish Royal Family still have their principal residence. Eventually, in 1963, Erskine built a new family house on the island with a separate studio alongside. Irregular patterns on the facade and the unusual fenestration gave hints about the remarkable interiors inside. The front of the house was dominated by a barnlike, double-height living and dining room arranged around a white floating fireplace. Within this generously proportioned space, the compact kitchen was designed as an open-sided rectangular box, complete with a curtain that could be drawn across for a light sense of separation. Perched on the top of this box was Erskine's study, which floated on a mezzanine gallery looking out over the playfully decorated communal zone below.

Villa Spies

Staffan Berglund
Torö (SE), 1969

During the late Sixties, the flamboyant Danish entrepreneur Simon Spies launched an architectural competition to find a fresh design for mass-produced vacation cabins that could be prefabricated easily and cheaply assembled on site. The winner of the competition was the Swedish architect Staffan Berglund (1936–2016), who invented a circular building largely made of fiberglass that could be assembled in almost any tourist-friendly location. Unfortunately for Berglund, Spies decided against production and, instead, asked the architect to build just one house for the hedonistic entrepreneur himself. Situated on the island of Torö, part of the Stockholm archipelago, Villa Spies was a tomorrow home. The futuristic building sat at the top of a cliff, overlooking the sea, with a ribbon of windows framing the panorama. The fluid all-white interiors, with neatly integrated furniture and fittings throughout, offered an ultramodern stage set for Spies's eccentric performances. The most theatrical feature was a round seating platform at the center of the plan that rose from the floor at the touch of a button to reveal a circular dining table bordered by a sunken fitted banquette upholstered in ruby-red cushions.

Mathsson House

Bruno Mathsson
Tånnö (SE), 1965

The mid-century Swedish designer Bruno Mathsson (1907–1988) is best known for his innovative and original furniture. He adopted an ergonomic approach to his work, designing chairs, sofas, and recliners that were comfortable as well as elegantly crafted. Yet Mathsson was also a much-respected architect, focusing in particular on residential design. During the mid-Sixties Mathsson designed a lakeside home, which became his principal residence, situated within a rural setting at Tånnö, just south of the town of Värnamo. For the interiors, Mathsson created just four rooms: a bedroom and a study to the rear, a service core to the center, and then a generous, sociable, and multifunctional living space. Graced with green mosaic tiles that echoed the colors of the lawns and landscape beyond the window, this single enticing space held various zones for dining and relaxing, with both loose and fitted furniture by Mathsson, including banks of bookshelves either side of the brick fireplace, and his sculptural bentwood Pernilla chaise longue, dressed with a brown sheepskin. Colorful curtains in a vibrant Josef Frank fabric added a playful note to certain parts of the house.

Lagerqvist Beach House

Kristin Lagerqvist
Varberg (SE), 2015

....

The picturesque town of Varberg sits on Sweden's west coast in an area renowned for its beach life. Kristin Lagerqvist, photographer and interiors blogger (under the Krickelins umbrella), enjoyed spending family vacations here as a child. Her love of the region was shared by her husband, Jonas, so the couple decided make a home for themselves and their children—eventually finding a Twenties period house. For the interiors, Lagerqvist was drawn to a beachhouse palette of blues and whites: "Blue has always been my color," she says. "There is something reassuring and comforting about the different tones of the sky and sea." Along with the wooden floors, this soothing palette helps unify interconnecting spaces such as the living room, kitchen, and study with gentle contrasts in tone and pattern exhibited in the choice of floral papers and paints. The Krickelins Haze Blue color for the walls of the living room was specially mixed, providing a compelling backdrop for art and furniture. Other key pieces, such as the rocking chair and coffee table, are auction finds, and the artworks are a mix of Lagerqvist's own photographs and those of friends, adding another layer of personality to the space.

Sørensen House

Friis & Moltke Architects & Vivian Bigaard Sørensen
Brabrand (DK), 1963

....

The Danish architects Knud Friis (1926–2010) and Elmar Moltke Nielsen (1924–1997) were best known for their rural buildings that had a sense of synergy with their surroundings. They took inspiration from not only Modernism but also vernacular typologies, like farmsteads, and often worked with traditional materials, such as wood, brick, and stone. This house in Brabrand, on the outskirts of Aarhus, was created in collaboration with interior designer Vivian Bigaard Sørensen, who commissioned the architects to build the home for her within a wooded garden. The architects designed two intersecting linear pavilions, with the smaller one holding the primary suite and the larger devoted to a spacious sitting room, as well as the kitchen/dining area. The interiors here have a sense of organic warmth, because of the timber ceilings and views of the garden via floor-to-ceiling glass. The larger pavilion is partially open plan, with the striking white-and-black brick fireplace partly separating the sitting room from the kitchen beyond. Much of the furniture, designed by Sørensen, is built-in, including a sofa and timber tables atop white-painted brick plinths. Dressed with shaggy throws, timber-and-leather Spanish chairs (1959) by Børge Mogensen add additional natural textures.

Gunnløgsson House

Halldor Gunnløgsson
Rungsted (DK), 1958

The seaside house that Danish architect Halldor Gunnløgsson (1918–1985) designed for himself and his wife, Lillemor, in the neighborhood of Rungsted, on the Øresund coast north of Copenhagen, has an air of simplicity and order. Yet, at the same time, the architecture has a highly thoughtful design and approach to flexible modern living. The aesthetics of this single-story pavilion were influenced by a honeymoon trip to Japan. Not long afterward the Gunnløgssons found this magical spot on the coast, and the architect began developing designs for a house that embraced the natural beauty of the setting. The entrance hall is reminiscent of a Japanese *genkan*, featuring a neatly aligned bank of storage cupboards and wardrobes. Beyond this, the house opens up with a free-flowing plan in which the sitting room, dining area, and study occupy one open space, lightly delineated by a monolithic fireplace. The small kitchen and the bedroom can also be perceived as part of this one expansive space, although sliding doors (echoing Japanese *shoji* screens) can be drawn across for privacy as needed. Gray stone floors and dark timber-paneled walls unify the interiors and provide an elegant backdrop for Danish mid-century furniture, much of it by Poul Kjærholm (below).

Kjærholm House

Hanne & Poul Kjærholm
Rungsted (DK), 1962

A stone's throw from the Øresund strait, the Kjærholm House offers the perfect fusion of engaging architecture and uplifting interiors. The designers of the house—Hanne Kjærholm (1930–2009) and her husband, Poul Kjærholm (1929–1980)—had the right combination of skills to achieve such harmony: Hanne was an influential architect, and Poul was one of the most innovative and accomplished furniture designers of the mid-twentieth century. In the neighborhood of Rungsted, north of Copenhagen, the couple acquired a parcel of land that was small but had the advantage of a waterside setting and sea views. They designed a one-story villa with the entrance, bedrooms, and kitchen all positioned to the rear. The front, facing the water, was devoted to a spacious, open living area spilling out onto a veranda. The Kjærholms collaborated on the interiors and introduced a number of celebrated furniture designs by Poul. In the living space, whitewashed brick walls, timber ceiling and paneling, and rush matting in a diamond pattern create a soft backdrop for a dining area at one end and a seating area at the other; a PK 111 wooden screen (1956) by Poul could be used as a light partition. Among Poul's other pieces were his sculptural PK 9 dining chairs (1960) and his PK 54 dining table (1963).

Peter's House

Studio David Thulstrup
Copenhagen (DK), 2015

Danish architect and designer David Thulstrup studied at the Danish Design School before working with architect Jean Nouvel in Paris and then Peter Marino (see p. 54) in New York. In 2009, he founded his own design studio, based in Copenhagen, developing a portfolio of work, including the 2018 interiors of René Redzepi's restaurant, Noma. Peter's House, also in Copenhagen, in the Sturlasgade neighborhood, encompassed an unusual project to convert a former garage into a house and studio for the photographer Peter Krasilnikoff. The interiors contrast semi-industrial materials —including the original raw-brick walls in the kitchen, dressed with African masks— with warmer and more organic choices, like the broad planks of Dinesen oak used to clad the walls in parts of the house. The living room features a collection of freshly upholstered furniture, including a Pierre Paulin Groovy chair in sunflower yellow. The dining room is one of the most dramatic spaces in the home, with a double-height bank of glass facing the atrium to one side and a vast curtain of Kvadrat purple velvet to the other. There is an elegant minimalism to the space, as its polished concrete floors contrast with the velvet and joinery; the wooden furniture and the chandelier assume a sculptural presence in this gallerylike space.

Denmark

Holm & Becker House

Jacob Holm & Barbara Bendix Becker
Copenhagen (DK), 2002

....

While Jacob Holm, the former CEO of the
Danish furniture company Fritz Hansen,
prefers country living, his wife, designer
Barbara Bendix Becker, favors city life.
The ideal compromise was the picturesque
coastal community of Klampenborg on the
northern edge of Copenhagen. Here the
couple came across a nineteenth-century
townhouse with something of an English
character, yet the interior treatment is distinctly and decidedly Scandinavian. White
provides a canvas for expression throughout. Walls, ceilings, and floorboards are all
painted crisp white, creating a soothing
sense of cohesion. This neutral backdrop
also allows the texture and form of furniture, lighting, and other pieces to shine out,
even when the materials are natural, such as
timber, leather, and wool. A prime example is
the sitting room, which doubles as a library,
with banks of bookcases framing the view
through the doorway to the hall beyond.
Furniture includes a China chair by Hans
J. Wegner and a steel-frame leather sofa
by Poul Kjærholm (see p. 183), two designers whose work is still produced by Fritz
Hansen. An insect-like, triple-headed standing lamp by Serge Mouille also stands out
here, as does the famous Poul Henningsen
Artichoke ceiling light that forms a glimmer-
ing centerpiece in the hallway.

Redzepi House

René & Nadine Redzepi
Copenhagen (DK), 2015

....

The Danish chef René Redzepi is well known
for his creative reimagining of Nordic
cuisine, which he showcases in his landmark Copenhagen restaurant, Noma. The
Copenhagen home that he shares with his
cookbook author wife, Nadine, and their
children is an inventive reworking of an
early nineteenth-century building that was
originally a blacksmith's workshop. The
house has two principal levels. The upper
story holds the children's bedrooms and a
spacious primary suite, where exposed roof
beams supporting the pitched ceiling lend
character and patina. With the exception
of two additional bedrooms, much of the
ground floor is devoted to a large open-plan
kitchen, dining, and living area. Here the
space partly revolves around the original
blacksmith's furnace, which now serves as
a fireplace. The white walls combine with
the texture of various complementary
natural elements, including the original
exposed beams of the timber frame, the
Dinesen oak floors, and the custom joinery
of the kitchen island and cabinets, stacked
with earthy ceramics. Alongside the kitchen
is the dining area, anchored by a custom
family-size table with a low-hanging copper
ceiling lamp overhead. It is a sociable
arrangement, well suited to family life but
also to entertaining in style.

Mogensen House

Børge Mogensen
Gentofte (DK), 1964

A number of Børge Mogensen's (1914–1972) most successful and enticing furniture designs were essentially intelligent reinventions of traditional pieces. The Spanish chair (1959), for example, with its distinctive timber frame and leather seat and back, was inspired by a generic Iberian design; his Hunting chair (1950), similarly, took inspiration from lightweight, portable vernacular examples. Mogensen's own house at Gentofte, on the northern edge of Copenhagen, could also be regarded in a similar way and seen as a characterful reworking of a Danish farmhouse, fusing familiarity and modernity. At the cusp of the Sixties, Mogensen asked architects Arne Karlsen and Erling Zeuthen Nielsen to help him draw up plans for the house, which embraced a sloping garden site. Some four years later, Mogensen added a glass-walled, brick-floored summer room at one end of the pitch-roofed house and a balcony at the other, both enhancing the relationship between house and garden. Naturally, the furniture was by Mogensen, who treated the family home as a testing ground for his work. The set of Spanish chairs and wooden dining table—inspired by traditional Shaker tables—were all designed by the Danish master. The pendant lamp, though, was by fellow Danish designer Poul Henningsen.

Number 31

Sam Stephenson
Dublin (IE), 1958

Irish Brutalist architect Sam Stephenson (1933–2006) designed some offices and banks that sparked intense controversy because period buildings were destroyed to make way for them. Yet when it came to his own central Dublin home, a Georgian mews house, Stephenson decided to convert rather than demolish. Stephenson came across the disused stable building, hidden behind an elegant period townhouse and a courtyard garden, and decided to rework the existing structure to create a striking modern home. He enlarged windows and other openings, yet the character-filled texture of the original stone-and-brick walls can still be seen under the whitewash paintwork outside and inside. The architect radically transformed the interiors. Tucked away at the bottom of the building, the most inviting space was the expansive sitting room with a seductive mid-century aesthetic. Stephenson designed a sunken conversation pit with a large, integrated U-shaped leather sofa facing the fireplace and room enough at the center for a sizeable marble coffee table. The combination of the leather, the rough painted walls, and the timber ceilings and mosaic tiled floor created a highly inviting space for entertaining. The gatherings hosted here by Stephenson, a legendary raconteur, are still referenced widely.

High Sunderland

Peter Womersley & Bernat Klein
Selkirk, Scottish Borders,
Scotland (UK), 1957

In 1955, just as Bernat Klein's (1922–2014)
career as a textile designer was heading
into its golden period, he and his wife Peggy
were visiting West Yorkshire when they
spotted Farnley Hey by architect Peter
Womersley (1923–1993, see p. 193). Klein
was so impressed by the mid-century house
that he contacted Womersley and asked him
to design a new family home on a picturesque parcel of land he had acquired in the
Scottish Borders. Klein was a man of refined
tastes—his highly fashionable textiles were
taken up in the Sixties by fashion houses like
Chanel, Pierre Cardin, and Christian Dior.
His strong views on architecture, interiors,
and furniture all fed into the design of High
Sunderland. The most rounded and characterful space of the house was undoubtedly
the sunken living room, which was arranged
around a fireplace. Womersley and Klein
collaborated on the interiors that featured
travertine floors and timber-paneled ceilings combined with many built-in elements,
including bookshelves and seating. The
room's predominantly neutral color scheme
was punctuated by Klein's own-designed,
vibrantly colored tweed cushions, which
brought an American West Coast vibe to
the room.

Dumfries House

David Mlinaric & Piers von Westenholz
Cumnock, Ayrshire, Scotland
(UK), 2011

During the 1750s, the Earl of Dumfries, William Crichton-Dalrymple commissioned architect Robert Adam (1728–1792) to design one of the finest neoclassical houses in Scotland. The enlightened earl spared no expense on both the house's architecture and interior decoration, which included a collection of Thomas Chippendale furniture. During the early-nineteenth century the house passed to the Marquess of Bute, who, in 2007, put Dumfries House and its contents up for auction. The story caught the attention of Prince Charles, who acquired the house and its estate with the aim of opening it to the public. Working with a team of designers and curators, David Mlinaric and Piers von Westenholz designed a suite of rooms for Prince Charles's personal use. In contrast to the formal grandeur of spaces like the Tapestry Room, the modestly scaled private living room features walls painted in soothing Vert De Terre paintwork from Farrow & Ball. A chintz linen from Christopher Moore, known as Bannister Hall, was used for both the curtains and the upholstery for the sofa and armchairs, which are arranged around the fireplace, near to a 1759 William Mathie giltwood pier glass.

Rhydoldog Manor

Laura Ashley
Rhayader, Powys, Wales (UK), 1973

In many respects Rhydoldog Manor in rural Powys encapsulated the Laura Ashley look. Laura Ashley (1925–1985) herself used her country retreat as a testing ground for her textiles and wallpapers, while the seven-bedroom house was also brought into service as the perfect backdrop for company catalogs and photo shoots. Ashley was born in Wales and was drawn back there again and again. Along with her husband, Bernard (1926–2009), the designer founded her eponymous company in London and the couple printed her first designs in their Pimlico flat during the early Fifties. By the late Seventies Laura Ashley was a global brand encompassing textiles, homeware, and fashion. Laura and Bernard Ashley bought Rhydoldog Manor in 1973, by which time the company was based in the nearby village of Carno. The house had last been reworked during the 1870s, lending it the picture-postcard look of a Victorian home. The Ashleys bedroom was decorated by Laura in an abundance of flower motifs— from the sofa upholstered in a rosebud print to the canopied bed dressed with full-blown Victorian roses. A natural progression from garden to house, the enchanting conservatory was designed by Laura herself: "a composite of all the Gothic-style conservatories I had ever seen," she said.

Malator House

Future Systems
Near Druidston, Pembrokeshire,
Wales (UK), 1998

One of the key ambitions for the Future Systems–designed house near Druidston in Wales was invisibility. Created for the politician, barrister, and author Bob Marshall-Andrews and his wife, Gill, the house sits within a national park on the Pembrokeshire coast. Owing to its location, a statement house was never going to be a possibility; instead, architects Jan Kaplický (1937–2009) and Amanda Levete decided to burrow down into the cliffs, creating a building topped with earth and grass. The resulting Teletubby House, as it is sometimes called, disappears into the landscape, leaving only a long glass window wall. The house's interiors are highly original, infused with the High-Tech ethos for which Future Systems became renowned. Its white-tiled center was designed as one spacious room, framed by an open view of the sea, punctuated only by operable portholes in the large glass window wall. A fireplace sits at the center of the house, with half-moon-shaped seating and surrounding dining areas, while two brightly colored service pods to either side hold the kitchenette and bathrooms.

Farnley Hey

Peter Womersley
Near Huddersfield, Yorkshire, England
(UK), 1954

The Yorkshire-born architect Peter Womersley (1923–1993) designed a grand total of three houses for his brother John, the managing director of furniture manufacturers Arkana. The first and, arguably, the most accomplished of these was Farnley Hey, near Huddersfield. With its palette of natural and earthy materials, as well as its engaging connections with the surrounding gardens, the house has even been compared by English Heritage with the work of Frank Lloyd Wright. The heart of the house was a double-height living room with wooden floors and paneling, complemented by exposed lilac-tinged brick walls. Dubbed the "dance floor," owing to its polished floors, the space floated above the adjoining rooms, forming a kind of stage, but also connected with the terrace and garden. It was a theatrical, mid-century Modern space, and featured a number of sophisticated integrated features, including a fireplace and built-in sound system—radical for the time. Period pieces abounded, like a wicker hanging chair and sage-hued seating by H.W. Klein. Farnley Hey is now in the hands of new owners who have been lovingly restoring the house.

Siegel House
David Shelley
Nottinghamshire, England (UK), 1970

Architect David Shelley (1934–2012) designed a number of eye-catching modern houses in Nottinghamshire and Derbyshire during the Seventies. The most rounded and characterful of these is Siegel House in Nottinghamshire, which has the accomplished grandeur of a Californian mid-century classic. The vast majority of the house is arranged on an U-shaped upper level with terrazzo floors that meet the rear garden with its terraces and swimming pool. The relationship between indoor and outdoor living is particularly vivid, with bands of floor-to-ceiling glass looking out to the gardens but also across a sparsely planted courtyard and a fish pond. In 2003, the house was bought by Simon and Monica Siegel, the owners of Nottinghamshire furniture and lighting store Atomic Interiors. They embarked on a sensitive restoration, while carefully housing their own curated collection of mid-century furniture and ceramics, like a charming orange Bitossi cat. One of the house's greatest delights is the rosewood-trimmed conversation pit, with its curving, black leather sofa facing an integrated fireplace and overlooking the courtyard garden. The space can be lightly separated from the main living room with a ceiling-mounted curtain in a natural shade, transforming the pit into a more intimate den.

McNally House

Keith McNally & Ian McPheely
Cotswolds, England (UK), 2013

....

One of the greatest delights of dining in one of Keith McNally's restaurants, whether in London or New York, is the atmosphere and interiors offered by his escapist eateries. The first Balthazar in New York was especially alluring; it felt timeless, natural, and glamorous. The same is true of McNally's own homes, whether in the United States or England, where he has aspired to his own version of perfection: "By perfect, I mean imperfect and undesigned-looking." In the United States, McNally renovated and reinvented houses in New York and Martha's Vineyard (see p. 68); in 2011 he returned to England and bought a stone farmhouse in the Cotswolds. Working with his usual design collaborator, Ian McPheely, he began the careful process of making his own mark on the house. A partition wall was removed between the unfussy kitchen and dining area to create a more open and sociable space, while the living room became an inviting retreat layered with vivid art and textiles; wall sconces and table lamps were favored over overhead lighting. Salvaged and reclaimed materials give these spaces texture and personality. In the primary bedroom, on the dresser, a Rupert Lee painting from about 1924 is a focal point.

Ashley Hicks
Country House

Ashley Hicks
Oxfordshire, England (UK), 2012

Interior designer Ashley Hicks balances the lessons and principles offered by his famous father David Hicks (1929–1998, see p. 198) with his own individual aesthetic approach. It is a complex balancing act for a designer and author who has sought to protect his father's legacy while also forging his own successful career, which has encompassed interiors, commissions, and books as well as furniture and fabric collections. In some respects, Hicks's own country home provides the perfect example of this approach. The house sits alongside Hicks's parents' Oxfordshire estate and consists of a set of nineteenth-century farm buildings converted into an engaging family home. There is a bold and expressive use of color, texture, pattern, and decorative-paint effects throughout the continually evolving interiors of the historic house. The gray-and-white dining room, for example, features geometric floor tiles from the David Hicks by Ashley Hicks collection (produced by Popham Design), while the walls are decorated in a trompe l'oeil depiction of frangipani trees. Much of the furniture here is also by Ashley Hicks, including the large dining table with its distinctive sculptural legs, while double doors connect with the adjoining kitchen.

The Grove

David Hicks
Oxfordshire, England (UK), 1979

David Hicks (1929–1998) was one of the first designers to use his own homes as showcases for his work. His career was launched during the Fifties when *House & Garden* magazine published a feature on his London home. Two of the most famous Hicks residences were in Oxfordshire: Britwell House followed by the Grove. At the Grove Hicks—as in so much of his work—fused the elegant proportions, scale, and symmetry of neoclassical architecture with a more radical approach to color, pattern, and an eclectic choice of furniture. He set out the ground rules of interior design and then bent and broke them: "Rules give structure," he wrote, "but often at the expense of vitality." The Grove began life as a farmhouse but was extended during the late-eighteenth century on a grander scale. The drawing room featured a geometric Hicks carpet combined with rose-pink cotton walls with matching curtains. Portraits by George Romney from his wife, Lady Pamela Mountbatten's, family stood out boldly against this backdrop, while antique furniture sat alongside comfortable sofas populated by pastel cushions. Characterful and distinctive, the room epitomized the Hicks design philosophy.

Rucker-Wheeler House

Chrissie Rucker & Rose Uniacke
Buckinghamshire, England (UK), 2008

....

The White Company was founded in the Nineties by entrepreneur Chrissie Rucker, based on the idea that white and neutral tones offer an enticing foundation for calm and inviting homes. This was not about minimalism but a way of living that creates a rounded and textural canvas for daily life, whether in the town or country. Rucker's own family homes have gently suggested how such a design philosophy might be applied. Around 2007, Rucker and her husband, Nicholas Wheeler, bought this period country house, collaborating with designer Rose Uniacke on the interiors. The main living spaces retain much of their original seventeenth-century architectural detailing. In the drawing room, for example, the characterful fire surround and cornicing are picked out in shades of white, while linen curtains and cushions soften the space. Antique tables mix with Uniacke's comfortable sofas, while the central ottoman doubles as a display surface for books and vases. The sculptural chandelier's bronze branches and foliage are echoed by the weeping fig in one corner, along with other subtle displays of greenery, which shine out against such a restrained but elegant backdrop.

Ahm House

Povl Ahm & Jørn Utzon
Harpenden, Hertfordshire, England (UK), 1963

....

Through his work with the London office of Ove Arup & Partners, the Danish structural engineer Povl Ahm (1926–2005) worked with some of the great architects of the twentieth century. One of these, Jørn Utzon (1918–2008, see p. 244), designed Ahm's own mid-century house in Harpenden, making it the Danish master's only English project. Working with Utzon's plans, Ahm pushed the house widthways into the gently sloping suburban site, using a palette of brick, concrete, and glass. From the street, the house is largely closed and enigmatic but inside the building opens up dramatically as it steps upward toward the rear. The most enticing space is undoubtedly the spacious living room, which overlooks the back garden. There, exposed concrete beams, bare brickwork, and timber combines with a seating area arranged around a fireplace, and then, a step-up, a white-tiled garden room feeds out to an adjoining terrace. Sensitive furnishing here includes a collection of Arne Jacobsen Egg chairs and Poul Cadovius's Royal System shelving. Grade II listed in 1998, the interiors still retain extraordinary character, offering a touch of Denmark in the English suburbs.

Barton Court

Terence Conran
Berkshire, England (UK), 1971

From the early Seventies onward Barton Court in Berkshire was a constant presence in Sir Terence Conran's life (1931–2020). This substantial Georgian house suggested how old and new might coexist in a harmonious way, offering an elegant and personal masterclass in twentieth-century living. The eighteenth-century building, which had served time as a boys' school, was derelict and in need of revival when Conran bought it. The designer, entrepreneur, retailer, and restaurateur fell in love with the house's proportions and symmetry and recognized that it could and would become a much-loved family home: "I could see how I could make it simple and modern . . . with contemporary furniture mixed alongside antique finds and my collections," said Conran. Key spaces at Barton Court included the spacious kitchen/dining room, Conran's study and the generously scaled primary bedroom and bathroom. The large and inviting reception room housed self-designed pieces, such as the large L-shaped sofa that faced the fireplace, as well as antique and mid-century pieces, along with a glass chair by Thomas Heatherwick. The white walls and surfaces also offered a canvas for the art of display—another of Conran's many talents—with neatly arranged shelves hosting collections of glassware and smaller artworks.

Alidad Apartment

Alidad
London, England (UK), 1980

....

The design and decoration of Alidad's London apartment played a key part in his decision to become an interior designer. For many years he worked at Sotheby's auction house as director of the department of Islamic art and textiles. Indeed his deep-rooted love of pattern and color, influenced by his child-hood in Iran, fed into the creation of the key living spaces at his London home. They included the library, where Alidad painted both the walls and ceilings in a distinctive red-and-gold design that draws on a number of Islamic reference points, and the dining room, where the walls were clad in shimmer-ing panels of hand-painted and silver-leafed leather. A mix of thoughtful opulence and an English focus on comfort helped to define Alidad's approach to interiors throughout, as seen in the drawing room. Here, the focal point is a seventeenth-century Flemish tapestry floating on pale yellow walls, while the sofa below is upholstered in linen from Pierre Frey. The vertical moldings on the walls, inlaid with small mirrored disks, help to frame the arrangement of pictures and paintings. The apartment has subtly evolved over the years, but the ethos behind it remains the same: "The art of doing a suc-cessful job is when a home looks natural, as though that's the way it should be."

Newson-Stockdale Apartment

Marc Newson & Squire and Partners
London, England (UK), 2010

....

The interiors of designer Marc Newson's London home were informed by chalet style. In particular, the mountaintop home featured in Alfred Hitchcock's classic 1959 thriller *North by Northwest* helped inspire Newson's approach to his spacious apartment on the second floor of a former mail-sorting depot. Newson and his partner, fashion editor Charlotte Stockdale, worked in collaboration with London architects Squire and Partners, and wanted to preserve the existing sense of open space and volume while avoiding the cold minimalism of many loft conversions. In the double-height living room, Newson coated the walls around the navy-hued central fireplace with rounded river rocks. An antler-style ceiling light hovers over two deep, large sofas covered in a verdant, mid-century Josef Frank fabric produced by Svenskt Tenn, while two of Newson's own Micarta chairs join the arrangement around the fireplace. A number of other pieces of furniture by the multi-faceted, Australian-born designer populate the apartment, including his Low Voronoi console situated in the adjoining dining area. The units in the kitchen beyond share a particular shade of pistachio green that was also used on the bodywork of Newson's vintage Aston Martin DB4.

Gurney House

Claud Cecil Gurney
London, England (UK), 2014

Claud Cecil Gurney is a house collector. The founder of de Gournay, which produces handcrafted chinoiserie wallpapers as well as ceramics and textiles, Gurney has homes in England, France, Russia, and Croatia. Among them is an elegant London mews house. The origins of de Gournay (taken from the Francophone version of the family name) lie partly in Gurney's early passion for collecting Chinese porcelain. He was increasingly attracted to the fine artisanal traditions of China and spotted an early opportunity to collaborate with the country's craftspeople on historically influenced contemporary wallpapers. A number of de Gournay wallpapers are evident within the interiors of Gurney's mews house, which he rebuilt and remodeled according to his own design. A prime example is the spacious living room on the top floor of the house, which benefits from large windows and balconies. Here a willow-print wallpaper provides an ethereal pattern around the glass fireplace, while the same design has been applied to the diaphanous window curtains. Gurney had a copy made of his original George III–period sofa to create a matching pair for the fireplace seating.

Dr. Rogers House

Richard Rogers
London, England (UK), 1969

For Richard Rogers, this house in Wimbledon designed for his parents—Dr. William and Dada Rogers—was a key project in terms of the evolution of his career as an architect and his thinking about design. The single-story, steel-framed house encompassed many of the themes explored further in later projects, including the Pompidou Center (1977). There is a lightweight but super-strong steel frame, an exposed structure painted in bold colors, and a powerful degree of openness and transparency. The home, which was later lived in by Rogers's son Ab, maximizes the sense of transparency offered by its floor-to-ceiling banks of glass, front and back, while providing a striking sense of connection with the gardens. Inside, the kitchen was pushed to one side behind a sunshine-yellow unit— which Rogers's ceramicist mother, Dada, used to display her art—and the bedrooms to the other, leaving the central living space open and fluid, dotted with bright pieces of furniture. Vivid lemon hues were used for the steel framework, adding a playful note to a serious building. Like Michael and Patty Hopkins' home in Hampstead (see p. 204), Rogers's house became a key exemplar in the development of the UK's influential High-Tech movement.

Kiely House

Orla Kiely
London, England (UK), 2011

....

The Irish-born designer Orla Kiely founded her own fashion and homeware label in 1997, together with her husband Dermott Rowan. The playful patterns and motifs of the mid-century period, in particular, served as a key influence upon her work. Many of Kiely's colorful designs appear in her Victorian terraced family house in Clapham, south London. While the four-story house retains a number of original period features, there is a vibrant mid-century thread running throughout. Kiely made some substantial changes, including at lower-ground level, where the couple created a more fluid sense of connection with the rear terrace and garden. Here, the shift in floor level has allowed Kiely to create a subtle sense of distinction between the sunken seating area at one end and the kitchen/dining area at the other, while still retaining an open plan. The two zones are further defined by changes in flooring and pattern. A mustard rhododendron print forms a focal point within the lounge area, while the move to a pea-green floor helps to characterize the rest of the space. The sculptural wood-burning stove by Malm offers another vibrant element, as well as warming the space. The distinctive island, with a matching storage unit suspended above it at mid-height, also has a characterful mid-century quality.

Hopkins House

Michael & Patty Hopkins
London, England (UK), 1976

....

Discreetly positioned among the quiet and leafy residential streets of Hampstead, with their Georgian and Victorian building stock, the Hopkins House is a key exemplar of the High-Tech movement, which came to the fore in the UK during the Seventies and Eighties. Michael and Patty Hopkins had outgrown their previous family home in Highgate, but also needed space for their new architectural practice. The Hopkinses used a steel frame to create a two-story rectangular home, infilled with metal panels to the sides but opening up dramatically to the rear garden via an expanse of glass. Their specially developed grid layout was highly flexible. Simple partitions arranged in a fluid formation divided up the downstairs family bedrooms with the garden-facing kitchen, dining area, and living room. The furnishings were minimal yet chosen to impact—such as the living room's bright-yellow Maralunga sofa by Vico Magistretti for Cassina, and the dining room's Eileen Gray E1027 Side Table and collection of Eames mesh office chairs. Steelwork, including the central spiral staircase, was a vibrant blue tone, adding a touch of playfulness to the house that functioned as the original architects' showcase.

Hoppen House
Kelly Hoppen
London, England (UK), 2015

....

The "East-meets-West" approach to interiors developed by Kelly Hoppen during the Nineties and noughties made her one of the most successful designers of the time. Her spaces were suffused with a sense of order and calm. Hoppen's own homes feature in a number of influential design books and have played an important part in the evolution of her work. The most ambitious of these spaces is undoubtedly the former Phillips auction house in the Bayswater area of London that Hoppen converted into a private residence. The building had a sense of volume and scale that allowed Hoppen's focus on texture and light to be seen at its best. One of the open-plan living area's most dramatic elements is the dining zone. Soaring ceilings add to the luxurious sense of open space and wooden-parquet floors provide warmth (it reportedly took six months to create the right shade). Hoppen contrasts white walls and ceilings with a number of black notes, as seen in the Marc Newson (see p. 202) chair, stools, and artworks. A geometric, custom lighting installation hovers over the custom 20-foot-long (6-meter) dining table, topped in bluestone and flanked by seating from Christian Liaigre (see p. 152).

Pawson House

John Pawson
London, England (UK), 1999

The fascination with the kind of minimalism espoused by architect and designer John Pawson is not simply to do with design but a way of living. Can it really be possible to live so simply and calmly, with clean lines and uncluttered surfaces, given all the complexities of daily life? The question was particular apposite when it came to the subject of Pawson's own London family home, which was widely published around 2000. The remodeling of Pawson's nineteenth-century, four-story terraced house involved the retention of the original facade but the reinvention of almost everything behind it. Any decoration and ornament was stripped back, while a new staircase was tucked to one side and services discreetly hidden away. The lower-ground floor was devoted to a family kitchen and dining room, while the crisp-white counters pierce the glass wall to the garden and continue outward. Upstairs in the living room, banks of cupboards create storage walls, while the fireplace is reduced to a neat, dark rectangular aperture in a creamy-white wall, flanked by a choice of elegant Danish furniture. The emphasis was on a pleasing and enviable sense of order and serenity, yet to achieve such perfection required discipline by design. As Pawson says: "It is very complex to make something simple."

Housden House

Brian Housden
London, England (UK), 1965

Despite its period gentility, Hampstead is home to a number of Modernist surprises, including 2 Willow Road (1939) by Ernö Goldfinger, Michael and Patty Hopkins' eponymous home (1976, see p. 204), and Housden House, an extraordinary 1965 Brutalist gem overlooking the southern edges of Hampstead Heath. In designing one of the most remarkable houses of the Sixties, Brian Housden (1928–2014) let his imagination run free, inspired by a brief conversation with Gerrit Rietveld and drawing inspiration from other Modernist greats, such as Pierre Chareau. Tucked between the neighboring buildings, the concrete-and-glass-brick house is arranged over three principal levels. Raw concrete and exposed pipes and services are balanced with a playful approach to color, as seen on the lower-ground floor. Here, Housden defined the dining zone within a lightly sunken white circle, bordered by a blue, mosaic-tiled floor. The dining table was designed by Housden himself, while a blue curtain on a ceiling track could be drawn around to lightly separate it from the kitchen and living room. A pinky-red hue is used in the steel window frames for the operable glazing, which sits between the banks of translucent glass brick.

Collett House

Anthony Collett
London, England (UK), 1982

For many years, interior designer Anthony Collett was nervous about using strong colors in his work. But, then, during the Eighties he began collecting vibrantly glazed nineteenth-century studio pottery, picking up one or two pieces at a time at Portobello Market. As his collection of ruby-red, cobalt-blue, and sunflower-yellow vases began to grow, so too did Collett's confidence about blending rich hues together: "Collecting these vases made me realize that if colors were good enough they could be put together and can go with virtually any other." The testing ground became Collett's own family home in West London. Collett and his wife Julia Pines bought the Victorian terraced house around 1982 and began transforming it into a family home. On the ground floor Collett knocked the two reception rooms to create a spacious living room, with light spilling in from both front and back. The walls were partly coated in shimmering gold leaf, which became the perfect backdrop for his pottery collection, which inhabits surfaces and sconces throughout. Self-designed furniture is mixed with Arts and Crafts pieces, as well as contemporary art by Gilbert & George and others.

Little Venice House

Studio Mackereth
London, England (UK), 2011

After many years of searching for a site to create a new home, Sally Mackereth's client eventually came across a modest Victorian coach house with an accompanying workshop. Situated in Little Venice in West London, the project involved the conversion of the coach house into a spacious primary-bedroom suite, while the semiderelict workshop was replaced with a new building looking out onto a hidden courtyard garden. Both architect and client were seduced by the original workshop's sense of scale, proportion, and volume. Mackereth sought to preserve the intrinsic sense of grandeur offered by the open space, while creating a fresh, original, and characterful home. In the double-height living space, top-lit with skylights, Mackereth placed the seating area around a monolithic brick fireplace and hearth. A Draw rug by Kate Blee for Christopher Farr floating on the concrete floor helps to define the lounge zone, along with the furniture itself, which includes two Forties armchairs covered in lilac mohair, a Florence Knoll sofa, and a Fifties semicircular white Ico Parisi sofa, all arranged around an aluminum table by Barber Osgerby for Established & Sons. Semiindustrial textures and finishes are contrasted with softer notes—like the George Nelson wooden side tables—throughout this dramatic and extraordinary room.

Packham House

Richard Dewhurst & Jenny Packham
London, England (UK), 2008

When it comes to interiors, key reference points for fashion designer Jenny Packham include the legendary U.S. designer Dorothy Draper, the English master David Hicks (see p. 198), and Hungarian-French, Op art–maestro Victor Vasarely. Such influences fuse and combine in the spaces of Packham and her partner Matthew Anderson's family home in Hampstead, north London—a four-story Victorian terraced home with pleasing proportions throughout. For help with the house Packham turned to interior architect Richard Dewhurst, drawing on the experience of many years of working together on the design of Jenny Packham stores and showrooms. On the ground floor, Dewhurst and Packham removed a dividing wall between the living room and dining area to create a more open and fluid space. The walls were coated in a textural denim-colored grass cloth (by Altfield), with soft-blue paint for the fire surround and dado rail. Bursts of color and pattern come from Op art prints, ceramics, a geometric rug, and a curated choice of much-loved Seventies classics, such as the two red armchairs by Gae Aulenti. As Packham said, "If you buy pieces that you respect and think are a great design, then you are never going to get fed up with them."

Kemp House

Kit Kemp
London, England (UK), 2003/2013

Interior designer and hotelier Kit Kemp practices what she preaches. As design director of Firmdale Hotels, the group that she cofounded with her husband Tim Kemp, she has pioneered a distinctive warm and inviting aesthetic style with a strong sense of character. The Kemps' Edwardian family home in Knightsbridge has a similarly exuberant personality. A decade after moving in the Kemps decided to radically reconfigure the ground floor to create a more family-friendly layout, revolving around a new kitchen with an easy sense of connection to the living and dining room, which overlook the rear garden. More recently, Kemp refreshed the interiors once again. The roomy entrance hall was remodeled to welcome visitors with a pink chinoiserie wallpaper designed by Kemp (and produced by Andrew Martin). The spacious drawing room is similarly layered with bold texture and pattern, along with a curated collection of modern art with occasional antiques—like an eighteenth-century Spanish chest—and pieces of Africana. Full of life and color, Kemp's generous spaces have a joyful quality without ever being overly serious or pretentiously grand.

Reed Apartment

Jonathan Reed
London, England (UK), 2015

For interior designer Jonathan Reed context is everything: "If you are a good observer, then you can see what it is about a building or an environment that makes it special, and then you find that you have this wealth of reference and starting points to draw on." Keeping this in mind, it's no wonder that Reed's own homes over the last twenty years have been quite different from one another. His apartment in Marylebone is a case in point. It sits on the ground floor of a late-eighteenth-century townhouse that once housed the offices of a plastic surgeon. Reed secured change of use from medical to residential and began turning the former offices into a welcoming home. The interconnecting set of living spaces includes a spacious kitchen and—beyond a set of sliding glass doors—the combined living-and-dining room. A 2011 Bridget Riley screen print (reflected in the mirror) floats above the horsehair sofa designed by Reed Studio, while a 1948 Salerno rug by Barbro Nilsson adds warmth and pattern. With many integrated or custom pieces of furniture—such as the orange corner banquet—together with an emphasis on natural textures and earthy colors, the apartment is characteristically calm, ordered, and handsome.

Crosland House

Neisha Crosland
London, England (UK), 2007

Within an urban neighborhood such as Wandsworth, in south London, a secret courtyard offers an unusual way to introduce light, air, and greenery into a home. Textile designer Neisha Crosland has always loved the idea of courtyard homes: "If it was in France, then perhaps it wouldn't feel so special," says Crosland. "But here in London there is a surprise element and I love being able to look out onto the garden from any window." Crosland and her husband bought the site during the early Nineties, when it was occupied by a collection of garages and a yard used by a horticultural company. The design of the L-shaped house itself evolved over many years, built with help from architect Alex Greenway and landscape designer Sean Walter. The courtyard is one of the first things to be seen as you step into the entrance hallway, which doubles as a welcoming garden room. Here, glass doors retract to create an immediate sense of connection with the sheltered court, while the wall murals and indoor plants tie in with the verdant scene outside, together with the spectrum of greens seen in the choice of curtain textiles. The central, circular table is made of composite stone and holds a collection of ceramics, while the vintage wicker chair adds another organic textural note.

Walter Segal House

Walter Segal & Faye Toogood
London, England (UK), 1964/2018

During the early Sixties, the German-born architect Walter Segal (1907–1985) demolished his second wife's Highgate house. The plan was to replace it with a larger one of his own design. In the meantime, Segal designed and built a "little house in the garden" for their temporary use; the structure, which was never replaced, played a key part in the evolution of Segal's "self-build" housing system. Jumping forward fifty-plus years, the two-story Modernist home caught the attention of Matt Gibberd, cofounder of Modern House, the estate agency, and his wife, designer Faye Toogood (see p. 247). The house, which they went on to buy, neatly encapsulated the interests of both parties, who first met when they were both working at the *World of Interiors* magazine. Inside, existing elements such as the parquet floors, pine cladding, and brick walls were carefully restored. The living and dining room features a number of Toogood's designs—including the sycamore Silo cabinet and a tapestry above the sofa—as well as inherited pieces, like a Marcel Breuer chair. These calm, largely white spaces, full of texture and character embody an aesthetic approach the designer has described as "minimalist folk."

Floral Court

Studio Ashby
London, England (UK), 2019

Interior designer Sophie Ashby studied interior design at Parsons School of Design in New York before founding her own London-based design studio in 2014. She creates interiors that are rich in color and texture, but are also layered with art, which, she explains, "plays a central role in our inspiration and process." Floral Court in London's Covent Garden, is a prime example. The penthouse apartment sits at the summit of a new building designed by architects Kohn Pedersen Fox. Within the apartment, Ashby explored a rich palette of colors and textures, while fusing custom designs, antique pieces, and contemporary furniture. In the dining room, for example, Ashby and her team commissioned a custom dining table, with dried flowers set under its glass tabletop, while a sculptural lighting installation by Cox London above the table also echoes the floral theme, referencing the apartment's setting close to the former Covent Garden flower market. In the living room, similarly, artist Christabel Forbes was commissioned to create a focal point painting, by the crescent-shaped sofa, on the theme of an urban garden. Other artists represented in the space include John Bartlett and ceramicist Abigail Ozora Simpson, while the colorful rug offers another eye-catching custom design.

Avery Row

Nancy Lancaster & John Fowler
London, England (UK), 1959

....

The Yellow Room, in Mayfair's Brook Street, has been described as one of the most influential spaces of the twentieth century. This spacious, buttercup-yellow, barrel-vaulted room was like a theater set. Born and raised in the United States, Nancy Lancaster (1897–1994) settled in England after her first marriage to British politician Ronald Tree. She established her reputation as a tastemaker and guardian of English country-house style with a series of her own homes, including Haseley Court in Oxfordshire, designed in collaboration with John Fowler (1906–1977, see p. 221), who became her business partner in 1948 after she bought Colefax and Fowler.

After selling her London house in 1957, Lancaster took a long lease on the rooms above the Colefax & Fowler showroom. Lancaster herself reported that the statement buttercup-yellow color was suggested by her cousin, architect Paul Phipps (1880–1953). Antique bookcases anchored each corner of the room and grand Elizabethan portraits floated on the walls surrounded by a choice of comforting armchairs and sofas. Two Louis XIV chairs were upholstered in an 1840s chintz that became the firm's Old Rose fabric. Given Lancaster's status as a leading socialite, the Yellow Room soon became one of the best-known salons in the capital.

Bella Freud Apartment

**Retrouvius, Bella Freud &
Piercy&Company**
London, England (UK), 2018

....

The heritage-listed Helios building at the Television Centre in London's White City was completed in 1960 by architect Graham Dawbarn (1893–1976). The elegant drum-like building formerly housed the BBC headquarters before a long redevelopment process transformed it into an urban village, comprising a hotel, members club, offices, and apartments. This penthouse represents a collaboration between architects Piercy&Company, interior designer Maria Speake of Retrouvius, and the fashion designer Bella Freud. Speake and Freud have collaborated on a number of projects together, including the latter's own home and her London flagship store. With its vivid use of texture and color, the interiors of the duplex draw inspiration from the vibrant design scene of the Seventies. In the main living space, for example, Speake and Freud teamed emerald-green rugs and matching detailing for structural elements, such as the pillars, with a textural-hessian coating for the walls. Gloss-black sofas are graced with standout orange cushions, while the Seventies influence continues into the dining area, with its glass-topped table and a set of steel-framed, cantilevered dining chairs.

Capel Manor House

Michael Manser
Kent, England (UK), 1970

....

Architect and architectural critic Michael Manser (1929–2016) was the author of a series of original English mid-century houses influenced by the work of pioneering Modernists such as Ludwig Mies van der Rohe and Philip Johnson. Manser's sophisticated, steel-framed residential pavilions included Forest Lodge House, Ashtead, Surrey (1967) and, perhaps his finest achievement, Capel Manor House. The house was commissioned by politician John Howard and his wife, Maisie. The site alone was extraordinary, as the gardens and remains of a mansion designed in the 1860s by architect Thomas Henry Wyatt. The Modernist pavilion itself was built on the remaining historic terrace with its grand stone steps leading down to the elegant gardens. Internally, dark-brown brick walls helped to gently partition the component spaces of the house, including the central living room where the sunken seating area enjoyed open views from floor-to-ceiling windows. Capel Manor House is now owned by TV producer and entrepreneur Remy Blumenfeld, who redecorated with period-appropriate Seventies furniture, sculptures by his mother, Helaine Blumenfeld, paintings by Alex Nichols, and works by his partner, Henryk Hetflaisz.

Kent Reservoir House

Brinkworth
Kent, England (UK), 2011

Artist Dinos Chapman's work has often been experimental or even iconoclastic in character. When it came to the dream of finding a country house, he and his wife, designer Tiphaine de Lussy, finally settled on an equally decidedly unconventional disused 1930s concrete reservoir in the Kent countryside. "The experience of going into this old reservoir was quite amazing," said Chapman. "It felt cavernous and huge, but it didn't feel anything like a living space." With the assistance of architectural designer Kevin Brennan of Brinkworth, the family found a way of converting this empty box into an extraordinary home. The seating area, dining zone, and kitchen sit within a fluid triptych of interconnected spaces, partly defined by original concrete pillars and beams. Within this, Chapman and de Lussy layered the interiors with a mix of custom pieces, mid-century finds, and bold artworks that sing out against a white partition wall and shiny concrete floors. A blue shaggy rug adds warmth, as does a trio of overhead chandeliers, formed of reindeer antlers. The bedroom features an assortment of George Nelson's Bubble lanterns and gentle tones, seen, for example, in the vintage chaise longue and sage-hued curtains.

Blackbirds

George Buzuk
Farnham, Surrey, England (UK), 1968

Mid-century architect George Buzuk studied in Poland before settling in London just after World War II. He worked with Murray Ward & Partners for many years and designed a number of original houses in and around Surrey and the Home Counties, including his own family house in Farnham, known as Blackbirds. The house was built with a modest budget but was packed with original ideas. Positioned on a gently sloping site, it features multiple shifts in floor level, including a workshop, guest bedroom, and writing studio (for Buzuk's wife Sheilah) tucked under the main body of the house. The heart of the building is undoubtedly the central living room, which enjoys open views of the surroundings framed by a long ribbon window. The interiors are given warmth and texture by the use of many natural materials, including timber floors, ceilings, and wall paneling, along with stone blocks that form a plinth for the fireplace. With its distinctive vertical flue, the fireplace forms a focal point for the seating area, while a palette of lime greens—seen in a feature wall and sofa—and soft whites works well with the natural tones. The primary suite is positioned a few steps up at the far end of the house.

Hunting Lodge

John Fowler & Nicholas Haslam
Oldiham, Hampshire, England (UK), 1977

....

The Hunting Lodge at Odiham, Hampshire is full of history. It was built during the fifteenth-century for King Henry VII when the area was surrounded by woodland and it was said to be the first meeting place of the king's eldest son Arthur and his future wife Catherine of Aragon. Later, during the early-seventeenth century, the house was remodeled and its distinctive three-pinnacle Jacobean brick facade was added. Just after World War II, the lodge became the country escape of John Fowler (1906—1977, see p. 213)—interior designer and principal of the venerable London firm Colefax and Fowler. In 1977, interior designer Nicholas Haslam rented the house from the National Trust on a long lease. Haslam, who famously balances social playfulness and professional erudition, respectfully took the baton from Fowler. He honored the provenance of the interiors, restoring and replicating many elements from Fowler's time while adding additional layers of his own. One major change was the dining room, where two small rooms were combined to create a fresh space. The living room fuses comfort with Haslam's collections of art, antiques, and personal treasures (which were auctioned by Bonham's in 2019).

Ansty Plum

David Levitt & Sandra Coppin
Wiltshire, England (UK), 1962/2015

With its distinctive mono-pitch roofline, Ansty Plum offers a touch of mid-century charm to a quiet Wiltshire hillside. The house was designed by architect David Levitt, of Levitt Bernstein, for the structural engineer Roger Rigby, a director at Ove Arup & Partners, with Rigby himself much involved in the design and build of this family home. Later, Rigby asked Brutalist architects Alison and Peter Smithson to design a separate studio in the sloping garden. More recently, Ansty Plum has become home to another architect, Sandra Coppin (of Coppin Dockray), and her family. Coppin has lovingly restored and updated the building. The key space at Ansty Plum is the open-plan living area. Here, the wood-burning stove and its brick fireplace form a focal point for the seating area, which features a Hans J. Wegner sofa and a leather armchair that came with the house. Flagstone floors and sloping timber ceilings, along with exposed brickwork, unify the space, which also includes a dining area facing the ribbon window; the tabletop is a reclaimed zinc roof panel. The adjoining kitchen is tucked under a cozy, timber-clad mezzanine bedroom.

Kasteel Van's-Gravenwezel

Axel Vervoordt
Schilde (BE), 1988

Since the 1980s the designer and curator Axel Vervoordt has built a global following; his interiors have a famously timeless quality derived from his love for the patina of history and a respect for the Japanese philosophy of *wabi-sabi*, which embraces the beauty of imperfection. These influences combine with a modern sensibility and an appreciation of contemporary patterns of living. During the Eighties Vervoordt bought a twelfth-century moated castle in the semirural Belgian municipality of Schilde to the northeast of Antwerp. This enchanting home, which the sculptor-architect Jan Pieter van Baurscheit the Younger

(1699–1768) had remodeled in the eighteenth century, gave Vervoordt the chance to explore his ideas on a grand scale. The castle offered more than fifty rooms with varied characters. Certain rooms, including the kitchen and living spaces, have a sense of organic simplicity, with wood or stone floors and limewashed walls. Other spaces, such as the peaceful, almost monochrome tea room, feature more neoclassical features and detailing; the white walls here are populated with a series of decorative sconces holding part of the designer's extensive collection of blue-and-white Ming dynasty china.

Maison Emery

Agnès Emery
Brussels (BE), 1996

....

When designer Agnès Emery (see p. 338) decided to move from rural Belgium to Brussels, she brought the colors of the countryside with her. Her company, Emery & Cie, is well known for its collections of paint colors, tiles, and textiles, which draw upon influences from the Art Nouveau and Arts and Crafts movements, as well as the vernacular design traditions of North Africa. The move to a Brussels townhouse offered a golden opportunity to combine these elements within the well-proportioned, elegant spaces of her new home, conceived as an urban sanctuary. Throughout, the palette inspired by the natural world, with Emery employing a small assortment of greens and blues within a purposefully narrow tonal range, which enabled her to create subtle contrasts while retaining a sense of overall cohesion—pearlescent greens and deep moss hues mingle with sea-blue shades, for example. In the dining room, a variety of mismatched mirrors helps to circulate light while reflecting and enhancing the pale green of the walls. Fairytalelike touches abound, seen in objects like the twin toadstools, used as a doorstop, and taxidermy bunny. Throughout the house, the overall effect is that of a cocoon.

VDC Residence

Vincent Van Duysen
Near Kortrijk (BE), 2010

The Belgian architect and designer Vincent Van Duysen has often worked at the intersection between past and present. His houses and rooms, in particular, have a contemporary quality that have been described as "minimalist," yet there is a characterful quality that comes of respect for history and a considered, layered approach to materiality, texture, and patina. The VDC Residence, near the city of Kortrijk to the west of Belgium, is a prime example of his ability to work within this borderland between the old and the new. The original villa was built in the Fifties and has a distinctive grandeur that references the neoclassicism of the eighteenth and nineteenth century. Van Duysen was asked to sensitively update the residence for modern living but also to extend the residence into the gardens, originally designed by landscape designer Russell Page. The home now offers a choice of spaces, designed for use partly depending on the time of year. There is, for example, both a winter living room and this summer living room, where the paneled walls and ceilings are painted a crisp white and the fireplace and surround a deep black. Black and white contrasts prevail throughout the space. In this context, modest bursts of color seen in the choice of cushions and art stand out vividly. "The palette is calm and serene but never dull," says Van Duysen.

Ungers House III

Oswald Mathias Ungers
Cologne (DE), 1995

The three houses that the influential German architect Oswald Mathias Ungers (1926–2007) designed for himself and his family in Cologne have been described as an autobiography. He began in 1958 with a house of brick and concrete that was full of complex ideas and multiple shifts in proportion, volume, and scale. Around thirty years later Ungers extended the house and added a second building alongside it known as the Cube, which was a much more precise and geometric structure designed to house the architect's extensive library of books and sculptures. Six years later, this journey toward architectural purity and abstraction culminated in Ungers House III (a.k.a. Haus Kämpchensweg). "The new house is cold, rational, monochrome, and pared to the bone," Ungers wrote. Ungers House III was an exercise in disciplined mathematical precision of a kind that Ludwig Wittgenstein might have enjoyed. The architect designed it as a crisp rectangle with a flat roof. In the sitting room a collection of boxy sofas, desks, and chairs in dark lacquered wood—all designed by Ungers and his wife, Liselotte Gabler—stand out against the white walls. Within each minimalist space of the home, the furniture, orthogonal in form, is exactingly adapted to the scale of each of the rooms.

Rams Residence

Dieter Rams
Kronberg (DE), 1971

Dieter Rams, head of design at Braun from 1961 to 1995, coined the maxim "Less is better." Naturally, simplicity reigns in his design of the Doppelbungalow he has shared with his wife since 1971. During the early Seventies, Braun offered Rams a site to build a house on a parcel of land the company acquired not far from its Frankfurt headquarters. Here he was able to express his design principles—and memorable maxim—on a large scale. The L-shaped building is embedded into a hillside site and oriented around a swimming pool and Japanese-style gardens. The main living spaces are all on one level and set out in an orderly manner, with white ceramic tiles and white walls. "The composition of these rooms represents the basic intention behind my design: simplicity, essentiality, and openness," he once remarked. The sitting room features a collection of leather Sesselprogramm 620 armchairs, designed by Rams for Vitsœ, framed by a rug and facing a neat fireplace. Rams's famous Vitsœ shelving system, which he designed at age twenty-eight, is a focal point; the flexible modular system is still in production and much in demand today. Color comes from the books and personal effects the shelves hold, including Japanese lacquer bowls.

Schloss Untersiemau

Gert Voorjans
Near Coburg (DE), 2014

There is a dreamlike fantastical quality to the work of Belgian designer Gert Voorjans. After studying interiors and art in Belgium, Italy, and England, Voorjans went to work with Axel Vervoordt (see p. 223) for eight years then, in 1997, he created his own Antwerp design studio and began to forge his own distinctive direction. Alongside multiple fashion stores for Dries Van Noten, among other projects, major residential commissions included the reinvention of the Bavarian castle, Schloss Untersiemau. Situated near the historic town of Coburg, in Upper Franconia, the property has a fairytale quality owing to its stone gate-houses, circular towers, and the moat. The oldest parts of the building date back to the sixteenth century but required both renovation and modernization to create a home suited to twenty-first century living. The dining room is a hymn to color, with its tartan-style fabric created for the walls and dining chairs. Other living spaces offer grandeur and open proportions, as seen in the circular colonnaded drawing room, with its skyscape ceiling mural and pale-pastel upholstery. The surreal quality to the space is found throughout many of the statement rooms within this extensive project.

Bavarian Dacha

Studio Peregalli
Bavaria (DE), 2019

There is a timeless and often dreamlike quality to Studio Peregalli's residential architecture and interiors . They have a sense of belonging, tied to history and the genius loci, and yet there is often an element of theatrical fantasy. This Bavarian *dacha* (cottage), for example, feels so natural because of how it has been woven into its bucolic forest setting. The client wanted to create an escape, or refuge, within the grounds of a larger property and identified the site of an existing guesthouse as a possibility. Finding that the existing building was too fragile to save, Studio Peregalli decided to build a new timber-clad *dacha* on the site of the old building. Inside, the atelier made the most of extraordinary pieces of architectural salvage and period elements to lend the *dacha* character and delight. For example, the sitting room features reclaimed eighteenth-century Tyrolean wood paneling, whose decorative paintwork conjures a feeling of faded grandeur. A comfortable ruby-red corduroy sofa specially designed by Studio Peregalli anchors the room, which is also decorated with antiques, like the Chinese low table, and Expressionist artworks from the client's collection.

Tsarkoe Selo Chinese Village Pavilion

Kirill Istomin
Saint Petersburg (RU), 2015

....

The Russian interior designer Kirill Istomin studied at the Parsons School of Design in New York before working with the American design legend Albert Hadley (see pp. 85 and 98) during the Nineties. He opened his own studio in 2002, developing a portfolio of projects characterized by a playful love of color and pattern. The Tsarskoe Selo Chinese Village near Saint Petersburg was built during the eighteenth century, for the Russian royal family, according to a master plan developed by Scottish architect Charles Cameron. Istomin's client helped to finance the restoration of the village, as well as adopting this pavilion as a weekend retreat. None of the original interiors had survived, giving Istomin free rein to invent his own version of "whimsical eighteenth-century architecture" with a Chinese-inspired theme. In the living room, the focal point is the eye-catching fireplace mantel, based on a seventeenth-century Dutch design, topped with twin Chinese dragons and complemented by vintage wall-mounted sconces and ceramics. The white walls here form a subtle backdrop for the more expressive colors of the curtains, cushions, and upholstery, including sage velvet by Cowtan & Tout for the sofa.

Wood Patchwork House

Peter Kostelov
Konakovsky District, Tver Oblast (RU), 2009

....

Within his residential work the Russian architect Peter Kostelov has referenced both the vernacular ideal of the *dacha* and the Soviet era ethos of making do and getting by. During the Soviet period standard materials were often in short supply, so a culture of working with whatever might be available developed over time, leading to a host of characterful patchwork buildings. Such thinking lay behind the design of this three-story vacation and weekend house in Konakovsky District, Tver Oblast, a small village to the northwest of Moscow and not far from the Volga River. The interiors—arranged around a central timber staircase—feature a range of timber with different textures and tones, creating the sense of a patchwork. Various kinds of wood and oriented strand boards are used throughout—not only for the walls, floors, and ceilings but also for integrated elements, such as the bookshelves and the seating zone, where striped cushions in deep pink and brown tones are laid directly on a raised platform. A low table, also in timber, is one of just a few items of furniture here, while storage is cleverly tucked below.

Izba Apartment

Denis Perestoronin
Moscow (RU), 2011

Across Russia and the Slavic countries an *izba* is a simple log cabin. Usually part of a rural farmstead, these vernacular cottages were made by hand using local materials and decorated according to folk traditions. Denis Perestoronin, a designer and antique dealer with a particular interest in folk art, decided that he would like to create an *izba* in central Moscow. Perestoronin found a rather unpromising apartment building that offered him a blank canvas to do as he wished. Drawing on a rich collection of antiques and architectural salvage, Perestoronin employed the rescued log wall of an *izba* to separate his living room and library, while adding a timber ceiling and an elegant parquet floor of his own design. Other key elements include the traditional tiled stoves, also common to Russian *izbas* and cottages, placed in the living room and bedroom. The kitchen is custom, with painted cupboard doors inspired by folk-art patterns and motifs. Much of the antique wooden furniture is also painted, creating layers of natural texture and warmth within this rustic escape at the heart of the city.

Sidorov Dacha

Gabhan O'Keeffe
Rublevo-Uspenskoye (RU), 2012

London-based designer Gabhan O'Keeffe is known for his fearless and friendly use of color and pattern, evidenced by landmark projects such as his flamboyant spaces for Mourad Mazouz's Sketch gastrodome in Mayfair in London. The word "dacha" usually suggests a modest cabin in the woods, but Russian entrepreneur Vassily Sidorov's home is a rural escape to the west of Moscow, offering O'Keeffe plenty of scope to create something out of the ordinary here. The double-height drawing room and the adjoining dining room, for example, features walls coated in a shimmering raffia and silk wallpaper. One of the most compelling spaces is the library, which has a more intimate sense of proportion and scale. Yet, here too, O'Keeffe has layered the space with an exuberant choice of textures and patterns, with just enough in the way of tonal links to tie it all together. Custom elements prevail including the L-shaped sofa with an array of striped cushions and bolsters, along with a custom zebrano coffee table, and beneath boldly patterned rugs, while the wenge timber bookshelves are stained a fresh sea blue.

Europe
South

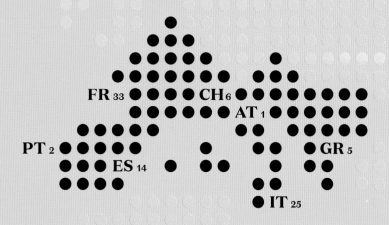

Casa Na Areia

Aires Mateus
Comporta (PT), 2011

Casas Na Areia resulted from Portuguese architect Manuel Aires Mateus's highly imaginative response to a unique site-specific natural setting. Hotelier João Rodrigues acquired two former fishermen's huts among the Comporta dunes, where rice paddies and the Sado Estuary Natural Reserve lie in one direction and the beach and open sea in the other. Rodrigues asked Aires Mateus to create a retreat there that was contemporary, yet drew inspiration from the original huts and the local vernacular. Rather than designing one large building, Aires Mateus created a handful of modest cabanas with unshowy timber decks arranged around a swimming pool. As well as a small service building, there are three cabins devoted to bedrooms and bathrooms, offering a degree of privacy. A fourth cabin, made with thatch and straw, holds the main living room and communal spaces. While the natural textures of the walls and ceilings echo local traditions, the banks of glass and contemporary furniture lend a twenty-first century feel to the space. Most enticing of all is the way Aires Mateus invited the dunes inside by loading the floors in loose sand, introducing another element of natural texture.

Casa Nina

Jacques Grange
Comporta (PT), c. 2000

The Portuguese word *comporta* means a water gate, yet over the years the word has also become synonymous with a stylish retreat on the Herdade da Comporta peninsula at the mouth of the Sado Estuary. Like Trancoso in Brazil and Essaouira in Morocco, Comporta is a destination that draws architects and designers in particular, including Jacques Grange. Grange first came to Comporta in the late Eighties to visit his friend Vera Iachia. Thanks to strict building regulations, this beachside enclave had remained quiet and undeveloped over the years. Grange was soon seduced: "You walk to the beach over the dunes and often it is empty," he has said. "You wake up and you see a stork fly above you. That is luxury." The French designer eventually bought a house here, Casa Nina, which once belonged to Iachia's mother and comprised four traditional thatched huts among the dunes. Grange used a light touch in keeping with the rustic charm of the house, with its white walls and exposed beams and ceilings. The living room in the primary cabana is informal and relaxed, featuring a mix of Fifties French seating and comfortable sofas, a farmhouse-style teak dining table, and rugs and cushions from Morocco.

Pinto Coelho Residence

Duarte Pinto Coelho
Madrid (ES), c. 1961

"A house should, at the end, look as if a designer had never set foot in it," said the celebrated designer Duarte Pinto Coelho (1923–2010). The irony, of course, was that Pinto Coelho became one of the most influential interiors designers in Iberia, commissioned to design palaces, embassies, and country estates. Born in Portugal, he settled first in Paris, where key influences on his choice of vocation included Madeleine Castaing (see pp. 269 and 277) and fashion designers such as Elsa Schiaparelli formed part of his social circle. During the Fifties, the designer lived and worked in Spain, eventually moving into an apartment on the principal floor of the Palacio Pinohermosa. The home became a setting for his collections of art, ceramics, and antiques, drawn from Spain and Portugal, as well as other parts of Italy. The grand salon was characteristically refined and exuberant, with a palette dominated by blues and golden yellows, with space enough for both a grand piano and a baroque Aragonese organ. It was a room for entertaining in style, with his extraordinary guest book including Ava Gardner, Truman Capote, and Oscar de la Renta. Following his death, Pinto Coelho's collections of art and antiques—from the Madrid apartment and his country house in Trujillo—were auctioned by Christie's.

Castillo Duplex

Lorenzo Castillo
Madrid (ES), 2008

The noble building that holds interior designer Lorenzo Castillo's duplex has seen many changes over the years. Built in the seventeenth century, it served as a convent before being transformed during the eighteenth century into a prestigious private residence. During the Spanish Civil War, it was divided up into apartments, and, by the time Castillo discovered the building, it had been stripped of much of its finest period detailing. This did not deter Castillo, a designer and well-connected antiques dealer. The spacious, well-proportioned duplex offered an opportunity to create not just a home but also a studio and showroom, encircling a central courtyard with a distinctive black-and-white checkerboard floor. Covered by a glass canopy, the enchanting courtyard became a pivotal outdoor room within Castillo's private realm, layered with statuary and plant life. The walls are lined with mirrors that help refract the sunlight, and Sixties daybeds create a lounge atmosphere. Elsewhere, Castillo used a similar mixture of architectural salvage, antiques, mid-century treasures, and self-designed pieces to create a sophisticated and eclectic blend of the old and new, which—like the building itself—evolves over time.

Silicon House

Selgascano Architects
Madrid (ES), 2006

Architects José Selgas and Lucía Cano live
and work in a garden on the green edges of
Madrid. For many years they were based in
the center of the city, but eventually suc-
cumbed to the leafy charms of La Florida
where they embraced the opportunity to
build a home and studio for themselves.
Among the acacias, laurels, pines, and plane
trees, Selgas and Cano designed three low-
slung, single-story pavilions that seek a vivid
sense of connection with the surrounding
landscape. Their atelier is based in one of
the pavilions, while the house itself is divided
into two complementary adjoining structures, one for daytime use and the other for
the nighttime. Arranged around a sunken
courtyard, both feature extensive ribbons of
glass that frame the greenery. Color plays an
important part inside and outside the largely
open-plan daytime unit, which features
a silicon roof and ceiling beams in bright
orange. A shift in floor level lightly separates
the dining area from the seating area, where
a custom steel fireplace is flanked with fitted
banquettes. A choice of bright and playful
mid-century furniture adds further bursts of
color—oranges and yellows—which sing out
against the gray floors and white walls.

Catalan House

Michèle Van Hove & Nicolas Vanderbeck
Celrà (ES), 2013

Barcelona's Fins de Siècles Gallery, run by
Belgian furniture dealers Michèle Van Hove
and Nicolas Vanderbeck, specializes in
twentieth-century design from the Art
Deco period through to the mid-century era.
Van Hove and Vanderbeck wanted a
Catalonian country escape as an alternative
to city living, and in 2013 they came across
an eighteenth-century farmhouse that had
been modernized during the Seventies by
Spanish architect Cristina Lopez Pavia.
The house was a hybrid but full of character. There were spaces with Catalan-style
vaulted ceilings, as well as pieces of integrated furniture from the Seventies renovation. Importantly, the white walls and simple
terra-cotta floor tiles created a gentle
backdrop for Van Hove and Vanderbeck's
own distinctive layers of furniture, textiles,
lighting, and art. They chose a white-and-
black scheme along with repeated red and
crimson notes. Sculptural floating fireplaces
and dynamic designs in dark tones stand out
like silhouettes against the white walls, while
upholstery and cushions add brighter tones.
This is true of the main living spaces but
also the master suite, which has its own
study area complete with a futuristic red-
and-white Ron Arad rocking chair and a
plush rug with a Sixties-style floral motif.

Casa de Verano

Ricardo Bofill
Girona (ES), 1973

There is a highly ambitious, fantastical, and even epic quality to much of Ricardo Bofill's work (see p. 241). His residential complexes and apartment buildings feel like postmodern dreamscapes, layered with surreal flourishes and allusions. Casa de Verano, in the rural Catalan village of Mont-ras, is a rare example of a private family house that still has a striking sense of scale and complexity. Bofill designed this summer house for his parents, as well as visiting family and friends. Casa de Verano resembles a small village, with a series of brick pavilions arranged around a central pool with a pool house, both clad entirely in deep-red ceramic tiles. In the main residence Bofill designed an inventive central atrium that served both as a focal point and a living room, with twin Maralunga armchairs by Vico Magistretti for Cassina and cushions in plum tones laid out on a ziggurat of steps that ascend toward adjoining spaces. A mezzanine level, accented by gold balustrades, is accessed by a spiral staircase. Each room seems to coexist within one fluid and semi open-plan space, with neutral-hued curtains used to create privacy as required.

The Factory
Ricardo Bofill
Sant Just Desvern (ES), 1970s

....

Around the same time that Ricardo Bofill
designed and built Casa de Verano for his
parents (see p. 239), he was working on an
extraordinary home for himself in Barcelona.
La Fábrica, which also hosts the offices and
studios of his architectural practice Taller
de Arquitectura, is a dramatic and unconventional house created within the vast
concrete shell of a former cement factory.
Bofill purchased the derelict factory after
realizing that few people cared what happened to it: "The half-ruined factory was a
magic box of wonderful, surreal elements,"
explained the architect. "The biggest challenge was to preserve the complex, which
seemed halfway between a ruin and a clois-
ter." Bofill's factory home balances dramatic
open volumes with rooms of a more intimate
scale. A key element of the intrinsic sense
of theater is the juxtaposition between the
industrial—raw concrete, unembellished
walls with carved-in windows—and the
domestic—comfortable, white sofas and
diaphanous linen curtains. Just as the building's exterior has surrendered to encroach-
ing nature, greenery also abounds in the
interior space—albeit in the form of an army
of pot plants.

La Ricarda

Antoni Bonet
Barcelona (ES), 1963

In 1949 the Gomis family commissioned Spanish architect Antoni Bonet i Castellana (1913–1989) to design a house for them while he was still based in Argentina, where he had settled during the Spanish Civil War. This may help to explain why the house took so long to complete, although things did speed up when Bonet moved his practice to Barcelona in 1963. Situated not far from Barcelona, close to the sea and a lagoon, the house was designed around the landscape, with a series of single-story pavilions among the trees rather than one imposing residence. There was a bedroom pavilion for the parents, one for the children, and then a communal pavilion as well as canopied fresh-air spaces and connecting walkways. The master pavilion was designed to be spacious enough to host not only family gatherings but modest concerts, as the family were great music lovers. Like other parts of the house, this pavilion featured a Catalan-style vaulted roof, distinctive sun-screens, and mosaic-effect windows made from a mixture of clear- and colored-glass blocks. In the main living space, most of the furniture was made by Bonet, including distinctive doubled-sided sofas arranged around an imposing blue fireplace.

Tagliabue Apartment

Benedetta Tagliabue
Barcelona (ES), c. 2008

....

Spanish architect Benedetta Tagliabue and her late husband Enric Miralles (1955–2000), founders of the practice EMBT, took an instinctive and intuitive approach to the design of their family home, a vast but neglected space in Barcelona's Gothic Quarter, hidden away behind the stone facade of an eighteenth-century building. During the substantial restoration project many original and long-lost features were uncovered and recovered, as the architects carved out a two-level home. The main living room is the most generously scaled space, complete with the ghostly outline of a Gothic arch found under the plasterwork of one wall. Although many of the buckling floors had to be replaced, Tagliabue and Miralles saved as many of the decorative tiles as they could, creating a patchwork of ceramic and parquetry. Other "found" elements included two weathered paintings discovered hanging in the courtyard and an ornate salvaged stove that now serves as a window screen and cupboard. Brighter bursts of color and pattern come courtesy of mid-century Josef Frank textiles, used to upholster the cushions on armchairs designed by Alison and Peter Smithson. A sliding wood panel, designed by Tagliabue, is used to store books.

Solo House

Pezo von Ellrichshausen
Cretas (ES), 2013

....

Designed by Chilean architects Mauricio Pezo and Sofia von Ellrichshausen, Solo House is the first in a sequence of landmark houses in the rural enclave of Cretas in Matarraña, situated on the edge of a natural reserve. With the ambition of creating something unique, Pezo von Ellrichshausen were given carte blanche by developer Christian Bourdais. The square concrete house is positioned on top of a hill. The house itself is perched on a plinth and is reached by a spiral staircase contained within the plinth. The unique structure of the house is designed to break down the traditional borders between indoor and outdoor space. In the center of the house is an outdoor courtyard containing a square swimming pool. Four entryways lead beyond the courtyard's walls to separate living spaces with fitted furniture and storage units. These living spaces are themselves hybrid spaces where the glass walls to the exterior retract fully into the floor, transforming each space into a veranda, or loggia, floating above the landscape below. Simple raffia rugs and a carefully edited choice of loose furniture complements the integrated elements in each space without detracting from the purity of these indoor/outdoor rooms and the drama of the open panorama.

House for a Photographer

Carlos Ferrater
Alcanar (ES), 2004

For many years, the photographer José Manuel Ferrater enjoyed spending time in a modest cottage in the middle of an orange grove within the Catalonian coastal enclave of Alcanar. Eventually, an opportunity arose to buy a strip of land facing the beach, so Ferrater decided to build a weekend house here, about two hours' drive northeastward from his home in Barcelona. Naturally the photographer asked his brother, the much-respected Spanish architect Carlos Ferrater, to design this fresh residential retreat. The architect created three small pavilions within a Cubist composition, consisting of a primary pavilion and a studio with the main suite sitting placed within the third; the terraces between the pavilions serve as a partially sheltered outdoor room. The master pavilion is essentially an open-plan living space, with a kitchen island to the rear and a seating zone to the front. White walls and ceilings, along with polished concrete floors, create a calm setting for José Manuel Ferrater's collection of furniture gathered in Africa and Asia. A deep shelf over the picture window forms a gallery in miniature hosting an assembly of sculptures, but the focus is on the window itself, providing a framed view of the avenue of palm trees planted in the garden.

Can Lis

Jørn Utzon
Majorca (ES), 1972

The Danish architect Jørn Utzon (1918–2008, see p. 200) and his family first visited Majorca during the late Sixties. As the son of a naval architect, Utzon loved the idea of living by the sea and managed to buy a parcel of land on the clifftops near Porto Petro on the island's eastern coastline. Utzon famously experimented with ideas for the house at a local café where he used sugar lumps to represent the local sandstone blocks used in the final build. The eventual design comprised a series of four stone pavilions facing the sea, interspersed by outdoor rooms including twin loggias arranged around an open courtyard. For the interiors of Can Lis, which was named after the architect's wife, Utzon sought to replicate some of the atmosphere he had discovered when viewing the sea from inside a nearby cave. The living room echoes this feeling with its combination of stone walls and carefully placed windows, which contrast the blues of the open water and the sandy colors and natural textures of the walls. Sparsely furnished, it features a semicircular sofa accented in glossy black tiles and a large simple fireplace.

Casa La Huerta

Anders Hallberg & Moredesign
Majorca (ES), 2018

....

The Swedish photographer and filmmaker
Anders Hallberg created not just a home for
himself and his family in Majorca but a farmstead that makes the most of the setting and
sunshine. Casa La Huerta, or the "orchard
house," is surrounded by fruit trees and vegetable and herb gardens, while the family
also has its own flock of sheep. The interiors,
too, have a suitably organic, natural, and
textural quality. Hallberg was based in New
York for many years but eventually settled
in Majorca after enjoying a number of family
vacations on the island. The family pieced
together their farmstead after buying two
neighboring parcels of land and embarking
on a lengthy process of restoration and sensitive modernization of the seven-bedroom
farmhouse. Collaborating with Oro del Negro
of Moredesign, Hallberg created a sequence
of inviting communal spaces with rippling
pebble-stone floors, white walls, and exposed
timber beams. The relaxed kitchen and
lounge is one of the family's favorite spaces.
Here, fitted sofas around the edges of the
room face the open fireplace, with cushions
coated in locally sourced sunshine-yellow
textiles, while integrated wall niches display
candles and ceramics.

Majorca House

Ágatha Ruiz de la Prada
Majorca (ES), 2000

....

Spanish fashion designer Ágatha Ruiz de
la Prada credits Majorca as a key influence on her famous love of color, especially
fuchsia pink and magenta. The fashion world
impresario began visiting the island with
her parents as a child and was introduced
to a family friend's white house with a pink-
walled courtyard designed by Francisco
Muñoz Cabrero. Ruiz de la Prada would later
purchase the property to serve as her own
much-loved family retreat. Situated on a
hillside overlooking the sea and backed by
mature trees, the two-level house was built
using Sixties-style clean lines, combined with
expanses of glass connecting the adjoining
terraces. Existing white walls, ceilings, and
floors had created a fresh and neutral foundation, but the pink courtyard offered a particular opportunity to Ruiz de la Prada: "My
biggest must have is color and pink is my
favorite," the designer has said. The fuchsia
thread travels through the house, in indoor
chair cushions, artworks, textiles, and even
the pool sun-lounger pads. These modest
touches of vibrant color provide a striking
foil for the Mediterranean context.

Casa Paloma

Faye Toogood
Ibiza (ES), 2017

London-based Faye Toogood served as an editor at *World of Interiors* for many years before embarking on a multifaceted career encompassing fashion, furniture, home-ware, and interiors (see p. 212). One of her most accomplished residential projects is Casa Paloma in Ibiza, where Toogood was commissioned to renovate and reinvent a substantial Seventies villa in a quiet, rural setting. Externally, windows were replaced, the house was painted a soft, sandy tone, and the garden was redesigned by Stephen Woodhams. Internally, the house became a characterful showcase for Toogood's approach, which adopts a subtle and restrained color palette, rich in textural shifts and contrasts. The result is cohesion and calm. The combined seating and dining area has gentle white-and-cream walls and floors that are complemented by the natural tones of exposed wooden beams. A generously sized Toogood-designed dining table is surrounded by iconic Superleggera chairs by Gio Ponti, while a triptych of large, abstract artworks hangs on nearby walls. Other pieces include a comfortable Piero Lissoni sofa and mid-century designs by Bruno Mathsson and Pierre Paulin. A wall of glass to one side slides away to connect to the adjoining terrace.

Château du Champ de Bataille

Jacques Garcia
Normandy (FR), 1992

As a young child, Jacques Garcia visited Château du Champ de Bataille with his father and declared that one day he would own this palatial estate. Years later, in 1992, the interior designer fulfilled his promise and began work on the monumental task of restoring the house and its grounds. The château was built in the seventeenth century for the comte de Créqui but had served as a hospital for forty-five years. There were just three rooms where Garcia was able to find the original period detailing underneath the layers of paint, and the designer used these spaces as a guide for the sensitive restoration of the building. Neoclassicism has long been a strong influence on Garcia's work, but he did not want the reinvention of the château to involve a slavish re-creation of the past. Sumptuous spaces have the formal grandeur one might expect, and he decorated them with the results of decades of collecting. A hundred pairs of antlers are on the walls of the hunting salon, where there are also numerous stuffed jungle cats and Empire chairs. Other rooms are more personal and even intimate, with an eclectic mélange of treasures and a greater focus on comfort and leisure; a pool table, for example, adds a dash of modernity to Garcia's childhood dream house.

La Datcha

Pierre Bergé & Jacques Grange
Normandy (FR), 1989

La Datcha was first conceived when Pierre Bergé (1930–2017) and his partner, Yves Saint Laurent (1936–2008), owned their Normandy retreat, Château Gabriel (1983). During the Eighties, Bergé commissioned local artisan Pierre Poulain to build a modest *dacha* (log cabin) on the grounds of the neo-Modernist château and asked his friend, interior designer Jacques Grange, to design the interiors with a suitably romantic Chekhovian atmosphere. Following the death of Saint Laurent in 2008 and the subsequent sale of Château Gabriel, Bergé kept the *dacha* and surrounding grounds, deciding to extend the house, which originally consisted of little more than a "great room" and a small kitchen. He added two bedrooms, while Madison Cox redesigned the gardens. At last, the house could function independently. The *dacha*'s interiors were inspired by the jewel colors and Modernist geometry of Ballets Russes costumes and stage sets, the emotive work of Léon Bakst. In the grand salon, the wood walls and floors contrast with the opulent exuberance of the stained-glass windows and doors, as well as the Orientalist tiled fireplace that serves as the room's focal point. The rug in front of the fireplace is Russian, while the antique Austrian armchairs and vintage hunting trophies add an Alpine quality.

Maison Bordeaux-Le Pecq

Claude Parent
Normandy (FR), 1965

....

The Sixties was a time of radical experimentation with architectural form. Increasingly, architects began to break away from the rectangle and the square to explore unconventional geometries. In France one of the leaders of this new shift was Claude Parent (1923–2016), who railed against the right angle and, with Paul Virilio (1932–2018), pioneered the idea of the *fonction oblique*. Parent applied his ideas to churches and shopping centers, as well as a small number of houses, including Maison Bordeaux-Le Pecq. Parent's client for that residence, Andrée Bordeaux-Le Pecq (1910–1973), was an artist, art dealer, and curator with a suitably adventurous sensibility. She had once owned a "bubble house" by the organic architect Jacques Couëlle, and her later home by Parent was a kind of futuristic pagoda. The interiors were equally avant-garde. The exposed ceilings, punctuated with skylights, offered sweeping surfaces of concrete echoed—in the main living room—by a vast custom concrete fireplace by Parent. The fireplace served as the centerpiece of a seating zone with wire chairs by Warren Platner and an Arco lamp by the brothers Pier Giacomo and Achille Castiglioni, suitably sculptural pieces for a house that resembled a sculpture itself.

Maison Deniot

Jean-Louis Deniot
Chantilly (FR), 2002

....

Interior designer Jean-Louis Deniot (see p. 364) has a portfolio of homes in Europe, North Africa, and America, yet this house in Chantilly to the north of Paris was one of his first loves. Given the beauty of the woodland setting, the charming scale of the house, and the pleasing proportions of the rooms within, it is not hard to understand why. With seven bedrooms arranged over three floors, the original farmhouse was built in the 1820s but extended around 1900 when two wings were added and the facade was remodeled to give the house a grander, neoclassical character. By the time Deniot acquired the building it had fallen on hard times. The initial restoration offered a welcome opportunity to bring the house and gardens back to life. Achieving balance is a guiding light for Jean-Louis Deniot, who combined period features and modern elements, including the new, custom country kitchen and breakfast room as well as larger and more inviting bathrooms. The house has continued to evolve over time, blending the serious and the playful, as seen in the central reception room where a mid-century Sputnik ceiling light found at a Paris flea-market takes center stage and instantly makes the space more inviting and interesting than the room's period provenance might first suggest.

Château de Wideville

Valentino Garavani & Henri Samuel
Crespières (FR), 1995

....

The Italian fashion designer Valentino Garavani, commonly known as simply Valentino, has a passion for houses and interiors. "I am only good for two things in this world: designing dresses and the decoration of houses," he once said. Valentino's portfolio includes homes in Italy, Switzerland, England, France, and the United States, and he has worked with interior designers including Jacques Grange, Renzo Mongiardino, Peter Marino, and Henri Samuel (1904–1996, see p. 264). In 1995 Valentino bought Château de Wideville, which is west of Paris, not far from Poissy. Originally built for one of Louis XIII's ministers, the seventeenth-century château is surrounded by extensive gardens; a *pigeonnier* (dovecote) on the grounds has been restored and converted into an additional retreat. Valentino asked Samuel to work with him on the interiors of the château, which became one of the master designer's final projects. One of Valentino's favorite spaces at the château is the winter garden, which features vaulted brick ceilings and a triptych of French doors offering views of formal gardens to the rear of the house, where pristine lawns are punctuated by topiary. Valentino chose an Eastern theme for the room, with blossom tree murals and eighteenth-century English chinoiserie mirrors on the walls. The room is spacious enough for a variety of seating and dining areas, with a mix of cane furniture and more robust, formal Portuguese chairs and tables.

Villa Windsor

Stéphane Boudin
Paris (FR), c. 1963

British king Edward VIII (1894–1972) abdicated the throne in 1936 in order to marry American socialite Wallis Simpson (1896–1986). The couple, who became Duke and Duchess of Windsor, settled in Paris after World War II and took up residence in a grand villa in the Bois de Boulogne, originally built in 1859 for the celebrated Paris city planner Georges-Eugène Haussmann. The interior design of Château Le Bois, or Villa Windsor, came under the jurisdiction of the Duchess, who had famously strong opinions about decor, fashion, and social etiquette. Having first consulted with American actress turned interior decorator Elsie de Wolfe (1859–1950), she eventually settled on Stéphane Boudin (1888–1967, see pp. 123 and 282). He was the head of the Parisian design firm Maison Jansen and later, in 1963, part of the team Jackie Kennedy commissioned to design the private rooms at the White House. Boudin was known for his use of bold colors and did not disappoint here. Photographs of the house that Horst P. Horst took for *Vogue* show her seated in the library, which is dominated by golden yellows for the walls and furnishings, tones matched by her sunshine satin ensemble. The couple's social hub, the dining room, adopted a blue palette reputedly inspired by the "Wallis blue" created for her wedding dress.

Garouste Residence & Studio

Elizabeth Garouste
Paris (FR), c. 2002

The designer Elizabeth Garouste is best known for her fantastical, whimsical, highly collectable furniture. Her sculptural pieces are often biomorphic, with legs that might take a table scuttling away, or with branches and fronds. Garouste caused a stir with Mattia Bonetti during the Eighties with their design of Christian Lacroix's couture salons, as well as their furniture collections. Garouste has worked alone since 2002 from her home studios in Paris and at her country house in Normandy. The Parisian live/work space is a nineteenth-century former mirror workshop. There is space enough here for Garouste's own atelier, which has high ceilings and skylights, but also plenty of room for the living spaces that she sometimes shares with her husband, the artist Gérard Garouste, when he is not in Normandy. The most dramatic space is certainly the grand salon, which combines a semi-industrial character, with its exposed beams and framework, with the feel of a greenhouse. The space is layered with plants and eclectic artworks, along with self-designed pieces in vivid colors and patterns, such as the overlapping rugs in crimson hues on the floor and the golden textiles and cushions flowing upon the twin sofas.

Apartment Haussmannian

Sarah Lavoine
Paris (FR), 2012

....

The Parisian interior and furniture designer Sarah Lavoine is known for her imaginative use of color. In many projects—including her design of her own family apartment—she has used color in a geometric and graphic way, creating vivid contrasts and striking juxtapositions. Shared with her actor husband, Marc, and their three children, her spacious four-bedroom apartment is in a nineteenth-century Haussmannian building near the Louvre and the Jardin des Tuileries. During a renovation of the apartment, Lavoine preserved the original period detailing while the fireplaces and parquet floors

were restored. The living room is a daytime space, with a black-and-white treatment. But the adjoining dining room is a space for the evenings and for entertaining, where Lavoine introduced blocks and bands of vivid sunflower yellow on the walls within a framework of black and white, rather like a Mondrian painting. The dining table is a custom piece, and Lavoine designed the benches alongside it, adding to the layers of interest that give this space the feel of an intimate and sophisticated brasserie in miniature.

Baudoux Apartment

Florence Baudoux
Paris (FR), 2009

Interior architect, art director, and furniture designer Florence Baudoux makes her home in Paris. Looking for a family-sized space for herself, her husband, and their two children, Baudoux—the head of the Parisian design agency Luma—came across a spacious first-floor apartment within a nineteenth-century mansion in the Trocadéro neighborhood. The apartment benefits from soaring ceilings, tall windows, and period detailing, such as the cornicing and other neoclassical flourishes. Undertaking a major renovation, Baudoux balanced the need for private hideaways with the luxury of open space in areas such as the expansive sitting room, which connects to the adjacent dining room via a double doorway. Dark-wood floors and a palette of specially blended soft grays for the walls create an atmospheric backdrop here, while helping to accentuate the detailing of the moldings and carved columns. Within this high drama but restrained setting, splashes of color stand out vividly, as seen in twin Saint Germain sofas in a papal-purple velvet, designed by Baudoux and produced by Gilles Nouailhac. Similarly, the modest splashes of color in the ceramics and art have a significant impact, because of the subtlety of the background tones.

Putman Apartment
Andrée Putman
Paris (FR), 1976

....

With her homes, hotels, and furniture, designer Andrée Putman (1925–2013) pushed the boundaries of convention, as seen, for example, in her conversion of a nineteenth-century water tower in Cologne into a hotel (Hotel im Wasserturm, 1990) and her groundbreaking designs for Ian Schrager's Morgans Hotel in Manhattan (1984), described as the first truly modern boutique hotel. Putman's own home in Paris is similarly avant-garde. During the early Seventies, while she was living next door, Putman had her eye on a late nineteenth-century building that housed a printing workshop. Eventually, in 1976, Putman was able to buy a large, semi-industrial space here and turn it into one of the first Parisian loft apartments. "I designed the apartment too early to be respected for having made a good decision," Putman remarked. "At the time I received condolences. 'Poor Andrée,' people said to me, 'when do you plan to have a real home?'" Putman created a new paradigm for loft conversions, maintaining an open-plan space as much as possible, unified with polished concrete floors and white walls. She zoned this supersize room with a careful arrangement of her furniture, rugs, and screens, with the bedroom separated by breezy gauze curtains; only the bathroom and the kitchen were upstairs, the latter situated in a conservatory of sorts, which leads onto a rooftop garden.

Avenue Montaigne Apartment

Joseph Dirand
Paris (FR), 2017

....

Joseph Dirand creates "frameworks for living" infused with a strong sense of narrative. His work has been described as minimalist, precise, and understated, yet increasingly—in his homes, hotels, and restaurants—Dirand has sought to infuse his spaces with narrative threads. In this respect, cinema is an important influence and also photography; both his father and brother followed the profession and this apartment in central Paris has been compared to an extraordinary stage set. Dirand's client acquired two separate apartments within a grand nineteenth-century building. This generous client offered Dirand carte blanche to create a dream apartment, where Dirand embraced the architectural challenge of turning two apartments into one welcoming home. There is a grandeur to the proportion and scale of the spaces, as well as a nobility to the choice of materials and finishes. A timeless quality comes from the fusion of nineteenth-century elements, mid-century classics, contemporary furniture, and modern art. A predominantly soft and gentle color palette ties these elements together, while creating a soothing atmosphere throughout. One of the most visually arresting spaces in this context is the kitchen/dining room, where Dirand combined gray-and-white geometric-tiled floors with the extensive use of marble—both for the kitchen units and the sculptural dining table and bar, bordered by a quartet of Warren Platner wire-rod chairs.

Kenzo Apartment

Kenzo & Ed Tuttle
Paris (FR), 2010

The fashion designer Kenzo Takada (1939–2020)—commonly known as simply Kenzo—was born in Japan but launched his career and his eponymous label in France. Architect Ed Tuttle (1945–2020) was an American best known for his work in Asia, particularly with the Aman hotel group. These two friends from different backgrounds and different parts of the world both settled in Paris, where they collaborated on the design of Kenzo's apartment in Saint-Germain-des-Prés. In many respects, the apartment was intended as a fresh start. During the Nineties Kenzo sold his fashion house to LVMH and then let go of his former home in the Place de Bastille, while auctioning its contents. He then found the Saint-Germain-des-Prés apartment. Located on the top floor of a nineteenth-century building, it offered extraordinary views across the city. Kenzo asked Tuttle to help him transform a warren of rooms into a light, bright home with an aesthetic of old meets new and East meets West. In the key living spaces, dark lacquered parquet floors contrast with the white walls, which accentuate the period detailing and plasterwork. The sitting room features a painting by Kenzo above the fireplace and a screen designed by him, emblematic of his second career in the world of interiors.

Rivoli Apartment

Isabelle Stanislas
Paris (FR), 2011

Height and light lend drama to this captivating living room, which forms the heart of a Parisian home owned by architect and designer Isabelle Stanislas. Close to the Louvre, the apartment sits within an elegant eighteenth-century building, once serving as the offices of a local brasserie until its conversion into a family home, shared with Stanislas' husband and children. Well known for her residential work and also stores for fashion labels such as Cartier and Zadig & Voltaire, Stanislas preserved original detailing as far as possible, restoring elements such as the floors, plaster moldings, and fitted mirrors. Yet, at the same time, the designer created a comfortable and contemporary home, including marble-lined bathrooms and soothing bedroom retreats. For the living room, Stanislas was blessed not only with the elegant period detailing but the tall windows and double-height ceilings. This created the opportunity for a mezzanine gallery and library at one end of the space, accessed by a sculptural staircase, while the more intimate zone below hosts a dining area to one side and a games table to the other. A neutral backdrop allows the darker blues and purples of the curtains and seating to stand out. The main seating zone features twin sofas by Stanislas and a coffee table originally designed for Céline.

Méchiche Apartment

Frédéric Méchiche
Paris (FR), 1996

....

The interior designer Frédéric Méchiche aimed for a natural, simple, and timeless feeling at his apartment in the Marais. "I wanted to give the impression that I had just arrived here and found it like this," said Méchiche, "and I added my books, sculptures and paintings." Méchiche succeeded in his ambition but, in truth, the entire apartment was an original invention. The project was a kind of elaborate jigsaw puzzle, with Méchiche gathering together multiple pieces of architectural salvage including wall paneling from an eighteenth-century stage station, as well as fireplaces, mirrors, and moldings, which were all integrated into the design. These elements formed an elegant, textural backdrop, with a dominant palette of creams and whites, along with bare reclaimed floorboards. Beyond this, Méchiche introduced a blend of period and mid-century furniture, as seen in the living room where the designer introduced a Louis XVI daybed juxtaposed with twentieth-century classics: twin Barcelona chairs by Mies van der Rohe and Lilly Reich, and a slender black LCM chair by Charles and Ray Eames. The space is also home to some striking works of art, particularly the black-and-white abstract sculpture by Jean Dubuffet floating on a wooden plinth.

Grange Apartment

Jacques Grange
Paris (FR), 1990

"I try to offer another manner of presenting the past for today, which is a modern attitude," Jacques Grange once said. In some respects, he took inspiration from his mentors Madeleine Castaing (see pp. 269 and 277) and Henri Samuel (see pp. 250 and 264), however he also brought a completely fresh eye to his interiors. Famously, Grange became Yves Saint Laurent and Pierre Bergé's designer of choice, collaborating on multiple residences around the world. Balancing past and present can be delicate, as Grange found with his own Parisian apartment. Overlooking the Palais-Royal gardens, the home had once belonged to one of the designer's heroines, the iconic French writer and actress Colette (1873–1954). Naturally, Grange wanted to respect the spirit of Colette and the provenance of the building. Yet he had to make his own mark, alongside the remaining nineteenth-century period detailing and the small bust and portrait of Colette left as mementoes. Grange began layering the space with his own lovingly curated collections, introducing pieces by Alberto Giacometti, Pablo Picasso, and Edward Burne-Jones. In 2018, he bought the apartment upstairs and created a duplex, allowing the interiors to evolve and mature once again.

Paris Apartment

Mathias Kiss
Paris (FR), 2011

....

The Parisian créateur Mathias Kiss works at the borders of art and design. His career started with a long apprenticeship in the field of decorative painting, focused on restoration projects, but Kiss began to find this world too constrained and wanted to explore other, more contemporary, creative strands. His work now encompasses multiple mediums, including painting, sculpture, furniture, and interiors. These elements combine with originality in the rooms of a Parisian apartment for a private client who had a passion for yoga and a love of mid-century furniture—in particular a collection of pieces by Jean Prouvé (see p. 268). Kiss's client had acquired a flat in an 1850s building that had been converted into residential use during the Seventies, but was in need of modernization and reinvention. Kiss's treatment of the interiors balances the need for relatively calm, open, and light spaces with the ambition to create an almost gallery-style setting for the owner's furniture collection including pieces by Kiss himself. The spacious living room, which connects with the adjoining kitchen, features a number of Prouvé classics such as the dining table and armchairs, but also a two-toned green Igloo sofa by Kiss and a blue custom rug that combines splashes of color with deconstruction.

240505 120336 220370

Samuel Apartment

Henri Samuel
Paris (FR), c. 1974

When it was first covered in magazines in the mid-Seventies, the Parisian penthouse of Henri Samuel (1904–1996) came as something of a surprise. Samuel was widely accepted as a key arbiter of a twentieth-century version of classic French taste and style, with a focus on period provenance and neo-classical grandeur. Samuel was particularly associated with his work for the French branch of the Rothschild family and grand châteaux for clients such as the fashion designer Valentino (see p. 250). Yet the interiors of Samuel's own penthouse were very different. The Paris penthouse was on the top floor of a building on the Left Bank that also housed Samuel's offices, offering a sophisticated equivalent of living above the shop, and was designed with a decidedly Seventies vibe. Samuel's "smoking room," or library, in particular, caused a stir with its thick, creamy shag rug and off-white leather sofas encircling a futuristic glass-and-plastic coffee table by François Arnal. The white walls offered a backdrop to an array of modern artworks, including colorful pieces by Arthur Aeschbacher and Guy de Rougemont, as well as an Alexander Calder mobile. Most unusual of all, for such a master of tradition, was Samuel's decision to mount one of de Rougemont's abstract artworks on the ceiling.

Pilati Duplex

Stefano Pilati
Paris (FR), 2006

Before founding his own fashion label, Italian-born designer Stefano Pilati worked at Giorgio Armani, Prada, Yves Saint Laurent, and Ermenegildo Zegna, where he was head of design. He settled in Paris in 2000, when he first came across this nineteenth-century duplex apartment surrounding a courtyard garden. After a period of renting, in 2006 Pilati bought the apartment and enlisted architect Bruno Caron to help him renovate and remodel. Pilati adopted a typically eclectic approach to the interiors. The dining room, for instance, features a bucolic wall mural by Mathias Kiss (see p. 262) and Olivier Piel, which complements garden views framed by the windows. The decor mixes mid-century velvet-upholstered armchairs by Gio Ponti with collections of vintage Lalique glassware. One of the most strikingly bold spaces is the sitting room, where Pilati chose a vibrant teal for the walls and the integrated seating alcoves flanking the fireplace. Artworks by Giorgio de Chirico and Sonia Delaunay hang above the mantelpiece, while Pilati opted for a corn yellow for the cushions on his pair of Frank Lloyd Wright timber-framed chairs. The room also serves as a gallery for a collection of African masks, and Pilati created an abstract, geometric ceiling sculpture using sconces by mid-century master Charlotte Perriand.

Frey Apartment

Pierre Frey & Marika Dru
Paris (FR), 2012

Ever since he was a student Pierre Frey, director of international relations for his family's fabric house founded by his grandfather, has lived on the top floor of a sixteenth-century building that serves as the company's headquarters. It is not hard to see why, given its enticing location close to the Palais-Royal and the Louvre. The apartment itself evolved most dramatically around 2012 when Frey decided on a complete reinvention of the interiors to create a more spacious and open home for himself and his wife, Emilie, enlisting the assistance of Parisian architect Marika Dru of Atelier MKD. The heart of the apartment is now the airy living room, with ceilings reaching up to the exposed roof beams. The space is generous enough in scale to hold a seating area, a dining zone, and also a library within an alcove to one side, while other spaces—including the kitchen—sit alongside. A number of crimson notes, as seen in the Braquenié rug and some of the fabrics on the custom sofa, stand out against the white walls and pale wooden floors. The spiral staircase next to the seating area is a focal point in itself, having been designed by Gustave Eiffel and discovered in a Paris flea-market.

Turenne
Humbert & Poyet
Paris (FR), 2019

Designers Emil Humbert, from Paris, and Christophe Poyet, from Monaco, take inspiration from the opulence of movements like Art Deco and Memphis-style postmodernism. They also pay heed to the design principles of classicism and Modernism. The result, seen in their homes, hotels, and restaurants, is a sense of rigor fused with a love of color and character-filled, luxurious materials. This Parisian apartment in the Marais neatly encapsulates the aesthetic approach of the design duo's firm, Humbert & Poyet. Home to a creative family, the apartment spans two floors of an elegant seventeenth-century *hôtel particulier* that had also served as a jewelry workshop. The architects sought to regain a sense of grandeur in the duplex, introducing terrazzo for the hallway and stairs, parquet floors for the key living spaces, and a variety of pared-down moldings and paneling. The well-proportioned sitting room sees such elements coming together harmoniously. A fireplace with a dark marble surround stands out against the neutral tones of the walls and, topped by a mirror over the mantelpiece, forms a vivid focal point. The most playful element is the Humbert & Poyet Grand Theodore sofa in a deep blue. With its echoes of Vladimir Kagan's theatrical mid-century seating, the sofa is bold, comfortable, and sinuous, adding a ribbon of color within this ordered space.

Yovanovitch Apartment

Pierre Yovanovitch
Paris (FR), 2009

It was, in part, Pierre Yovanovitch's design of his own home that initially led him into the interior design profession. His first career was in fashion, and he spent eight years designing menswear for Pierre Cardin before his former apartment, near the Elysée Palace, caught the attention of friends and word spread. Before long he had an expanding list of clients asking him to design homes, and he set up his own atelier. In 2009 Yovanovitch decided to move from his duplex to the top floor of a seventeenth-century mansion in Paris's seventh *arrondissement*. The exposed beams and wooden floors of this rooftop escape offered a strong framework for Yovanovitch's relaxed but elegant vision. The heart of the apartment is the spacious open-plan living room, with matching pairs of dormer windows to either side. Here Yovanovitch created two distinct zones, with just a hint of separation provided by a screen by Shigeru Ban. A clover-shaped coffee table is at the center of the sitting-room zone, which is anchored by a floating rug. A fireplace and a wall of color-coded books lend something of a library, or den, feel. The comfortable seating includes a self-designed sofa in white wool and a vintage Danish armchair by Flemming Lassen, which both fit into the natural color palette.

Maison Prouvé

Jean Prouvé
Nancy (FR), 1954

The French designer and engineer Jean Prouvé (1901–1984) was one of the great innovators of the mid-century period. With his furniture, Prouvé took industrially manufactured materials like steel and plywood and created pieces that were both practical and poetic. With his buildings, Prouvé explored affordable and flexible prefabricated construction systems using kits of factory-made components that could make houses, or shelters. Yet, despite his undoubted talents and many successes, Prouvé's business struggled during the early Fifties and his financial backers eventually took control of his factory. The designer was forced to make a fresh start and his own self-built family home in Nancy was emblematic of this essential renaissance. The house was made of a melange of custom elements and leftover ingredients from Prouvé's past projects, including wall units from his Métropole houses in Meudon and "porthole panels" from the Maisons Tropicales. The living room toward the center pushed outward to meet the view, which was framed with walls of floor-to-ceiling glass. This key family space was arranged around a custom fireplace and a selection of the designer's own chairs and other furniture, while the house as a whole became a powerful showcase for Prouvé's ingenuity.

Maison Louis Carré

Alvar Aalto
Bazoches-sur-Guyonne (FR), 1959

One of the finest mid-century houses by the Finnish master architect and designer Alvar Aalto (1898–1976) was not in Scandinavia but in rural France. The art dealer Louis Carré (1897–1977), who first met the architect at the 1956 Venice Biennale, commissioned the house, which is on a hillside southwest of Paris. Carré and his wife wanted a modern and original building but one that would also be in tune with the natural beauty of the surroundings, constructed with largely natural or traditional materials rather than concrete. Carré also wanted to be able to entertain clients and friends here while displaying his art collection of work by European Modernists such as Picasso, Paul Klee, and Juan Gris. Aalto, characteristically, applied himself to every aspect of the interiors, down to the leather-wrapped doorknobs. The dramatic but welcoming entrance hall, with its curvaceous ceiling of Finnish red pine, sets the tone. Half a dozen steps lead down to the airy sitting room, where wood floors and ceilings enhance the sense of warmth. Like other spaces in the house, the light-filled main seating zone features the furniture of Artek—Alvar and his wife, Aino's, company—much of it custom created for Carré, including nesting fan-legged side tables and hanging A338 pendant lights overhead.

Maison Jean Cocteau

Madeleine Castaing & Jean Cocteau
Milly-la-Forêt (FR), 1947

Madeleine Castaing (1894–1992) was one of the most inventive and eclectic interior designers of her generation, while the same could be said of Jean Cocteau (1889–1963) and his impact upon the worlds of literature and art. Within her work, Castaing fused a range of historical and more contemporary influences with a playful approach to pattern and color. Similarly avant garde, Cocteau was an auteur in the widest sense, turning his hand not just to art but poetry, plays, and film. One of their most rounded projects was Cocteau's own refuge situated in the picturesque town of Milly-La-Forêt, to the south of Paris. Here, he bought a seventeenth-century house at the end of a quiet cul-de-sac, with extensive gardens intersected with waterways, lending the setting a semi-rural character. For the sitting room on the ground floor, Castaing chose a floral wallpaper but applied it in reverse, creating a more abstract pattern. Bronze Chinese fawns sit either side of the fireplace while the choice of furniture is typically wide ranging, with—for instance—a baroque sofa juxtaposed with a leather armchair suited to a gentleman's club. Upstairs, in Cocteau's study, Castaing introduced a leopard-print wallpaper: a favorite pattern repeated in a number of key projects, including her own country home.

Château du Grand-Lucé

Timothy Corrigan
Le Grand-Lucé (FR), 2009

The American designer Timothy Corrigan is a dedicated Francophile. In recent years, he has undertaken a series of projects in France on an increasingly ambitious and complex scale. The Château du Grand-Lucé in the Loire Valley stands high among them, with its three stories, eighteen guest bedrooms, and 80 acres (32 hectares) of gardens and parkland. The house was originally designed by Mathieu de Bayeux for Baron de Lucé and was completed in the late-eighteenth centurycentury. It served time as a military hospital during World War II and then as a sanatorium before Corrigan eventually managed to purchase the house, in 2003, to begin the long process of transforming the property back into a home. A key challenge throughout this process was the need to balance the restoration of the neoclassical grandeur of the house, which is heritage listed, with the ambition of creating a home suited to contemporary living. Prime examples include the "grand salon," overlooking the formal gardens, where Knole sofas and George Smith armchairs offer comfort among the restored splendor of the room. Similarly, the guest bedrooms offer layers of soothing colors—including shades of blue—gentle patterns, like in the antique Portuguese rug, and lounge-style seating to soften the space and create a sense of welcome.

La Reinerie

Serge Royaux & Cristóbal Balenciaga
Near Orléans (FR), c. 1955

Even to other couturiers, such as Christian
Dior, Cristóbal Balenciaga (1895–1972) was
known as "the master." The Spanish-born
fashion designer combined great technical
mastery with a gift for sculpted lines, sur-
prising silhouettes, and fluid forms, creating
highly original designs that captured the
imagination of celebrity clients, including
Grace Kelly and Audrey Hepburn. Balenciaga
moved from his native country to France
during the Spanish Civil War, and in 1937
he opened his eponymous Parisian house of
couture, which flourished during the Fifties
and Sixties in particular. During this golden
age of success and productivity, Balenciaga
had homes in both Paris and Normandy, as
well as Madrid, Barcelona, and the Basque
Country. For his country house, known as La
Reinerie, Balenciaga enlisted the assistance
of the influential French interior designer
Serge Royaux (1924–2016). Like Balenciaga,
Royaux had a reputation for discipline,
restraint, and meticulous attention to detail.
The choice of period furniture at La Reinerie
was largely in keeping with the neoclassical
character of the manor house. The paint and
curtains were mostly neutral in tone, as seen
in the dining room and sitting room. Pattern
and color were introduced primarily with the
carpets and upholstery; occasional touches
of playfulness—such as a life-size pair of
bronze stag heads in the sitting room—also
offered welcome moments of warmth.

Château de Champgillon

Christian Louboutin & Bruno Chambelland
Vendée (FR), 1988

....

Famed shoe designer Christian Louboutin and his business partner, Bruno Chambelland, share a bucolic country retreat in the Vendée, a largely rural region in western France. The oldest parts of the château, which once belonged to one of Chambelland's ancestors, date back to the thirteenth century, but the character of the residence was largely defined during a major rebuild during the eighteenth century. The house and its grounds had suffered from periods of neglect, so after the two men purchased it, there was considerable restoration work to be done both inside and outside before turning to the interiors. Louboutin wanted to respect the provenance of the building and to work with the generous scale of the main reception rooms, including the music room and sitting room that flank the central hallway. Much of the period furniture was bought at auction in Paris, but more contemporary elements and pieces of furniture were also introduced, gathered on Louboutin's travels in North Africa and other parts of the world. The choice of colors had a strong impact on the personality of these spaces, with a soothing lavender hue for the music room and an optimistic mustard yellow for the sitting room.

Chalet La Transhumance

Noé Duchaufour-Lawrance
Saint-Martin-de-Belleville (FR), 2010

....

La Transhumance was formerly a restaurant in the picturesque Alpine town of Saint-Martin-de-Belleville in Les Trois Vallées ski region of France. After the restaurant closed its doors, the character-filled building caught the attention of Antoine and Isabelle Ernoult-Dairaine. Having fallen in love with the setting, the couple eventually purchased the former restaurant and a semiderelict barn alongside it. Antoine persuaded one of his favorite interior and furniture designers, Noé Duchaufour-Lawrance, to turn these two buildings into one welcoming home for the couple and their four children. On the top floor is the communal family living space, which offers the best mountain views, ideally absorbed from a hanging Perspex orb chair. Duchaufour-Lawrance designed the open-plan space with smooth concrete floor, up in the eaves, combining a seating area, dining zone, and kitchen. Many of the key elements here are integrated custom designs, including the boomerang-shaped dining table and sculptural central fireplace and chimney, characterized by the designer's use of fluid forms. The cohesive result is simultaneously dynamic and soothing.

Villa G

Studio KO
Luberon (FR), 2007

....

Villa G is a prime example of the cohesive, character-filled fusion of architecture and interiors of Karl Fournier and Olivier Marty, founders of Studio KO. The partners are much respected for their creative adaptations of existing buildings for restaurants and hotels around the world, including André Balazs's Chiltern Firehouse (2014) hotel in London; but they are equally deft at building from the ground up—as is the case with Villa G. Thierry Gautier, formerly the director of jewelry company Van Cleef & Arpels and now the head of David Morris, commissioned the studio. He had owned a farmhouse in the Luberon region of Provence for a number of years, but he wanted a modern, custom-designed rural retreat. Studio KO placed the house, with a swimming pool alongside it, discreetly within the landscape—a green roof atop the stone-and-concrete building makes it nearly disappear into the hillside. The main living room looks out over the pool and open landscape. This room is furnished with a mix of contemporary pieces, such as the Living Divani sofa; mid-century pieces, like the Bruno Mathsson (see p. 181) chaise longue; a shaggy ottoman; and more rustic elements, including a Moroccan Beni Ourain rug. The combination of the soothing backdrop and natural textures helps to fulfill the client's desire for a contemporary refuge.

Armani House

Giorgio Armani
Saint-Tropez (FR), 1996/2009

....

"People always ask me how I have fun," Giorgio Armani once said. "I have fun with my homes." With houses in Milan, the Italian island Pantelleria, Antigua, Saint Moritz, Switzerland, and the Côte d'Azur in France, the Italian fashion designer has certainly indulged his passion for property, while using his self-designed interiors as testing grounds for the extensive offerings of Armani/Casa, his company's line of home-wares and furnishings. Armani bought a house in Saint-Tropez, France, in 1996, renovating and expanding the nineteenth-century-style villa in 2009, adding guest rooms and a spacious loggia that forms a harmonious transition between the rear of the house and the gardens, terraces, and swimming pool beyond. While the main living room, with its banks of bookcases, floors, and ceiling dark African teak, has the feel of a sophisticated library, the loggia alongside it is vibrant and breezy. The inspiration here is not only Provençal but also Asian, with ultra-fine white fabrics forming a sunshade over the ceiling; the gong, supported by two figures, is from Thailand. Softened with a colorful mix of rugs and oversize cushions in gentle pinks and greens, the seating by Armani/Casa is low-slung and informal.

Palais Bulles

Antti Lovag & Pierre Cardin
Théoule-sur-Mer (FR), 1989

....

The futuristic Palais Bulles, on the French Riviera, feels as though it has grown from the cliffs. With its countless eyes and aper-tures sitting upon a rounded body of inter-secting pods and spheres, the bubble palace is a house like no other. This surreal home fuses the work of Finnish-Hungarian archi-tect Antti Lovag (1920–2014), a pioneer of organic architecture, with interiors and furnishings by Pierre Cardin (1922–2020), who had long been influenced by space-age aesthetics and science fiction. Lovag settled in France and built a number of houses near Cannes during the Seventies, including the Maison Bernard and the Palais Bulles. When Lovag's original client for the bubble palace passed away before the house was complete, Cardin stepped in and continued the project: "I've always been fascinated by circles, spheres, and satellites," he said. "I knew it would correspond perfectly with my universe." Given the fluid nature of the twenty-eight-bedroom house, with scarcely a right angle to be seen, most of the fittings and furniture were specially designed by Cardin. Some elements, including desks, tables, and seating, are woven into the fabric of the house while others are free floating but often abstract and sculptural in nature. In many respects, Cardin and Palais Bulles were meant for each other.

Villa Santo-Sospir

**Madeleine Castaing, Jean Cocteau &
Francine Weisweiller**
Saint-Jean-Cap-Ferrat (FR), 1950

The French socialite Francine Weisweiller
(1916–2003) was a key patron of the antique
dealer and interior designer Madeleine
Castaing and the designer, artist, and
poet Jean Cocteau (see p. 269). Francine
Weisweiller and her American husband,
Alec, provided Castaing with a series of key
commissions, including their townhouse in
Paris and a country home in Mortefontaine
in northern France. The couple's residence
at Saint-Jean-Cap-Ferrat, Villa Santo-
Sospir, was the most unusual of their homes,
representing an eccentric collaboration
between Francine Weisweiller herself,
Castaing, and Cocteau. Castaing advised on
the decoration of the clifftop villa, with many
pieces of furniture and fabric sourced from
her own Parisian store. For the dining room,
Castaing suggested a textural patchwork
of woven wickerwork panels applied to both
the walls and ceilings, while the adjoining
sitting room was graced with a set of rattan
furniture topped with cushions upholstered
with a bold jungle-scape Feuillage pattern
by Castaing. But it was Cocteau who made
the boldest mark upon the house. He
painted a mural of the Greek god Apollo,
flanked by two handsome "priests of the
sun," above the fireplace in the sitting room
and then carried on using the walls of what
he called the "tattooed house" as a canvas
for his art. Two years later, in 1952, Cocteau
made a short film about his work at Santo-
Sospir and also filmed part of *Testament of
Orpheus* (1960), which was partly funded by
Weisweiller, at the house.

Villa Fiorentina

Billy Baldwin
Saint-Jean-Cap-Ferrat (FR), 1971

The dean of American decorating, Billy Baldwin (1903–1983), had an extraordinary client list. Among them, two of his strongest supporters were advertising executive Mary Wells Lawrence and Braniff International Airways founder Harding Lawrence (1920–2002). The Lawrences, one of the great American power couples of the Sixties and Seventies, commissioned Baldwin to design a total of four residences. "Billy liked working for us because I gave him complete control," Mary remarked. "He was quite simply a genius." Of the quartet, the most legendary was this retreat on the French Riviera, a 1917 mansion that, having been through a string of owners, had been substantially modified since it was first completed. Baldwin's most famous room at Villa Fiorentina was the blue salon, which took inspiration from the coastal setting. A sequence of French doors connecting the salon to the terrace filled the room with sunlight. Baldwin chose checkerboard-patterned David Hicks (see p. 198) rugs to anchor the space and sofas and armchairs upholstered in fresh blue linen, with Indian handkerchief pillows. The lacquered tables were by Charles Sevigny, who assisted Baldwin with the project, and blue notes were repeated throughout, as seen in the assortment of blue-and-white Chinese ceramics on the mantelpiece.

Panton House

Verner Panton
Binningen (CH), 1972

During the late Sixties Danish designer Verner Panton (1926–1998) formed a creative alliance with Willi Fehlbaum, the founder of Vitra. Together, Panton and Fehlbaum perfected the design and production method for the iconic Panton chair (1967)—Vitra's first piece of furniture and the first to be made from a single piece of injection-molded plastic, made available in a range of bright Pop colors. Perhaps given the success of this new partnership, Panton and his family settled on the outskirts of Basel, not far from Vitra's Swiss base. The exteriors of the period townhouse were hardly exceptional but inside Panton created a fantastical wonderland inhabited by his furniture, lighting, and textiles. The key living spaces were full of color, energy, and theater. The ceilings were transformed into vast lighting installations, reminiscent of a lunar landscape; the walls were tiled in vivid color mosaics; and rugs in Op art patterns were laid on the floor. The dining room featured a set of Panton chairs, while one of the designer's Living Towers doubled as both seating and a screen to the living room. Dramatic, daring, and delightful, the house was widely published at the time, serving—as the designer intended—as a showcase for the Panton style.

Villa Savoia

Jacques Lopez
Vésenaz (CH), 1973

....

Situated close to the shore of Lake Geneva, Villa Savoia has a flamboyant, decidedly Seventies aesthetic inside and out. The house's character is defined, in part, by the curvaceous design by Swiss architect Jacques Lopez. The Italian head of the house of Savoy and the Prince of Naples, Vittorio Emanuele IV (the son of the last king of Italy), and his Swiss wife, Marina Ricolfi-Doria, commissioned the residence. Lopez created a tiered, undulating modern house using sculpted concrete. The interiors of the three-story home, which is still owned by the family, have a futuristic quality throughout. The main sitting room, for example, features a built-in semicircular sofa, forming part of a tiered ziggurat stepping down toward the windows, the terraces, and the view, while the dining room has a blue-mirrored ceiling. A guest bedroom features lacquered bedside tables housing a sound system; the gleaming metal wall sculpture is by Peter Lobello, while a creaturelike Italian 1970s lamp holds court on the bedhead. Here, and elsewhere, family antiques and portraits are juxtaposed with modern furniture and lighting.

Gstaad Chalet

Thierry Lemaire
Gstaad (CH), 2020

....

The designer Thierry Lemaire opened his own atelier in 1986. While many of his early commissions were solidly architectural in character, Lemaire soon began spreading his wings and embracing interiors and furniture design. Many of Lemaire's most distinctive projects, which include fashion flagships and private residences, splice these three overlapping disciplines. Standout commissions within Lemaire's portfolio include a sequence of mountain chalets in Switzerland and Lebanon, embracing both conversions and new builds. This project in Gstaad, high in the Swiss Alps, marked a creative collaboration with Lemaire's sister, Sophie Prezioso, who is an interior designer based in Geneva. The building itself is a sixteenth-century farmhouse and the principal challenge was to conserve the original character of the building. Lemaire carefully restored the original timber walls, floors, and ceilings, which offer a setting for a curated assembly of old and new. In the living room, for example, the characterful woodwork provides the backdrop for a number of pieces of furniture designed by Lemaire himself. They include the Niko sofa, with echoes of the Sixties and Seventies seen in its dynamic form, and a Jeruk coffee table in bronze, reflecting Lemaire's love of noble materials and artisanal craftsmanship.

Usine Gruben

Antonie Bertherat-Kioes
Gstaad (CH), 2010

Architect Antonie Bertherat-Kioes and her family have a deep-rooted love of the mountains and winter sports. For many years they kept a winter chalet near Zermatt but were increasingly drawn to Gstaad. While looking for a place of their own, Bertherat-Kioes stumbled across a former stationmaster's house and its adjacent building, which housed an electrical transformer for the Montreux Oberland Bernois railway. The renovation process began with a deep clean to remove any pollutants from the building and garden, but the architect decided to keep the generators and control panels, which now form dramatic features in the family's combined kitchen and dining room. An impressive family living room offers a postcard view of the mountains and valley below thanks to a large picture window. The architect designed a custom-textile wall covering in association with Arpin, with a bold check pattern that helps warm the space. A vast black-and-white artwork by artist Ugo Rondinone adds another theatrical element, while a supersized L-shaped sofa by India Mahdavi is positioned to face both the window and the fireplace.

Saint Moritz House

Studio Peregalli
Saint Moritz (CH), 2011

There is a seductive escapist quality to Saint Moritz. The town floats above the rest of the world high in the Alps, and the winter sports are superlative. For those seeking refuge or a place to recharge in the mountains, then Saint Moritz is ideal, as Studio Peregalli's client concluded. Roberto Peregalli and Laura Sartori Rimini (see pp. 228 and 281) had already worked with the client, a publisher and his family, on three other residences. In Saint Moritz, the family acquired a former mid-century chalet split into apartments. Studio Peregalli were asked to convert the building into one spacious, cohesive mountain retreat. The designers created a family home that not only feels as though it belongs to the Alps but one that possesses a timeless quality, fusing both past and present. The chalet offers a sophisticated and high-crafted interpretation of Alpine living, using architectural salvage, characterful materials, and a curated blend of custom and antique furniture. In the primary bedroom, one of the most restful spaces, bookcases are used to lightly separate the space into areas for sleeping and for reading. Floor-to-ceiling timber paneling with subtly decorated carved patterns and motifs reinforces the romance of the chalet aesthetic.

Lugano House

Renzo Mongiardino & Studio Peregalli
Lugano (CH), c. 1991

This Swiss house close to the shore of Lake Lugano feels as though it must surely be centuries old, which is a testament to the talents of masterful Italian designer Renzo Mongiardino (1916–1998). In reality, the house and its interiors were completed just before Mongiardino's death, making it one of his last legacy projects. The project was unusual in many ways. His client asked for a "new" Palladian-style villa on a hillside looking across the lake. To fulfill the brief, Mongiardino enlisted the assistance of designer Roberto Peregalli and architect Laura Sartori Rimini, who had, by that time, left Mongiardino's studio to launch their own atelier, Studio Peregalli. The creation of such timeless spaces was, inevitably, the work of many years. The interiors—arranged around a central octagonal hallway paved with marble—required exceptional devotion to detail. In one bedroom, for example, Enrico Perroni-designed wallpaper is complemented by an antique Russian canopy bed. One of the most engaging rooms in this great country houses is the library. Parquet floors and ornate coffered ceilings are joined by a series of templelike bookcases in walnut and briarwood, along with an array of tables that offer surfaces for display and reading. It is an erudite space within a house layered with lessons drawn from the history of design.

Rainer House

Roland Rainer
Vienna (AT), c. 1965

Architect Roland Rainer (1910–2004) was drawn to the site of his third and final Austrian home in the Hietzing district of Vienna, near the Schönbrunner Schlosspark, partly on account of the mature trees that already inhabited the site. He wove the design of the new house around these trees, using large swaths of glass to frame them like living sculptures. The house was designed on one level and built with reclaimed brick and timber, which add to the organic character of the home. The sitting room itself spans two levels. A sunken zone, almost like a conversation pit, is partly defined by a Rainer-designed wraparound tan leather sofa, which faces the walled garden—designed by Rainer in conjuction with his wife—complete with courtyard spaces and pools of water. A long window seat makes the space even more convivial. A nearby platform features a striking round window; mid-century seating in the form of a fluid Bruno Mathsson chaise longue and fiberglass Eero Aarnio Ball chair, upholstered inside in bright orange; and a fireplace clad in glossy white tiles. Rainer also designed a white ash library wall, which lightly separates the sitting room from a study; the house is now owned by Rainer's daughter.

Villar Perosa

Marella Agnelli & Stéphane Boudin
Near Turin (IT), 1953

An eighteenth-century rural retreat in northern Italy, Villar Perosa has been in the Agnelli family for generations. Gianni Agnelli (1921–2003)—who eventually served as head of Fiat—inherited the house, and it became a constant presence in his life. In 1953 Gianni married Marella Agnelli (1927–2019, see p. 334), who was much respected for her sense of style and her appreciation of art, gardens, and landscape design. After the marriage, Marella worked on the interiors of the house in conjunction with the great French decorator Stéphane Boudin (1888–1967, see pp. 123 and 252). Together, they sought to balance their desire to respect the historical character of the villa with the need to create spaces that were suited to a more informal modern lifestyle. The intimate library is among the key spaces that Marella and Boudin shaped. Its walls are wallpapered in bold green-and-gold stripes, and a colorful Modernist painting by Emmanuel Gondouin sang out against this backdrop. In the *salone da gioco* (gaming salon), where card games are played, there is eighteenth-century Piedmontese portraits of a king and queen of Sardinia, with pizzazz added through luxurious, animal-themed prints and upholstery.

Mollino Apartment

Carlo Mollino
Turin (IT), 1960

A dandy with a love of downhill skiing, car racing, and erotic photography, Carlo Mollino (1905–1973) was one of the greatest showmen of mid-century Italian design, establishing himself as the leading proponent of Turinese Baroque. His furniture, especially, combined high standards of craftsmanship with the sculpted lines of an artist, at once flamboyant, fantastical, and often biomorphic. One of the last of his projects, which now houses the Museo Casa Mollino, was this apartment in a building on the banks of the Po River. The apartment became a showcase for the exuberant and distinctive Mollino style. The main living spaces form an enfilade running along one side of the building, overlooking the gardens below. The last space in line, the library is the most seductive room, with its screened bookshelves to one side and a long black leather sofa opposite, under the window. Most unusual is the far wall, where Mollino designed a small fireplace seeming to hover at mid-height surrounded by a bucolic nineteenth-century scene. The fireplace is occupied by a small terra-cotta figurine and flanked by two crimson slipper chairs, which shine brightly within the space.

Casa Tabarelli

Carlo Scarpa & Sergio Los
Bolzano (IT), 1968

The Tabarelli family's eponymous furniture company was first established in the 1880s and represented Thonet in northern Italy for many years. By the 1950s the company was based in Bolzano in the Italian Tyrol, not far from the Austrian border, and was run by Gianni Tabarelli de Fatis who promoted mid-century Modern furniture and formed friendships with many of the leading Italian architects, artists, designers, and manufacturers of the period. One of these friends was Italian master architect Carlo Scarpa (1906–1978), who was asked to design a new house for the family. Working with his colleague Sergio Los, Scarpa created a villa with an undulating roofline that drew inspiration from the terraced vineyards common to the region. Inside, Gianni Tabarelli and his wife Laura opted for spaces that spoke of the playful, colorful, and exuberant character of Italian design during the Sixties. In the combined living and dining room, great bands of yellow and ochre run across the wave-like ceilings, while the choice of furniture includes sofas by Gavina teamed with pieces by Marcel Breuer and Alvar Aalto. The vivid tapestry on the wall is by the Italian futurist artist Giacomo Balla, while the vibrant mobile by the Brionvega stereo unit is by Bruno Munari.

Villa Olda

Alessandro Mendini
Olda (IT), 2006

One of the great figureheads of Italian postmodern architecture and design, Alessandro Mendini (1931–2019) was able to turn his talents to many different strands of design while always adopting a light and playful touch. There were museums and houses, rugs and lamps, tables and chairs, along with a range of homeware for Alessi. Mendini was born in Milan, where he also studied, worked, and lived for much of his life. In 2006, Mendini, tempted by the Italian Alps, went in search of a vacation home within an easy distance of the city. He came across an elegant Art Nouveau–style villa near San Pellegrino Terme and fell in love with this retreat where he could walk in the mountains as well as work in peace. The villa offered a set of well-proportioned living spaces and a wealth of period details, including tilework, chandeliers, paneling, and moldings. This was no impediment to Mendini's introduction of a characteristic choice of vivid colors and bold pattens, as seen in the living room, where the walls are painted apple green. Here, armchairs coated in Mendini's Proust fabric and a Mendini cocktail table, along with a pair of bright ottomans by designer Anna Gili sit eclectically on a multicolored rug positioned on the polished parquet.

Vergiate Villa

Enrico Baj
Vergiate (IT), 1967

There was a dark, playful humor to the work of the avant-garde artist Enrico Baj (1924–2003). His irreverent collages and prints broke with all convention, while adopting elements of Surrealism and the absurd. Yet many of the themes explored by Baj, a co-founder of the Arte Nucleare movement, were often sombre and even disturbing. The heart of much of Baj's work and family life was this house in the town of Vergiate in Lombardy, to the northwest of Milan and not far from the southern tip of Lake Maggiore. Baj and his wife, Roberta, found the Art Nouveau–style villa in 1967 after deciding to step away from urban life in Milan. The interiors of the villa were layered with antiques, as well as a collection of paintings and drawings by other artists that Baj admired. The house also served as a gallery for many pieces by the artist himself. For example, the walls of the primary bedroom were covered by his work, including a selection from the Furniture series, in which Baj transformed a range of three-dimensional pieces of timber furniture to become almost two dimensional. Despite this rich context, a colorful semicircular headboard in a patchwork of ceramic tiles by the artist Ugo Nespolo provides an arresting focal point.

Missoni House

Rosita Missoni & Enrico Buzzi
Sumirago (IT), 1971

"A house must have the personality of the people who live in it," Rosita Missoni has advised and enacted at her home in Sumirago, northwest of Milan. Missoni, the matriarch of the family-owned eponymous fashion house, has kept a pied-à-terre in Milan and a vacation home in Venice, but the Sumirago residence has been a constant presence in her life since the early Seventies. Missoni grew up near here and this was where she and her late husband Ottavio chose to both live and work. The Missoni factory, designed by architect Enrico Buzzi, is close by and in 1971 the couple asked Buzzi to design them a six-bedroom family home set in verdant gardens. The interiors have been Rosita's domain ever since, reflecting a passion that also saw her develop a dedicated MissoniHome collection. As one might expect, this expressive house is bursting with color and pattern. The living room, which features a picture window framing a view of the grounds and a circular, wooden coffee table, includes Missoni designs and fabrics on the rug, cushions, and sofa upholstery. Also on display are Missoni's decorative mushrooms—a favorite motif that appears many times over in both ceramic and knitted versions.

Saronno Apartment

Studio Catoir
Saronno (IT), 2014

There is a cinematic quality to this pent-house apartment in the city of Saronno, not far from Milan. One of the key reference points for designers Elisa and Michael Catoir of Studio Catoir was the iconic 1955 Alfred Hitchcock film *To Catch a Thief*. The interiors fuse a touch of mid-century glamour with a powerful degree of individuality, partly derived from the custom furniture and custom finishes the Parisian atelier designed. The project was commissioned by an entrepreneur who had acquired this three-bedroom duplex apartment at the summit of a luxury condo building as his main residence. The apartment offers views of the Alps, yet the interiors were a blank sheet, requiring a good deal of imagination to bring them to life. The use of color and pattern—employed in a graphic manner—is particularly striking throughout. Several spaces feature a blue, white, and gray palette echoing the colors of the mountains, but the main sitting room has sunshine-yellow highlights, as seen in the curtains, cushions, and a number of pieces of furniture, many of which were designed by Studio Catoir. The strong sense of narrative is enhanced by de Gournay's (see p. 203) dreamy Views of Italy wallpaper, while the double-sided fireplace in Carrara marble provides a focal point.

Aulenti Apartment

Gae Aulenti
Milan (IT), 1973

One of the great Italian polymaths of the post-World War II period and beyond, Gae Aulenti (1927–2012) was one of the most influential Italian designers of her generation. Her projects spanned a huge variety of scales, ranging from the Musée d'Orsay (1986) in Paris to her sculptural Pipistrello lamp (1965)—the lampshade resembling bat wings—for Martinelli Luce. Aulenti's own home in Milan can be seen as a fusion of these multiple design disciplines, as well as an expression of her own taste and her desire to "take a stand against the ephemeral, against passing trends." From the early Seventies onward, Aulenti's office and apartment were both in a remodeled building near the Piazza San Marco, offering a neat and elegant live/work setup. The apartment itself revolved around a double-height living room that served as a library as well, with vast banks of bookcases running along a wall but also framing various seating zones within this loftlike space. The room features many of Aulenti's own pieces of furniture and lighting designs; more expressive bursts of color and pattern come from the vibrant rugs and the Roy Lichtenstein wall-mounted tapestry. A steel stairway and bridge traverse the space to access a sunroom on a mezzanine.

Milano Jenner

Dimorestudio
Milan (IT), 2019

The interiors designed by Britt Moran and Emiliano Salci have a particular sense of history, patina, and provenance. The rooms of the houses, apartments, and restaurants designed by their atelier, Dimorestudio, feel deeply rooted in the past, with multiple references to the mid-century period in particular, and yet they also have a characterful and contemporary warmth. The two friends and business partners have used their own shared spaces in Milan as a way of exploring and developing such ideas. Salci grew up in Tuscany and Moran in North Carolina, yet the two have much in common, including a mutual love of Milan itself, where they have lived and worked for many years. Milano Jenner is an apartment within a grand nineteenth-century building. Moran and Salci were enticed by the richness of the building's original detailing and characteristically opted for a seductive choice of hues, settling upon a predominantly green palette. The most dramatic room here is undoubtedly the living room, with its ornate plasterwork ceiling, timber paneling, and a feature fireplace with a carved wooden mantle and decorative detailing. The celadon colors of the walls are complemented by soft greens and blues for the textiles—such as in the upholstered twin Piero Portaluppi chairs—while the earthy hues seen within Moran and Salci's extensive collection of antique Asian ceramics also sit well with the focus on organic textures and tones.

Elkann Apartment

Lapo Elkann & Studio Natalia Bianchi
Milan (IT), 2014

Blue is Lapo Elkann's signature color. The entrepreneur and designer is often photographed wearing blue tones, and his Milanese apartment features a decidedly maritime palette. The interiors here are bold, personal, and playful, but also sophisticated, as one might expect of the grandson of the great Italian tastemakers Gianni and Marella Agnelli (see pp. 282 and 334). For Elkann, purchasing the duplex penthouse in a postwar building offered the opportunity to create a spacious new home with the benefit of a private rooftop garden on the adjoining terrace. Collaborating with architect Natalia Bianchi, Elkann opened up the interiors to create a more informal layout. The living room is a hymn to blue, with the floors custom painted in a vibrant blue zigzag pattern and the walls covered in a custom blue-and-white wallpaper. The palette continues in the choice of furniture, including the sinuous statement sofa by Ueli Berger, curving around a custom coffee table; a Memphis side table by Alessandro Mendini (see p. 285) sits alongside the sofa. Artworks include a quartet of flower prints by Andy Warhol that echo the garden beyond the window while also adding bursts of contrasting color.

Citterio Apartment

Antonio Citterio
Milan (IT), 1986

The Italian architect and furniture designer Antonio Citterio has worked all around the world, but he is deeply rooted in Milan. He grew up not far from the city, attended the renowned Milan Polytechnic, and opened his first design studio here when he was just twenty. Together with his wife, American architect Terry Dwan, Citterio bought the space that would become their Milanese apartment in the central Brera district during the mid-Eighties. They were attracted by the blank canvas offered by the uppermost levels of a historical building. "It's really a new 'house' in an old building," Citterio says. "The idea was to open everything up and bring in more light." With no period detailing to worry about in these atticlike spaces, Citterio and Dwan were free to do as they wished. They created a double-height loft at the center of the plan that serves as a spacious family living area, with ancillary spaces arrayed around it over two levels. The initial incarnation of this space was pared back and minimalist, but over the years Citterio has introduced multiple examples of his own furniture designs, along with family heirloom pieces and other treasures. Each of these layers, added over time, has enhanced the character of the space.

Colombo Apartment IV

Joe Colombo
Milan (IT), 1970

Flamboyant, dynamic, and original, Joe Colombo (1930–1971) packed an extraordinary amount of creativity into his too short life. His work embraced interiors, products, and furniture yet one of the key preoccupations of Colombo's career was the ambition to break down the boundaries between these disciplines. Colombo used his own apartments in Milan, of which there were a series during the Fifties and Sixties, as a way of offering a vision of a futuristic way of living. This apartment from 1970 is on the city's Via Filippo Argelati, where Colombo's design studio was also based. The main living area contained little more than two multifunctional elements designed by Colombo: a Roto-Living Unit (1969), intended to hold almost everything one might need for daytime living—rotating dining and coffee tables plus home technology, including a stereo and television; the other piece was a yellow Cabriolet Bed (1969), which, similarly, held everything required for the evenings and nights, including a fold-down canopy. The apartment generated a good deal of attention for Colombo's work and, a year before his death, the Museum of Modern Art in New York commissioned a Total Furnishing Unit (1971), which managed to pack every element of the home into one compact installation.

Villa Fornasetti

Piero Fornasetti
Milan (IT), c. 1955

....

This house of dreams and illusions has been called a *Wunderkammer* (chamber of wonders). It is filled with original designs that spilled from the feverishly creative mind of Piero Fornasetti (1913–1988), who translated his talents as an artist into pieces of furniture, ceramics, wallpapers, and interior spaces, including the rooms of this home of his. His father, a businessman, built the three-story Villa Fornasetti, located in in the Città Studi quarter of Milan, near the end of the nineteenth century. Much later, during the Fifties, the designer expanded the family house, while adding a design studio and offices alongside it. The home, which is now owned aby the designer's son, Barnaba, became a showcase for Fornasetti's work, which combined neoclassical motifs with touches of Surrealism and an endearing playful streak. The emerald-green sitting room is layered with Fornasetti designs, including a trompe l'oeil cabinet on one wall, surrounded by bookshelves. Upon the opposite wall is a sparkling collection of mirrors, below which is a Fornasetti side table and a blanket box, which now serves as a coffee table. In a primary bedroom, the walls are papered in the monochrome Nuvole pattern, a cloud pattern designed by Barnaba with Cole & Son, punctuated by an eighteenth-century Italian giltwood mirror.

Guadagnino Apartment
Luca Guadagnino
Crema (IT), 2015

Architecture and interiors have always played a strong part in Italian filmmaker Luca Guadagnino's movies, including *I am Love* (2009), which featured Piero Portaluppi's Milanese Modernist masterpiece Villa Necchi Campiglio (1935). Guadagnino launched Studio Luca Guadagnino in 2018, working on private residences, as well as a number of stores for skincare brand, Aesop. "In cinema, you are an imposter, in a way, because you can always edit afterward," Guadagnino has said. "You cannot do that with a house." His own home in the northern Italian city of Crema, to the east of Milan, is a spacious apartment on the second floor of a palazzo, dating back to the seventeenth century. The apartment had been empty for decades, requiring extensive restoration. Period detailing was carefully preserved, including the frescoes on the ceilings and the paintwork on the shuttered windows. Beyond this, color played a vital part throughout, as seen in the living room's deep-blue walls, one of the many tones mixed especially for the apartment. Mid-century and contemporary furniture also play a key role, as seen in the breezy dining room, with its Gio Ponti 699 Superleggera dining chairs and vintage Danish furniture, while the profusion of plants gives the space the atmosphere of a garden room.

Patrizia Moroso House

Patricia Urquiola
Udine (IT), 2010

This modern and original home in the city of Udine, in northeastern Italy, could be seen as the culmination of a long-term collaboration between architect and designer Patricia Urquiola and art director Patrizia Moroso. Spanish-born Urquiola founded her own studio in Milan in 2001 after studying there. One of her greatest patrons was Moroso, who commissioned Urquiola to design a series of successful pieces for her family-owned furniture brand. Within a modern, timber-clad, two-story home, the interiors balance order and warmth, with "much of the design and the palette . . . inspired by my husband's family home in Senegal," said Moroso, who shares the house with artist Abdou Salam Gaye and their children. Their home offers a choice of seating and relaxation zones, including a sunken conversation pit around a fireplace and a lounge area with its earthy, terra-cotta-hued floors. This space features a selection of key pieces for Moroso, including the modular purple Misfits sofa by Ron Arad and twin Op art-inspired leather ottomans by Nendo. The bold color combinations are carefully curated, with royal-blue and deep-red notes forming bright highlights against a darker backdrop.

Casa Sotto Una Foglia

Gio Ponti & Nanda Vigo
Malo (IT), 1969

Completed in the late Sixties, Casa Sotto Una Foglia (House under a Leaf) was a creative collaboration between one of the giants of Italian Modernism, Gio Ponti (1891–1979, see p. 323), and the avant-garde artist and designer Nanda Vigo (1936–2020), who had come into Ponti's orbit while establishing her own influential atelier in Milan after time spent traveling and working in America. During the Sixties Ponti had presented speculative plans for the house in *Domus*—the design magazine that he founded and edited for many years—inviting any interested parties to use the plans and build. The art collector Giobatta Meneguzzo decided to turn the house into reality. However, Meneguzzo wanted more space for his collection but Ponti declined to revise his design, instead putting forward Vigo for the job. The futuristic interiors were partly defined by Vigo's use of wildly contrasting textures, particularly the extensive use of floor-to-wall white tiling, including the casings of fitted furniture, alongside soft-gray shag-pile used on the stairways and the seating. The striking juxtaposition of hard and soft, along with Meneguzzo's collection of abstract art, gave the house a surreal sense of drama.

Palazzo Venier dei Leoni

Peggy Guggenheim
Venice (IT), 1948

The American art collector and gallery owner Peggy Guggenheim (1898–1979) was one of the greatest supporters of modern art during the mid-century period. She launched her first but short-lived gallery in London during the late Thirties, with an exhibition of drawings by Jean Cocteau (see pp. 269 and 277). After World War II and the end of her brief marriage to artist Max Ernst, Guggenheim spent an increasing amount of time in Italy and, in particular, Venice. Eventually, in 1949, she bought the Palazzo Venier dei Leoni on Venice's Grand Canal. The palazzo itself dates back to the mid-eighteenth century, yet it was never finished and it was only a succession of flamboyant twentieth-century owners—Luisa Casati, followed by Lady Doris Castlerosse and then Guggenheim—who gradually transformed the house into a sophisticated Venetian residence. Naturally, Guggenheim filled the palazzo with the extraordinary fruits of her own years of collecting, with work by artists including Alexander Calder, Jackson Pollock, Alberto Giacometti, Giorgio de Chirico, Pablo Picasso, René Magritte, and many others. Period photographs show Guggenheim sitting in the main salon, where a Calder fish mobile floated above a long, glass-topped coffee table next to a geometric sofa, hosting her resting dog.

Palazzo Orlandi

Sabrina Bignami
Prato (IT), 2007

The juxtaposition of old and new is a recurring theme for architect Sabrina Bignami. The Tuscan architect's practice, B-Arch, has tackled a number of residential commissions involving both the restoration and revival of historical buildings to make them suited to twenty-first-century living. One of the most dramatic examples of this juxtaposition is Bignami's own home in the historic cathedral city of Prato, to the northwest of Florence. When Bignami first came across the late-eighteenth-century palazzo, it was semiderelict. She focused her attention principally on the *piano nobile*, where she uncovered a series of frescoes under layers of whitewash. Painted by Luigi Catani around two hundred years ago, the frescoes offer a vibrant backdrop to the key living spaces. The colors, patterns, and trompe l'oeil scenography in the frescoes create a powerful, theatrical setting. Bignami used a light touch in introducing furnishings to avoid competing with Catani's work and the neoclassical grandeur of the rooms. In the main living room, she opted for a quartet of white chairs designed by Piero Lissoni, which can be used separately or combined to create sofas. Modern, geometric, neat, and pure, these pieces seem to float like art installations within the space but are also functional and comfortable.

Mispelaere House

Yvan Mispelaere & Stéphane Ghestem
Florence (IT), 2013

....

Although the Florentine home of Yvan Mispelaere—who works mainly in the fashion industry, as well as taking on occasional commissions for interiors—is almost at the heart of the city, it has the feel of a rural escape. This comes in large part from the fact that the French creative consultant's modest cottage sits at the edge of a private park, where it was built in the nineteenth century in grand neoclassical style to serve as a pool house—although the pool itself was never completed. The cottage—which he designed with architect Stéphane Ghestem—had previously been renovated and updated by the Italian architect Alberto Sifola di San Martino. Within its airy central portion, the kitchen is tucked away inside a black cube with a diamond-pointed exterior. A golden example of the designer's fondness for repurposing materials are the brass vases, made from unused World War I mortar shells, arranged on an Italian Fifties dining table. The white-painted concrete staircase leads to the primary bedroom, painted in a Dulux Valentine blue, which pops against the custom wood-floor tiles, while the graphic black-and-white bedcover is another Mispelaere creation.

Val d'Orcia Farmhouse

Elodie Sire & Matteo Pamio
Bagno Vignoni (IT), 2015

....

The Val d'Orcia is one of the most beautiful
and unspoiled parts of Tuscany. The influence of the vernacular is enticing, as seen
in this farmhouse updated and redesigned
by the French interior designer Elodie Sire,
in conjunction with Italian architect Matteo
Pamio. A Provence-based family who had
come to love the region over the course of
many summer vacations here, commissioned
the design when they came across a crum-
bling farmstead in need of major restoration.
Strict local planning controls necessitated
a sensitive treatment for the exterior, but
much more freedom was to be had inside, to
create a contemporary version of farmhouse
living. The main living spaces of this retreat
within a retreat were designed with a largely
informal layout with an interconnected enfilade consisting of the kitchen, dining area,
and family lounge, which features a collection of leather riding crops on one wall, complemented by a Gonzalo Rivera photograph
depicting a lasso on another. Just as enticing
are the bedrooms, particularly the primary
bedroom at the attic level, which has its own
private roof terrace. Exposed beams and
the simple oak sleeping platform here echo
the rustic character of the house, as do
the linens in natural hues. The two-tone curtains from Holland & Sherry and polished
concrete floors add a modern sensibility.

Fighine

David Mlinaric & Hugh Henry
Fighine (IT), 1999

....

Fighine could be seen as something of an Anglo-Italian fusion. This hilltop castello is clearly Tuscan, yet the owners are English and so are the two interior designers, David Mlinaric and Hugh Henry, who spent many years working on the restoration of the house and the design of its interiors, with the aim of creating a rustic and grand home suited to both family life and entertaining. The oldest parts of the castello date to the eleventh century, yet the house was largely remodeled during the sixteenth century. By the time Mlinaric and Henry's clients bought the residence, as well as the surrounding buildings, it was in a state of semidereliction. Much of the restoration work focused on the *piano nobile*. Here the central hallway with its checkerboard tiled floor and decorative ceilings was brought back to life and simply furnished with a mixture of rustic pews and a carved central display table. The music room and drawing room to either side were also revived, with the ornate nineteenth-century frescoes on the vaulted ceilings restored— zodiac panels were added in the roundels— and a blend of Italian, English, and Flemish furniture introduced. Elsewhere, a soothing sitting room, painted in a pretty lilac hue, has an avian theme. Throughout, different spaces are comfortable and welcoming, as well as refined.

Spello Loft

Paola Navone
Spello (IT), 2012

The Campi family has published the famous
Italian almanac *Barbanera* for over one
hundred years. The publication is devoted
to the changing seasons, good food, and
country living, so it seems fitting that the
family business and home are now in a
semirural setting on the outskirts of the
Umbrian town of Spello. In the former
agricultural building, publisher Feliciano
Campi and his wife, Andrea, created offices
and meeting rooms for *Barbanera* on the
ground floor. They enlisted architect and
designer Paola Navone to help create a
home on the upper levels. Navone designed
what could be described as an epic rural

loft apartment. The heart of the home is a
double- or triple-height space holding the
main living area bordered by a mezzanine
walkway and gallery. Navone painted the
walls and exposed beams white, while lightly
zoning the great room into various spaces
for seating and dining. The main seating
area is anchored by a Berber rug and a large
Navone sofa (produced by Linteloo), while
the central dining zone is on a "carpet" of
Navone-designed hexagonal gray tiles set
into the wood floor. Here a quintet of ethereal cotton lanterns hangs over the long,
rustic timber table.

La Torre

Renzo Mongiardino
Tuscany (IT), 1985

Renzo Mongiardino (1916–1998) was the interior designer of choice for many of the wealthiest families in Europe. Houses such as Vistorta (1960), his creation for the Brandolinis in the Veneto region of Italy, secured his reputation. By the Eighties, Mongiardino was in demand around the world. Popular with the fashion world, his clients included Valentino Garavani, Gianni Versace, Jil Sander, and the jewelry designer Elsa Peretti. Born in Florence, Peretti established herself in New York during the Sixties and Seventies working with fashion designers and, most famously, Tiffany & Co. Initially, Mongiardino worked with Peretti on her apartment in Rome but then began working on the interiors of La Torre, a former watchtower on the peninsula of Monte Argentario. Here, Mongiardino used trompe l'oeil on the interior walls to suggest a ruin in the landscape. The most famous room was undoubtedly the living room with its dramatic, open-mouthed fireplace. It's sculptural shape "recalled the original sixteenth-century *Mascherone Infernale* [infernal mask] at the Garden of Bomarzo," Peretti said. "The interesting thing was that he created the illusion of being inside the most spacious of rooms when in fact you were sitting in an extremely narrow and small space."

Rebecchini Apartment

Livia Rebecchini
Rome (IT), 2008

The spacious, central Roman apartment that interior designer Livia Rebecchini shares with her family is a striking blend of old and new. For many years Rebecchini lived in a modern apartment building, but was always hunting for a dream project with history. Eventually she came across a palazzo, dating back to the sixteenth century, almost at the heart of the city and close to the banks of the Tiber. Rebecchini acquired the top two floors of the palazzo, which is arranged around a central courtyard, and began turning them into a home. The lower level had been divided up into a warren of rooms over the centuries and demanded, in particular, a radical reworking in order to create a spacious and welcoming living room. Internal partition walls were removed and the spaces stripped back, revealing the original ceiling beams. The designer laid rustic terra-cotta tiles on the floor, while the walls were simply plastered to keep their natural tone. More contemporary interventions include the sculptural steel stairway that seems to float lightly at the center of the room while connecting the floor above. Similarly, modern art and furniture blend family antiques and period treasures within a careful melange lent cohesion by a subtle and restrained use of color and texture.

Fendi Apartment

Carla Fendi & Cesare Rovatti
Rome (IT), 2012

With her sisters, Carla Fendi (1937–2017) built the family fashion house into a global household name. She was also an avid art patron and collector, and the depth and sophistication of her art interests were very much in evidence in the spacious three-bedroom apartment in Rome that she shared with her husband, Candido Speroni. After the couple found the apartment in the Palazzo Ruspoli, a sixteenth-century former palace in central Rome, interior designer Cesare Rovatti drastically transformed the space over the course of around two years, including introducing a library, a billiards room, and an elegant bridge room. The most eclectic space was the spacious sitting room.Here, Fendi and Rovatti created a subtle backdrop with crisp white walls and ceilings, as well as custom-designed sofas, also in white. The space was then ready to display a key part of Fendi's art collection, including pieces by Lucio Fontana, Henri Matisse, Giorgio Morandi, and Enrico Castellani, along with Gio Ponti ceramics and animal bronzes by Claude and François-Xavier Lalanne. One of the most wondrous pieces here was another Lalanne creation —a sculptural bar table, complete with a vast bronze egg, which once belonged to Yves Saint Laurent and Pierre Bergé.

Spetses House

**Nikos Moustroufis & Isabel
López-Quesada
Spetses (GR), 2015**

The Madrid-based interior designer Isabel
López-Quesada has brought her distinctive
and engaging fusion of tradition and
modernity to projects around the world,
including the United States, Switzerland,
France, and Greece. On the small picturesque island of Spetses, which is near the
Peloponnese peninsula, López-Quesada
designed a new family vacation retreat that
has been compared to a village in miniature.
Situated on a hillside with a sea view and
surrounded by terraces and gardens, the
retreat comprises a number of complementary buildings designed by architect Nikos
Moustroufis to accommodate the various
generations of a family based primarily
in Athens. Punctuated by courtyards and
outdoor rooms, the thoughtful arrangement
of a triptych of whitewashed stone buildings allows the extended family to enjoy a
balance of privacy and conviviality. In this
spacious living room, the ceilings and floors
provide a soothing backdrop of whites and
pale blues. Characteristically, a calm foundation serves as a canvas for brighter splashes
of bolder patterns, such as the Kathryn
M. Ireland fabric chosen to upholster the
chaise longue, as well as textiles used for
cushions and the ottoman. Above the sofa is
a collage by Athens-born artist Irini Gonou,
complemented by Greek antiques, like the
small wooden captain's chair. Such joyful
elements lift the space and excite the eye.

Serifos House

Paola Navone
Serifos (GR), 2010

....

In a place like Serifos, the view is everything. This small, quiet island in the western Cyclades offers vistas across the Aegean Sea and an enviable sense of calm. For the Italian architect and designer Paola Navone, Serifos represents a refuge from her busy work life in Milan. "This is my private world," she says. "I feel completely at ease here." Using a Neo-Vernacular style, the Greek architect Yorgos Zaphiriou designed Navone's vacation home, which is on a hillside overlooking the coast. This contextually sensitive stone house, along with its terraces and outdoor rooms, steps gently down the slope toward the water and has a true sense of belonging. For the interior design, Navone embraced the feeling of simplicity offered by the exposed stonework and painted wood beams, and adopted a sensitive palette of whites and neutrals. The living room features Navone's Ghost chairs covered in loose wraps of white linen; decoration comes only from the white trompe l'oeil pattern painted directly onto the cement floor to resemble a carpet. The boldest statement here comes from the sea of blue framed by the two open windows.

Páros House

Mark Gaudette & Ioannis Mamoulakis
Páros (GR), 2010

....

The setting that American interior designer Mark Gaudette and Greek shipping executive Ioannis Mamoulakis chose for their airy island retreat is certainly sublime. The couple had spent a number of vacations on the island of Páros in the Cyclades, and having fallen for its many charms decided to buy 2 acres (0.8 hectares) of land on the coast, with views across the Aegean Sea to neighboring Naxos. Gaudette and Mamoulakis collaborated with architects Torsten Bessel and Dimitris Vathrakokoilis on the design of the house, which draws upon the local vernacular while making the most of the hillside location. Painted a crisp white, the single-story building features a central courtyard with an infinity pool and other outdoor rooms positioned to face the sea. For the interiors, Gaudette and Mamoulakis adopted a suitably uplifting blue-and-white color palette. White walls and pale Naxos marble floors give the house a sense of quiet cohesion that is not disrupted by a relatively eclectic choice of furniture in a similarly subtle tonal range. The dining room, for example, features a Swedish oval table and French balloon-back chairs upholstered in white cotton; the nineteenth-century ceramics and the paintings over the fireplace add pops of blue.

House in Patmos

John Stefanidis
Patmos (GR), c. 1967

Interior designer John Stefanidis has been predominantly based in England ever since he went to study at Oxford University as a young man. He founded his architecture and interior design practice in London in 1967 and has lived both there and in the West Country. But Stefanidis comes from a Greek family, and his homeland has played a constant role in his life and his career as designer, with multiple projects across the country. One of the most influential of these was the house on Patmos island that he adopted with his partner, artist Teddy Millington-Drake (1932–1994), during the mid-Sixties. The renovation and modernization of this house, which lacked running water and electricity when Stefanidis first arrived, were an ongoing labor of love. He decorated the interiors with an eclectic mix of furniture and antiques—wooden benches, lanterns, elaborately carved mirrors—from around the Mediterranean; much of the art was by Millington-Drake. But just as important were the multiple terraces that are an integral part of Greek living. They include this enticing space, where rush-seated stools and simple blue-and-white cushions rest against the sloping walls of the home; trees provide dappled shade with pops of color introduced through flourishing bougainvillea growing in terra-cotta pots.

Therasia House

Costis Psychas
Therasia (GR), 2012

The small island of Therasia lies just to the west of Santorini but is a world apart from its larger and more excitable neighbor. There are just a few hundred houses here, and the focus is on small-scale farming for grapes and capers rather than tourism. When the Greek hotelier and designer Costis Psychas spotted a disused warehouse on the coast of Therasia, he decided it would be the perfect spot for a hideaway. Dating back to the 1850s, the stone building had once been used as a storehouse and accommodation block for a pumice mine on the island but had long since fallen into disrepair. Psychas tracked down the owners of the building, bought the site, and began the long process of converting the structure into his four-bedroom retreat. He added a series of terraces and decks to the building, overlooking the sea and reaching out into the water. For the interiors, Psychas opted for rounded and expressive forms made with layers of sculpted white plaster. In spaces such as the living room, for example, these plaster walls morph into fireplaces, as well as seductive seating alcoves and window seats, padded with oversize cushions and purple-hued pillows. Low-slung dark-wood coffee tables complete the laid-back look.

Middle East

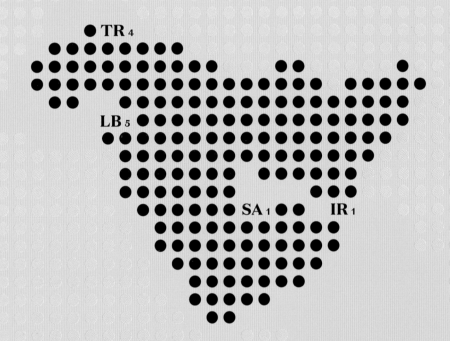

Khoury Penthouse

Bernard Khoury / DW5
Beirut (LB), 2014

Lebanese-architect Bernard Khoury likes to describe his three-level family home in Beirut as an independent house that happens to be perched on top of one of three new residential towers designed by his practice in 2013. Part of Khoury's attraction to this setting was the open vista across the city toward the distant Chouf Mountains. The design of the four-bedroom triplex, also known as the N.B.K. Residence, makes the most of these views. The spacious double-height living and dining room features oak floors and a wall of glass that connects with the balcony beyond. Khoury designed banks of elegant storage units topped with double-height bookcases, accessed by a steel walkway and bridge that doubles as a gallery to look down onto the communal space below. Apart from the custom dining table, much of the furniture was curated by Khoury's wife Nathalie, a designer, and includes a large sectional sofa by Piero Lissoni and a choice of sculptural chairs by Hans J. Wegner, Ib Kofod-Larsen, and Philippe Bestenheider.

Maison Gemmayze

Carole Schoucair
Beirut (LB), 2015

Lady Cochrane, a member of the influential Lebanese Sursock family, was a passionate defender of the characterful period architecture of the Achrafieh district of Beirut, owning a number of historic properties to protect them from redevelopment. One of these grand residences serves as a family home to business coach Carole Schoucair and her husband. Schoucair had long admired the Sursock villas and jumped at the chance to take a lease. Respecting the elegant architectural features of the house, including its elegant windows and tiled floors, Schoucair painted the walls in a palette of soft neutrals, allowing these elements to shine. She also introduced a more contemporary edge to the key living spaces, incorporating choice pieces of furniture and art. The living room hosts two white Ghost sofas by Paola Navone (see pp. 302 and 308), complemented by a selection of locally made coffee tables and vintage Scandinavian stools. Schoucair's emphasis on neutral tones creates a soothing space, with plenty of interest provided by the distinctive triptych of windows and a few grander touches, particularly the chandelier, which was a gift from her husband's family.

Daouk Villa

May Daouk
Beirut (LB), 2002

When interior designer May Daouk returned to her Lebanese homeland at the beginning of the Noughties, one of her first projects was a villa for herself and her family. Daouk had spent many years in the United States, studying in Boston and later working with the influential designer Bunny Williams (see p. 151), who became a design mentor. Having settled back in Beirut, Daouk managed to find an elegant nineteenth-century villa in Achrafieh, one of the most historic neighborhoods in the city. The villa is blessed with many engaging original architectural features, as well as rooms with a welcoming sense of proportion and scale. The glory of the house is undoubtedly the spacious living room, which runs from the front to the back of the house and includes a set of three arched windows leading to the adjoining terrace. For this dramatic space, Daouk opted for lavender for the walls and the coffered ceiling. This soft tone is echoed by complementary colors throughout: purples, lilacs, and blues seen in textiles, ceramics, and the chandelier's lampshades. The choice of furniture is purposefully eclectic. Fine and antique pieces rub shoulders with vintage finds, such as the wooden trestle table used to display blue-and-white vases.

Maison Habis

Pascale Habis
Beirut (LB), 2008

Creative director Pascale Habis's home in Beirut is a welcoming family abode that balances the old and the new, the traditional and the modern. Around 2008, Habis and her husband discovered a nineteenth-century villa in the historic quarter of Beirut—originally built for the wealthy Sursock family while awaiting the completion of the nearby Sursock Palace. It was spacious enough to accommodate the couple's five children, but also offered a refined backdrop for Habis's collections of modern art and furniture. The key space in the house is the central living room—as is often the case with historic Lebanese villas. Habis respected and preserved the architectural features of this grand, communal centerpiece, with its marble floors and partial screen formed by a triptych of internal arches. The original ceiling is ornately painted but the walls are in calming soft tones. Choice pieces of furniture include a sculptural coffee table by Lebanese designer Karen Chekerdjian, flanked by comfortable family-sized sofas. Other standout pieces include an Antonio Citterio (see p. 292) daybed and, from Lebanese Galerie Gabriel et Guillaume, a vintage chair with crimson-red upholstery that shines out against the dove-gray walls and floors.

Maison Raya Raphaël Nahas

Raëd Abillama Architects
Beirut (LB), 2010

....

Architect and designer Raëd Abillama is one of the leading lights of the Lebanese contemporary design world. When it comes to houses, his practice manages to cohesively fuse architecture and interiors with character, as seen in the renovation of the Beirut family home of banker and art collector Raya Raphaël Nahas and her husband Anthony. The house itself, which dates back to around 1910, had been in the family for many years but was in poor condition, having been split up into apartments, while the ground floor had been used as a painting studio by artist Nabil Nahas, Raya's uncle. As well as reuniting the internal spaces, the interiors are lent additional depth and personality by Raphaël Nahas's art and furniture collections. This is very much the case with the generously scaled living room, which flows out onto a marble terrace. Here, pale walls and stone floors form a gentle, gallery-style backdrop for mid-century furniture by Charlotte Perriand and Jean Royère, along with some shining, golden coffee tables by Karen Chekerdjian. Artworks include pieces by Walid Raad, Hiroshi Sugimoto, and, naturally, uncle Nabil Nahas.

Fadillioglu House

Zeynep Fadillioglu Design
Near Istanbul (TR), 1987

....

"For me," says Turkish interior designer Zeynep Fadillioglu, "the most important qualities in a space are soul, taste, and the rhythm between colors and objects." Her own home in Istanbul offers a sophisticated exemplar of her unique design approach, layered as it is with history and modern treasures. The house itself, built in the eighteenth century as the summer residence of the sultan's clockmaker, lies just to the north of Istanbul not far from the banks of the Bosphorus. Fadillioglu bought the house and the next-door orangery with her husband, restaurateur Metin Fadillioglu. While there was much work to be done on the interiors, Fadillioglu took great care to preserve the character of the building, including original features like the staircase as well as the patina of walls and surfaces. The interiors of the living spaces feature an extraordinary blend of antiques, ceramics, and textiles from both the East and West. Small splashes of crimson pink on a few choice armchairs, some cushions, and a tablecloth, demonstrate Fadillioglu's engaging use of color—just enough to captivate the eye and lift the space.

Tunca House

Asli Tunca & Carl Vercauteren
Istanbul (TR), 1997

The Turkish designer Asli Tunca and her husband, Belgian artist Carl Vercauteren, began the three-year renovation of their extraordinary home not long after the pair moved from Antwerp to Istanbul. It was Tunca who first discovered the neglected five-story building, which had once served as a grand residence in one of the most historic quarters of the city but had most recently been divided up into a series of workshops. As such, the reinvention and reunification of the house and garden, with its wide views out across the city to the Bosphorus, became a grand labor of love for Tunca and Vercauteren. The project was a spur for their collaborative creativity: the ground floor doubles as a gallery showcasing Tunca and Vercauteren's collections, including restored antiques and new pieces of furniture. One of the most dramatic and beautifully proportioned spaces here is the central hallway, with its stone floors and columns, which spills out onto the private terrace and garden via steel-framed French doors. It is a serene and magical setting for their subtly evolving choice of art and furniture.

Ezer Apartment

Hakan Ezer
Istanbul (TR), 2013

The Turkish designer Hakan Ezer has compared his interiors to journeys between the East and West. The ancient Silk Road, in particular, encapsulates many of his interests and passions. Ezer's own Istanbul apartment is inhabited by many treasures drawn from that part of the world: "Objects should have a story and those with mystery have always fascinated me." Situated on the top two floors of a Twenties apartment building in the historic Galata district, on the northern shore of the Golden Horn, his home enjoys open views across the cityscape. The designer used timber paneling and a number of pieces of architectural salvage, including doors and architraves, to enhance the sense of character. This view from the hallway on the top floor through to the combined kitchen and dining area provides a compelling example, with a black latticed screen and doorway offering a subtle sense of separation. The room itself features wraparound units arranged around the edges, while a series of skylights introduces natural light. Thonet armchairs and Twenties leather chairs by Verdat Tek flank the marble-topped dining table. The living room sits on the other side of the hallway, with free-flowing connections between these more social elements of the apartment.

Bodrum House

Rifat Ozbek
Near Yalikavak (TR), 2005

....

The Turkish-born designer Rifat Ozbek has enjoyed two careers. In around 2005, following a thirty-year period spent as a fashion designer, Ozbek launched a new Istanbul venture focused on textiles and homeware called Yastik, as well as taking on interior design commissions himself. The catalyst for this change of direction was, in part, his own home in Bodrum in southern Turkey. The house, built of local stone, sits in an olive grove near the village of Yalikavak, and was originally designed by the Turkish architect Ahmet Iğdirligil. Given the hillside setting, including views out over the Aegean, the property was a tempting prospect for Ozbek and his partner, Erdal Karaman. Inside, Ozbek indulged his love of textiles and color. In the living room, for example, the walls, floor, and ceilings are in neutral tones allowing the designer's choice of locally sourced rugs, textiles, and seating upholstery to stand out. Soft yellows complemented by gentle reds and touches of pale blue dominate, enhanced by glimpses of the terrace and gardens seen through the French doors.

Villa Namazee

Gio Ponti
Tehran (IR), 1964

....

During the Fifties and Sixties, the Italian architect and designer Gio Ponti (1891–1979, see p. 296) was asked to design a series of substantial overseas family villas, including an ambitious home in Tehran for government minister Shafi Namazee and his wife Vida. The two-story house was designed as an irregular rectangle that splayed slightly as it opened up to the rear garden. Outside, an integrated patio featured walls lined with decorative tilework by artist Fausto Melotti. Inside, Ponti explored multiple shifts in height and volume. One of the villa's most seductive spaces was the double-height living room in which Ponti engaged a vivid blue-and-white color scheme. He also introduced sofas and armchairs of his own design and a suitably patterned Persian rug to cover the marble floor. Curtains and screens followed the same palette, seen too in the Ponti-designed Hotel Parco dei Principi in Sorrento, Italy, made around the same time. The generously scaled space was also overlooked by a second living room on the upper-level mezzanine. The house was confiscated by the state in 1979 following the Iranian Revolution.

Prince Faisal's Majlis
Christopher Hall
Riyadh (SA), 2017

In Saudi Arabia and other parts of the Middle East *majlis* traditionally refers to a spacious salon used for entertaining and gatherings. *Majlis* might be part of a house, or a tent, and typically feature low seating, often consisting of cushions laid directly on the floor. One of the most striking modern *majlis* was designed by Christopher Hall in the grounds of Prince Faisal bin Sattam bin Abdulaziz Al Saud's palace in Riyadh. The New Zealand–born Hall has an Istanbul-based practice and has worked widely in the Middle East, including on a number of projects for Prince Faisal. Faisal's earth-toned grand salon features soaring ceilings with an aperture in the roof through which the stars can be seen at night. Every element was custom designed by Hall, including the low sofas, which are over 20 ft. (6 m) in length. One of the most dramatic elements is the sculptural fireplace, which is coated in burnt-orange ceramic tiles specially made in central Anatolia. A geometric antique 1930s bronze artwork, bought in Paris, dominates in the dining room beyond, separated from the grand salon by floor-to-ceiling sliding doors.

Africa

Gibbs Residence

Christopher Gibbs
Tangier (MA), c. 2000

The English antique dealer, interior designer, and dandy Christopher Gibbs (1938–2018) first visited Tangier when he was twenty years old. The city made a profound impression on him and remained an almost constant presence over the course of his successful career. In 2006 he relocated, or "retreated," to Tangier full time and lived here until the end of his life. Gibbs began putting down roots in the city when he acquired a modest house known as El Foolk on the Old Mountain, beautifully situated with a panorama over the Strait of Gibraltar. The former home of the American artist Marguerite McBey (1905–1999), El Foolk offered Gibbs a welcoming retreat that was never opulent or overbearing, but certainly layered with history and countless treasures. Some years later he built a larger villa next door, with Gibbs's grandson, Cosimo Sesti, designing its architecture, and Gibbs decorating the interiors in a sophisticated fusion style, blending antiques from Europe with Moroccan textiles and furnishings. The resulting spaces were calm and timeless, filled with pieces of provenance and personality. The lounge was a seductive space in the villa, with its terra-cotta colored walls, and comfortable seating overseen by a decorative fireplace—twin creatures standing guard add a touch of eccentricity.

Maison Pasti

Umberto Pasti & Roberto Peregalli
Tangier (MA), 2010s

The Italian writer, garden designer, and horticulturalist Umberto Pasti first came to Tangier during the Nineties. Together with his partner, French fashion designer Stephan Janson, he began work on the gardens at Villa Tebarek Allah, creating a multilayered world, complete with terraces, verandas, and a swimming pool. Pasti's residence also represents an autobiographical journey of a special kind. Sitting within the garden, the villa is composed of three pavilions, which have been restored, remodeled, built or rebuilt over many years, assisted by Pasti's good friend Roberto Peregalli from Studio Peregalli. One pavilion serves as a space devoted to sleeping and eating, while another is dedicated to guests, and a third is for daily living. Here, the main sitting room is layered rather than "decorated." The neutral tones of the plastered walls offer a canvas for a collection of Oriental textiles and curiosities, such as whalebone and gourds. A sixteenth-century Turkish carpet hangs above the fireplace; other pieces have their origins in the Middle East, Italy, Spain, and England. Framed tile panels—ancient *azulejos* from Seville and Portugal—cover the walls. Plants feature too, including exotic cultivars. These layers have evolved gradually and organically, adding to the sense of calm that permeates Pasti's home.

Gazebo

Veere Grenney
Tangier (MA), 2017

....

The New Zealand–born, London-based interior designer Veere Grenney lives just down the hill from Christopher Gibbs's former home (see p. 330). Gazebo, as Grenney's Old Mountain home is known, was a small cottage that once belonged to artist Marguerite McBey (1905–1999) and her family before becoming part of Gibbs's compound of buildings. Like Gibbs, Grenney was in his twenties when he first came to Morocco, and he has been coming back ever since. Gazebo offered him the chance to create a home here of his own, which involved a drastic extension of the one-bedroom cottage. Over the course of five years, Grenney extended the cottage and added a five-bedroom guest lodge alongside it, while architect Cosimo Sesti designed a "meditation tower" on the grounds. Decoratively, the most ambitious space is Grenney's elegant drawing room, where the garden seeps inside via the French doors. Connections to the natural world are amplified by the birdlife and creepers seen in the patterns of the chintz curtains and wallpaper. This spacious drawing room seems even more expansive and engaging because of the way it flows freely into the adjoining garden room, where the walls are lined with trelliswork, and twin rattan rocking chairs face an open view of the grounds.

Casa Tosca

Nicolò Castellini Baldissera
Tangier (MA), 2018

On the outside, Nicolò Castellini Baldissera's house in Tangier is painted a crisp Mediterranean white. But step inside, and the Italian interior designer's home is a hymn to color, pattern, and delight. Castellini Baldissera, who grew up in Milan, comes from a family of designers and has homes in Italy and England. Yet Morocco, and Tangier in particular, exerts a pull on his heartstrings and imagination. For some years Castellini Baldissera based himself near the medina, but in search of quieter surroundings he decided to move to a 1930s villa overlooking a quiet square in the Marshan district of Tangier. He began by adding a veranda overlooking the garden, which writer and horticulturalist Umberto Pasti (see p. 330) redesigned. Castellini Baldissera clearly relished the five-story house's many opportunities to experiment with color and texture in the interior design. The study is painted mauve and doubles as guest quarters, while a primary bedroom is painted blush pink and another in peacock blue. The antique turquoise bed frame was sourced locally. In the salon, which is designed around a new focal-point fireplace, twin stuffed parrots are perched upon the mantelpiece to form part of an avian theme. Naturally, Castellini Baldissera sourced the many fabrics in the house from the family textile firm, C&C Milano.

Villa Mabrouka

**Yves Saint Laurent, Pierre Bergé
& Jacques Grange**
Tangier (MA), 1999

....

Along with their famous home in Marrakech,
Yves Saint Laurent (1936–2008) and Pierre
Bergé (1930–2017) also acquired a house in
Tangier, called Villa Mabrouka. The couple
turned to their familiar and favorite team:
interior designer Jacques Grange and landscape designer Madison Cox. They were
tasked with, according to Cox, the instruc-
tion to "carry the spirit of having been
inhabited by a somewhat impoverished and
reclusive elderly English woman who loved
bold, overblown chintz and surrounded
herself with few possessions." The American
ex-pat designer Stuart Church was also
tracked down to restore the pavilion that
he had designed alongside the swimming
pool. Saint Laurent commissioned his friend,
sculptor and designer Claude Lalanne, to
design the striking mirror over the fireplace
in the main salon, while a decorative artist
who worked at Saint Laurent and Bergé's
Normandy retreat, Château Gabriel (1983),
was invited to Tangier to re-create a Monet-
inspired waterlily fresco on the walls of
the dining room. One of the most soothing
and delightful rooms was Saint Laurent's
bedroom, where the colors of the fabrics,
painted woodwork, and turquoise chandelier
shine out against the neutral shades of the
walls, curtains, and fire surround.

Smit House

Willem Smit
Essaouira (MA), 2017

....

Dutch designer and hotelier Willem Smit
is best known for his work on the interiors
of El Fenn, the character-filled boutique
hotel in Marrakech founded by Vanessa
Branson and Howell James. One of his most
personal projects was the design of his own
retreat on the edges of another Moroccan
city, Essaouira, on the Atlantic coast. The
retreat would provide an occasional escape
from the fast pace of life in Marrakech.
With this project, Smit was able to fulfill
a long-standing ambition to build a house
from scratch. He managed to find a former
farmstead that came with a very small
house but a very big view, across fields and
toward the coast. Smit designed his new
home to combine a primary pavilion, a guest
annex, and an outdoor living room within
a courtyard facing a swimming pool and
the sea. Inside, the center of the house is
devoted to a large living space; the main
seating area is anchored by a built-in
cast-concrete and brown leather banquette,
while the dining area and kitchen are just a
few steps lower down. The neutral textures
of the exposed-concrete frame and stone
walls form a backdrop to Smit's blend of
custom-designed elements—including twin
turquoise ottomans—along with vintage
finds and mid-century pieces, such as chairs
by Ray and Charles Eames.

Lagoon Lodge

**Danny Moynihan, Katrine Boorman &
Fabrizio Bizzarri**
Oualidia (MA), 2016

For many years Danny Moynihan and his
wife, Katrine Boorman, fulfilled their
love of Morocco via their riad in Marrakech.
But then they came across a derelict
cowshed in Oualidia, a picturesque village
on the Moroccan coast situated between
Casablanca and Essaouria. The setting is
certainly extraordinary. The former farmstead overlooks Oualidia's extensive natural
lagoon and dedicated ecoreserve, known
as the oyster capital of Morocco but also
rich in birdlife. This creative couple decided
to build a house of their own here. The
design of Lagoon Lodge makes the most
of the house's gently elevated position by
having the naturally filtered swimming pool
and terraces look across the coastal landscape. For the interiors, the family collaborated with ex-pat Italian designer Fabrizio
Bizzarri, who spliced contemporary elements with traditional materials and ways
of making, including the earthy *tadelakt*
(Moroccan plaster) walls and Moroccan
rugs. The sitting room revolves around
the stone fireplace and a spacious built-in
sofa layered with cushions and goatskins.
Natural textures prevail, while color comes
via the choices of textiles and art, including a Sixties abstract painting by Danny
Moynihan's father, Rodrigo.

Agnelli House

Marella Agnelli & Alberto Pinto
Marrakech (MA), 2006

As an influential patron of design and the
decorative arts, Marella Agnelli (1927–2019,
see p. 282) was associated with some of
the most inventive designers of the twentieth century, including Renzo Mongiardino,
Stéphane Boudin, and Russell Page. She
began work on Aïn Kassimou a few years
after the 2003 death of her husband, Gianni
Agnelli, the former chairman of Italian car
giant Fiat. The estate, which once belonged
to the famous Tolstoy and Hermès families,
is situated within the Palmeraie—a historic
desert oasis populated by thousands of date
palms—just outside the city of Marrakech.
Here Agnelli created a retreat within
a retreat, and a Madison Cox–designed
garden within a garden. For the interiors
of the reinvented and extended house,
Agnelli turned to the Moroccan-born, Paris-
based designer Alberto Pinto (1943–2012,
see p. 165). He refreshed the original parts
of the house that had once belonged to
Count Tolstoy, Leo Tolstoy's son, with a
palette of light, bright neutrals, including
cream tones and warm yellow highlights.
A menagerie of framed parrots and other
birds flutter around the fireplace in the
sitting room, while signature Agnelli touches
include sculpted rattan chairs by Boccaccini
arranged on reed matting.

Maison Loum-Martin

Meryanne Loum-Martin
Marrakech (MA), 2001

....

Falling in love with Morocco changed the direction of Meryanne Loum-Martin's life. Her first career was as a lawyer in Paris, yet after a number of increasingly regular trips to Morocco, and the city of Marrakech in particular, she eventually decided to relocate and embrace her long-held love of design. Loum-Martin and her ethnobotanist husband, Gary Martin, bought 7 acres (2.8 hectares) of land in the Palmeraie, a palm oasis just outside Marrakech. Here, Loum-Martin designed a hotel, Jnane Tamsna, within gardens that her husband created following sustainable principles. She also designed a new family home here, which—like the hotel—blends Moorish influences with a more contemporary aesthetic. Generously proportioned and inviting, the lemon hue–accented sitting room spills out onto the adjoining terraces via two arched doorways. Loum-Martin made good use of Moroccan artisanal craftsmanship while reinventing traditional decorative features, as seen in the elegant custom fireplace surround in polished *tadelakt* (Moroccan plaster) and the cornicing, inspired by a pattern on an old oven door that she spotted in a cart being driven through the medina. The comfortable seating and other furniture includes a number of pieces designed by Loum-Martin and made locally.

Riad Méchiche

Frédéric Méchiche
Marrakech (MA), 2013

....

For the interior designer Frédéric Méchiche (d. 2021), the decision to buy a house for himself in Morocco represented a homecoming of sorts. Although he has lived and worked in France for a number of years (see p. 260), Méchiche grew up in Algeria, and the architecture and atmosphere of Marrakech remind him of his childhood. He discovered a riad in the medina, near the Place des Épices, and set about transforming it into a personal sanctuary. The high rammed-earth walls of the riad date back to the seventeenth century, while the ornate plasterwork and vibrantly patterned tiles are largely nineteenth century. Yet much of the original character of the house had been hidden away during its time as a guesthouse, requiring a six-month restoration of the house itself, the central courtyard garden, and the rooftop terrace. One of the greatest lures of the riad was the unusually spacious salon, which looks out across the garden court. Here, Méchiche restored the original ceilings and other period detailing, including the hand-carved plasterwork decorating the doorways. He introduced a custom sofa in emerald green, as well as other furnishings—such as decoratively inlaid pedestal tables and chairs—from Morocco, Syria, and France, and nineteenth-century paintings with a North Africa or Orientalist theme.

Dowe-Sandes House

Caitlin & Samuel Dowe-Sandes
Marrakech (MA), 2015

Having decided to settle in Marrakech, Morocco, in 2006, American ex-pat designers Caitlin and Samuel Dowe-Sandes eventually moved to Guéliz, known as the "new town," settling in a two-story house, which offered space and, importantly, a welcoming garden for themselves and their young daughter. The move also provided Caitlin and Samuel an opportunity to use the renovation and interior design project as a laboratory for experimenting with the patterns, colors, and ideas explored within collections of their own Marrakech-based tile company, Popham Design. The designers layered their home with these dynamic color choices. The hallway sets the scene, with bold gray-and-white striped walls and vividly patterned blue, white, and gray cement floor tiles. This pattern carries on, via a pair of folding glass doors, into the main sitting room. Here the designers opened up the space to create an expansive salon with aqua-blue walls and a curated choice of antique, mid-century, and contemporary furniture gathered on many travels across Europe and in the souks and antique stores of Marrakech itself—twin 1970s chairs by Ingmar Relling, for example, and a sculptural ceiling light by Constance Guisset; the cocktail table's top was originally a ceiling panel in a 1970s department store. Additional layers of art, curios, and treasures on the walls create an eclectic mélange.

Riad Emery

Agnès Emery
Marrakech (MA), 1998

Belgian designer Agnès Emery has divided
her time between Brussels (see p. 224) and
Marrakech since the Nineties. Morocco
and its workshops have played an important part in the evolution of her collections
of tiles, furniture, and lighting, with Emery
taking inspiration from the process of
creative collaboration with local artisans,
particularly in Marrakech. Emery bought
her first riad here around the turn of the
century. The character of these traditional
townhouses—with their central courtyard
gardens and high boundary walls—suited
her well. Here, she was able to create a
secret oasis, layered with her own designs.
Some years later Emery was able to also
buy the house next door, and she combined
the two properties to create one substantial home arranged around twin gardens.
It is an oasis full of color and pattern, with
constant connections between inside and
outside space. Emery is instinctively drawn
to a palette of natural tones, such as greens
and grays, while vivid blues echo the sky
above. The patterns seen on her tile designs
throughout the house also take inspiration
from nature, with the designer's motifs
drawn from flora and fauna. Such tones and
tendrils lift the atmosphere of this character-filled urban escape, complemented by
the citrus trees and reflecting pools within
the two courtyards.

Dar El Sadaka

Jean-François Fourtou
Near Marrakech (MA), 2000

The 25-acre (10 hectare) farmstead just outside Marrakech belonging to French artist Jean-François Fourtou and his family offers him the time and space needed for creating his art installations, sculptures, and playful experiments with scale and perspective. One of the first things that catches the eye in the garden is a giant goat sculpture standing by the swimming pool, and just a walk away is the surreal sight of a full-scale two-story house at the edge of a field, upside down, resting upon its roof. As well as being a setting for art, Dar El Sadaka is a welcoming retreat with a house full of character. Fourtou first started spending time in Morocco during his early twenties, and his family decided to buy the farmstead and its olive groves in the mid-Nineties. The artist rebuilt the former farm buildings and extended, adding to the project again and again. Two of the key spaces here are the sitting room and dining room: airy, double-height spaces connected by a glass link that doubles as an entrance hall of the main residence. Tall windows frame views of the garden, complemented by lines of high clerestories adding extra light, while fireplaces anchor both spaces. A colorful, supersize modular seating system by Sandra Ancelot sings out against the white walls in the sitting room, while a Fourtou giraffe looks down upon the dining table next door.

Beldi House

Julie & Alex Leymarie
Near Marrakech (MA), 2012

....

Alex Leymarie and his family have created a destination retreat near Marrakech, known as the Beldi Country Club, which encompasses landscaped grounds, a pottery, and a glass factory, with a fusion of stylish living, sustainability, and artisanal craftsmanship. The same kind of fusion can be found in Alex and Julie Leymarie's design of their own private family home, built on the grounds of Beldi. The house sits within a secluded garden, which features roses and olive trees, as well as a choice of outdoor rooms and fresh-air escapes for the Leymaries and their children. The couple were able to draw on the teams of experienced artisans and carpenters who have worked on the evolution of Beldi for many years, constructing a highly organic and contextual house made of *pisé* (rammed earth); stone; and salvaged architectural materials, such as beams, doorways, and ceiling panels. One of the most character-filled spaces is the central sitting and dining room, with its high ceilings and layers of textural interest. Pieces such as the large sofa and dining table were custom-made at Beldi, while other items of furniture and art were gathered in France (where the Leymaries grew up) and India (where the couple lived and worked for many years).

Redecke-Montague House

Chris Redecke & Maryam Montague
Near Marrakech (MA), 2010

....

After many years of traveling and periods spent living in Nepal and Namibia, American ex-pats architect Chris Redecke and author and designer Maryam Montague settled in Morocco in 2001. After four years living and working in Rabat, they moved on to the Marrakech area, and Redecke was able to realize a long-held dream to build a house of his own on a farmstead not far from the city. The house fuses vernacular references with a more contemporary approach to space and light, as well as fluid connections to the terraces and gardens, which feature olive groves and have views of the Atlas Mountains. At the heart of the house is a spacious sitting room topped by a domed roof and a line of high clerestory windows. A fountain serves as the centerpiece of the room, and a line of French doors leads out to a veranda with views of the pool and gardens. The main seating area—including Frank Gehry Wiggle chairs dressed with vintage Indian belts—encircles the fireplace to one side; Berber rugs partially cover the polished concrete floor. The interior has been layered by Redecke and Montague with the fruits of their travels, as well as finds from the souks of Marrakech.

Villa D

Studio KO
Al Ouidane (MA), 2004

French designers Karl Fournier and Olivier Marty of Studio KO have designed numerous projects in Morocco, including the Musée Yves Saint Laurent in Marrakech and a sequence of contextually sensitive rural villas characterized by their distinctive minimalism combined with the use of traditional materials. One of the most striking of these is Villa D, a family home near Marrakech set within a walled farmstead. "The clients wanted a house that was elementary, something that was very close to nature, using earth and water," Marty says. The clients also wanted to avoid large apertures, leading to an almost sculptural, semiabstract form with windows that are mostly slots incised in the earthen brick walls. The interiors are minimalist—polished concrete floors, earthy plaster walls—yet depth and character are achieved through texture in particular, as well as the way that light entering the space is manipulated to create a dramatic atmosphere. The primary suite is set apart from the rest of the house on a modest upper level, with its own adjoining roof terrace beyond sizable glass doors. The built-in bed holds center stage within the space, backed by a brown leather banquette that looks across the farm.

Ourika Valley House

Liliane Fawcett & Imaad Rahmouni
Ourika Valley (MA), 2009

....

Gallerist Liliane Fawcett first fell in love with Morocco when she visited the country as a student. Some years later, after moving from Paris to London, she began visiting every year with her husband, Christopher, until eventually, they bought a parcel of land in the Ourika Valley and decided to build a family home of their own here. The Fawcetts commissioned architect Imaad Rahmouni to design the new house, which is a contemporary reimagining of a rural farmstead. Rahmouni created a house of generous proportions with a fluid relationship between the main living spaces and the adjoining courtyards and verandas. He also designed a series of guest pavilions set among the landscaped gardens. Liliane designed the interiors of the house herself, drawing on her long experience running her London design-and-art gallery, Themes & Variations, and curating collections of postwar and contemporary furniture. Standout pieces by Vladimir Kagan, Tom Dixon, and others anchor the main living spaces. Fawcett balanced neutral tones for the circulation spaces with bursts of color in the key communal spaces, including the sitting room and dining room, as well as the bedrooms. Contemporary art introduces additional layers of color and character.

Nile Riverboat

Christian Louboutin
River Nile (EG), 2004

French fashion designer Christian Louboutin was first introduced to the city of Luxor, Egypt, by a friend, archaeologist François Larché. After many visits to the ancient city, Louboutin decided to create a house here of his own. Inevitably, being so close to the Nile, he was also drawn to the river, which led him to eventually commission a houseboat as an adjunct to his new home, so he could explore the country using the great waterway. Known as *dahabeahs* (or *dahabiehs*), this type of traditional flat-bottomed sailing barges became popular during the late nineteenth and early twentieth centuries, when they served as passenger boats for tourists taking Nile cruises. Louboutin's own version is elegant and substantial, requiring a crew of ten to keep the *dahabeah* in motion and in good order. Its canopied upper deck is well suited to relaxation or entertaining with an ever-changing view; a choice of bedrooms and more social spaces are situated below deck. Louboutin collaborated with interior designer Amr Khalil on key rooms, such as the grand salon, blending Egyptian antiques and other treasures from Mali, Mauretania, Panama, and India. With its echoes of an Agatha Christie classic, the houseboat offers a very different way of living than Louboutin's other homes, such as his château in the Vendée (see p. 273).

Nairobi House

Maia Geheb & Rob Burnet
Nairobi (KE), 2004

Artist Maia Geheb grew up in Kenya with her Scandinavian parents, then studied art and illustration in England before returning to Kenya. The interiors of her home on the green edges of Nairobi, shared with her husband, Rob Burnet, and their two children, fuse various elements and influences of her background. There are touches of English colonial architecture, but also Nordic notes, seen in the white walls and painted floors in the sitting room, dining room, and library. Remarkably, given the multiple layers of historical references in Geheb's home, the house itself was a new creation. Geheb took the lead with the interiors, creating a calm, neutral backdrop, which she then layered with art, Scandinavian furniture, and antique pieces collected in East Africa, while textiles provide modest splashes of bolder colors. Anchored by fireplaces, the main indoor living spaces are soothing and restful. Elsewhere, one of the most important living spaces for this house is the archetypal Kenyan veranda, which offers a strong sense of connection with the garden and the wider surroundings while providing an all-weather space graced with rattan armchairs and a sink-in sofa.

Tangala

Giles & Bella Gibbs & Fred Spencer
Zambezi (ZM), 2000

....

The history of Tangala stretches back to the late Eighties, when Ben Parker settled in Zambia and decided to run safaris along the Zambezi River developing a number of safari lodges, which became known as Tongabezi. Following his marriage to math teacher Vanessa Parker, the family continued to develop the resort while also establishing a local school, known as Tujatane. The Parkers asked South African architect Fred Spencer to draw up plans for a new house, named Tangala, for themselves and their three children in the late Nineties, and invited interior designers Giles and Bella Gibbs to help them. The design of the four-bedroom waterside home—just along the Zambezi River from Tongabezi—fuses influences from both Africa and Europe. The use of indigenous materials, such as thatch, give the house an earthy quality. Some spaces, such as the semicircular veranda, suggest the influence of African rondavels while others, such as the kitchen and living room, introduce touches of Europe. In the latter, for example, a fireplace anchors the seating area, which features comfortable sofas and armchairs, yet at the same time the sculpted, organic quality of the interiors continues in elements such as the built-in shelves and banquettes and the winding staircase alongside.

Casa Comprida

Designworkshop & Interdeco
Vilanculos (MZ), 2015

....

The picturesque Mozambican coastal town of Vilanculos and its tempting beaches look eastward across the Mozambique Channel. Here, within a game reserve, Liz and Lloyd Mitchell have built a contemporary beach house that takes inspiration from this extraordinary setting and vernacular architecture. The family commissioned architect Andrew Makin of Designworkshop to design their new home: a steel-and-concrete-frame building supported by a series of pillars embedded in the dunes. The form is essentially a modern version of a long house (*casa comprida* in Portuguese), with bedrooms at one end and a spacious living room at the other. The traditional pitched and thatched *jekka* roof means the building blends into the landscape. Connections with the coast are maximized throughout, with key living spaces leading out onto a long veranda and pool terrace facing the beach. Designed in collaboration with Durban–based Interdeco, the interiors fuse natural textures—seen in the pendant lights, which are made from repurposed baskets—with contemporary furnishings, while elements such as polished concrete floors are practical for beach-house living. The use of subtle, muted tones throughout, punctuated with occasional pops of color, means that the star attraction remains the framed ocean vista.

The Observatory

**Rory Sweet & Silvio Rech +
Lesley Carstens
Leobo Private Reserve, Waterberg
(ZA), 2012**

It's no wonder Rory and Lizzy Sweet
chose to call their South African home the
Observatory. Perched upon the brow of a
hill, the house offers sweeping views across
the open landscape of Limpopo province.
Factor in the copper-domed tower that
holds a celestial observatory, and the name
is even more apt. The residence is part
of the Sweets' compound of pavilions and
other buildings that form a unique village
in miniature. The British entrepreneur
and adventurer Rory Sweet began buying
land here around the turn of the millennium, after falling in love with the Leobo
Private Reserve. The family accumulated
about 1,980 acres (800 hectares) and asked
architects Silvio Rech + Lesley Carstens
to design an organic house that would sit
comfortably within the landscape. Rech and
Carstens used largely natural and recycled
materials, such as stone, thatch, and timber.
The primary suite occupies a dedicated
"rondavel": a modern reinterpretation of a
vernacular circular hut with a conical roof.
This storybook-like space features a four-
poster bed, a swing seat hung on a thick
industrial chain, swaths of white linen curtains, and an egg-shaped bath tub, all facing
views of the bushveld savanna.

Westcliff Poolhouse

**Silvio Rech + Lesley Carstens
Johannesburg (ZA), 2011**

From within, this garden pavilion designed
by the architects Silvio Rech + Lesley
Carstens looks as though it is surrounded
by an untamed landscape, yet the setting
is actually Westcliff, an affluent suburb of
Johannesburg. The clients requested a new
building within the generous grounds of an
existing residence, to serve as a pool house
along with guest rooms and a choice of
inside and outside spaces for entertaining.
In its eco-conscious design, the architects
slotted the pavilion into the site's undulating
topography. The building was constructed
using a combination of a rammed-earth wall,
with the indoor pool adjacent, and recycled
timber for the structural framework and
cladding. The pavilion is spacious enough
for a kitchen at one end, a dining area
at the center (arranged around an existing
eucalyptus tree, which grows through the
building), and a lounge at the opposite end,
positioned a few steps down from the main
floor level. Here a built-in, semicircular
sofa in apple-green leather upholstery faces
a suspended fireplace and views of the
surrounding treescape through a folding
wall of glass. There are echoes of a Seventies-
inspired conversation pit and traditional
East African *baraza* seats, but the overall
aesthetic remains decidedly contemporary.

Beyond

SAOTA
Cape Town (ZA), 2018

When it came to designing his own family home, Cape Town architect Stefan Antoni of SAOTA seized the opportunity to experiment with some fresh ideas. While visiting a client in the neighborhood of Clifton, known for its quartet of sandy beaches beneath Lion's Head mountain, Antoni stumbled across a steep site that offered unimpeded views of the ocean. He embraced the challenge to build a new home here. The main living spaces, right at the top of the house, are the crowning glory of the villa, with a collection of both indoor and outdoor spaces that make the most of the ocean vista to the west. Chief among these communal family zones is a double-height, glass-sided pavilion with space enough for a combined kitchen, dining area, and lounge. Furnishings include a family-sized OKHA seating system and sculptural mid-century plywood chairs by Hans J. Wegner, while a collection of Central and West African masks populates the end wall behind the kitchen. When the glass at either side of the pavilion slides away, the space seamlessly flows out to the adjoining roof terrace and infinity pool.

Du Toit House

Pius Pahl
Cape Town (ZA), 1974

The German-born architect Pius Pahl (1909–2003) studied at the Bauhaus under Ludwig Mies van der Rohe before setting up his own practice in Mainz, Germany, after World War II. In 1952 Pahl and his wife emigrated to South Africa, where he established a new practice in Stellenbosch, near Cape Town, and began teaching at the University of Cape Town's School of Architecture. One of his most pleasing residential commissions was this house in the town of Paarl, which is near Stellenbosch and within one of South Africa's prime wine-growing regions. Completed in 1974, the L-shaped house was graced with a courtyard and terrace that made the most of the hillside site. Architectural historian Dicey du Toit and her family eventually acquired the residence and restored it with a light touch, assisted by Malherbe Rust Architects. The open-plan sitting and dining room is the lynchpin of the house. Natural textures and tones prevail here, seen in the sloping timber ceiling and dark brick floors, while the whitewashed brick walls form a backdrop for art and furniture, including a steel artwork by landscape artist and sculptor Strijdom van der Merwe, a white leather upholstered Barcelona chair by Mies van der Rohe and angular blue table lamp by Dokter and Misses. Pahl's custom geometric fireplace, also in brick and slatted timber, provides a key focal point for the space.

Karoo Homestead

Gregory Mellor
Cape Karoo (ZA), 2012

Having lived and worked in Sydney, Australia, for many years, interior designer Gregory Mellor eventually returned to his native country, South Africa, establishing his own practice in Cape Town. He also created a retreat for himself and his partner in the Karoo, a semiarid region where the Drakensberg mountains meet the veld (or scrub). The project began when Mellor came across a modest Cape Dutch–style cottage, which had once served as a small farmhouse, together with an adjoining barn. Attracted by the elegant simplicity of the architecture, with its painted white walls and tin roof, as well as the setting and garden, Mellor decided to reinvent the cottage as a charming rural retreat. The most dramatic and spacious room in the house is the sitting room, situated in the former barn, where part of the delight comes from the sense of volume and the high ceilings, with their traditional reed coating. Mellor has retained the semirustic character of the space, using bare plaster on the walls and raw concrete floors, while creating a welcoming, warm seating area around the fireplace. The rustic modern aesthetic is enhanced through the restrained use of color, seen in the choice of art and the olive green used for the wooden doors to the bedrooms beyond.

Asia

Great (Bamboo) Wall

Kengo Kuma and Associates
Near Beijing (CH), 2002

Japanese architect Kengo Kuma was one of ten Asian architects who were each invited to design a house within a new development in a forested enclave near the Great Wall of China. As an innovator who has long sought out ways to frame the natural world rather than impose statements upon it, as seen in his 1995 Water/Glass house in Atami, Japan (see p. 362), Kuma was an apposite choice for the project, given the natural beauty of the rural setting. With the twin aims of respecting the landscape and using local materials, Kuma decided to design a pavilion principally made of glass and bamboo. The single-story pavilion forms a process of interrelated spaces moving across the topography like a kind of wall—specifically inspired by the Great Wall of China, in terms of that wall's connection to its environment. Internally, the lattices of bamboo serve not only as a way of filtering light and glimpses of the views, but also as a unifying design feature used along the walls as well as ceilings and screens. The main living room and dining room form a key part of the enfilade of spaces, where sofas and other Western furniture sit against the natural, textural backdrop; the kitchen sits on a mezzanine level alongside those rooms, with another lattice of bamboo pillars creating a subtle line of demarcation.

Hong Kong House

Fiona Kotur
Hong Kong (HK), 2015

American fashion designer Fiona Kotur began her career in New York, working with major brands, such as Ralph Lauren. In 2002 she relocated to Hong Kong with her husband, and a few years later she launched her own label, Kotur, specializing in handbags, shoes, and other accessories. Initially, Kotur and her family lived in an apartment near the Victoria Peak, but they were lured to the Western District when they discovered a six-story tenement building dating back to the Sixties. Working alongside Hong Kong–based architect and interior designer Alexander Stuart, Kotur converted the semiderelict building into an inviting and spacious home, complete with balconies bordered by planters and a rooftop pergola. The house deftly accommodates shifts in scale, with large spaces, such as the double-height living room, balanced with more intimate hideaways. Among the most vibrant of these is the library. A hymn to blue, the library pairs walls and ceilings in a light sky tone with the deeper blue-black of the woodwork and library shelves. Yves Klein's acrylic cocktail table, filled with Klein Blue pigment, appears to float upon a blue and cream Berber-style rug, and a pair of Christian Liaigre (see p. 152) armchairs and a custom sofa by the window all tie in with the predominant palette.

Hong Kong Apartment House

Mattia Bonetti
Hong Kong (HK), 2015

....

Designer Mattia Bonetti could be described as a "maximalist." His interiors, furniture, and lighting are so inventive, they sometimes feel more like art installations. Born in Switzerland, Bonetti settled in Paris during the Seventies. He formed a famous creative partnership with Elizabeth Garouste (see p. 252) known as Garouste & Bonetti, which designed residences, restaurants, and furniture. Since 2002 Bonetti has worked alone, attracting a devoted following, including clients in Hong Kong who commissioned Bonetti to design this multigenerational family apartment complex. Color and pattern are everywhere, nowhere more so than in Bonetti's surreal furniture. The most theatrical area is the communal sitting room, where the extended family comes together in a double-height space with huge banks of glass—softened by Bonetti's candy-stripe curtains. Sofas, rugs, and stools are all unique designs by Bonetti; a central cocktail table displays a Naum Gabo artwork. The colorful hoops of a lighting installation hover overhead, with the circular motif replicated in the pattern of the wool rug below. Elsewhere, a Slawomir Elsner painting hangs on an ombré wall in a living room, spiced up by orange accents and polka-dotted Yayoi Kusama gourds.

Opus Apartment

Yabu Pushelberg
Hong Kong (HK), 2012

Canadian designers George Yabu and Glenn Pushelberg have produced a number of interiors for projects in Hong Kong and mainland China, including hotels, fashion stores, and residential projects, each time bringing their signature aesthetic cocktail of sleek and monumental design to the table. This lush apartment occupies an entire floor in Hong Kong's landmark Opus building, designed by Frank Gehry. A sequence of interconnected living spaces offers views out across the city and of the dramatic Peak District landscape. Given the distinctive shape—based on the bauhinia flower—of the building, the floor plan is composed of a series of "petals." Yabu and Pushelberg embraced these zones, using them to help shape the identity and function of various living spaces without the need for solid walls and partitions. Instead, spaces such as the sitting room, dining room, and breakfast room are zoned by a clever use of bronze-finished screens and sheer curtains, as well as the placement of custom silk rugs that pick up on the circular and semicircular motifs within the architecture. The bathroom is framed with marbled Bruno Elegante stone from Brazil.

Southside Home

André Fu
Hong Kong (HK), 2013

....

Hong Kong–based interior architect and product designer André Fu describes his work as a hybrid of Oriental and European influences, traditions, and aesthetics. He grew up in Hong Kong but studied in England, and has continued to travel constantly between Asia and Europe. The designer is best known for his work on luxury hotels, including the St. Regis in Hong Kong and the Waldorf Astoria Bangkok, but he has done occasional residential projects as well, including his own home in Hong Kong. Fu's home is situated in an apartment building in the city's Southside, with views over Deep Water Bay and the South China Sea. The key living spaces are flanked by expansive banks of glass framing open vistas; double-height zones in both the living room and dining room not only create a sense of volume and drama, but also draw natural light deep into the home. Neutral tones and natural textures prevail, which is characteristic of Fu's work. In the peaceful dining room, a Fu-designed display unit takes advantage of the high ceilings and hosts an ever-changing collection of favorite treasures. The circular oak dining table and upholstered oak dining chairs are designs from Fu's own furniture collection.

Gyedong Hanok Residence

Teo Yang Studio
Seoul (KR), 2020

....

A *hanok* is a traditional Korean courtyard house, with a design history stretching back to the fourteenth century. There are many regional variations in shape and size, but *hanoks* were generally built using natural materials, such as timber and rammed earth, with pitched tiled roofs. Crucially, the living spaces were arranged around a central courtyard that offered light and air as well as a private, sheltered outdoor space. Interior designer Teo Yang finds inspiration in such vernacular designs, looking to "bridge present and past." He founded his eponymous design studio in Seoul in 2009. When a client asked him to design a modern *hanok* in the city, on the site of a former courtyard house that had been demolished many years before, Yang embraced the opportunity. The elegant courtyard garden is, naturally, the focal point of the house. Most of the key living spaces on the ground floor, including the sitting room and library/study, look into the garden and connect with it via sliding walls. The sitting room, in particular, suggests the fusion of Asian and Western influences in the choice of furniture and art. Yang also created a discreet lower ground level, where he tucked away the media room, garage, and other service spaces.

Nest House

Keisuke Maeda/UID
Near Hiroshima (JP), 2008

In a forest near Hiroshima, Japan, the Nest House is an innovative hybrid of house and garden. Japanese architects and designers have traditionally blurred the distinctions between these two realms with courtyards, gravel gardens, water pools, and outdoor rooms, yet Hiroshima-based architect Keisuke Maeda has gone a step further with his concept of a nesting place in the landscape. Designed for a woman and her two teenage daughters, the house was embedded into its site, with a concrete plinth holding semisubterranean spaces, including the main bedroom and bathroom. Most of the family's daily life happens on top of the plinth, where a rectangular timber-clad case, or "lid," as Maeda describes it, protects an open-plan living space with an integrated garden at the center. Featuring trees, like Japanese maples, and other plants growing upward toward a roof aperture, this garden is the focal point of the house, and it doubles as an entrance and hallway. To one side of the home is a combined kitchen and dining area, and on the other side is a spacious study and living area. These spaces are sparsely furnished but key pieces include Hans J. Wegner Wishbone chairs and twin stools by Alvar Aalto upholstered in a striped fabric. A series of large windows and skylights connects the house to the forest outside.

Koshino House

Tadao Ando
Near Ashiya (JP), 1984

Koshino House is a sublime example of what the Japanese architect Tadao Ando has described as "site-craft." Fashion designer Hiroko Koshino commissioned the residence, which is tucked into the topography of a site near the city of Ashiya, Japan, situated on the coast between Osaka and Kobe. Formed of a series of interconnected pavilions, this house, or "landscraper," almost becomes part of the hillside itself. "The goal," as Ando put it, "was a house in which the power of nature that penetrates it is made conspicuous by a thorough purification of the architectural elements." One of the pavilions holds a run of bedrooms; another houses Koshino's atelier. The central pavilion contains the main family living spaces, including a double-height, strikingly stark living room—its walls look just the same inside as out—along with ancillary spaces and a primary bedroom suite to the rear. In the living room, light filters into the space and spills across bare concrete walls, and the sloping terrain can be glimpsed beyond the windows. The interiors are minimally furnished, enhancing the sense of purity and abstraction. Koshino has used the house as not only a family home but also an art gallery for exhibiting her own paintings.

Ring House
Takei-Nabeshima-Architects
Karuizawa (JP), 2006

Situated in a forest, the Ring House represents a radical reinterpretation of the traditional cabin in the woods. The site is part of an exclusive planned community in the Japanese town of Karuizawa, and came with a number of restrictions related to height and position, as well as overwhelming desire to protect the pine-and-cherry-tree forest itself. Takei-Nabeshima-Architects embraced the magical atmosphere of the woodland and felled just three trees to build a three-story tower. A modest ground floor is largely devoted to a guest room; the main living spaces are at midlevel, with the family sleeping spaces at the top of the house. Each elevation is articulated in alternating bands of cedar and glass, ensuring a strong sense of connection with the forest. The most open and generous space is the open-plan family living space. Here, furniture for dining and seating floats on the timber floor, but all other elements are affixed to the horizontal bands, including the custom kitchen and wood-burning stove, which hover a few feet above the floor. The ribbons of glass frame views of the forest, its appearance constantly changing according to the time of day, the weather, and the season.

Paper House

Shigeru Ban
Near Lake Yamanaka, Yamanashi
(JP), 1995

Japanese architect Shigeru Ban is famous for experimenting with a variety of unusual materials and building blocks. For example, he used polycarbonate sheeting and polyethylene noodles to create the translucent Naked House (2000) in Kawagoe, Japan, and he designed a series of "furniture houses" using cupboards and bookcases as structural elements, as well as spatial partitions. Ban has also employed cardboard and paper in multiple projects, including the Paper House (a.k.a. Paper Tube Structure 05) near Lake Yamanaka, not far from Mount Fuji. A series of structural cardboard tubes winds its way through what is essentially a square pavilion, holding up the roof and demarcating different zones of the house. At the center of the pavilion is an open-plan living, dining, and kitchen area with the single sleeping space alongside; a screen can be drawn across to separate these two principal areas. Ban explores the theme of transparency: the glass walls that surround the pavilion are also retractable, enabling an intimate sense of connection with the woodland landscape beyond. Seen together, the cardboard tubes and trees seem to echo one another.

Water/Glass

Kengo Kuma and Associates
Atami (JP), 1995

Japanese master architect Kengo Kuma explored the theme of transparency to the full in his design of the Water/Glass house, one of his most influential residential projects. The house is high on a hillside overlooking the coastline and the waters of Sagami Bay as part of the Izu Peninsula. Kuma made the most of this dramatic vantage point, as he sought to nearly erase boundaries between the architecture and the natural world. The three-story house's main entrance is accessed at midlevel via a walkway extending out from the hillside. Bedrooms and living spaces on the lower levels feature floor-to-ceiling windows framing panoramas of the sea and the landscape, and the staircase is made of structural glass. But the pavilions on the uppermost level provide the most complete expression of Kuma's ideas. Here, a pod with a glass floor and walls contains the dining room, whose dining table and chairs are also translucent. The pod is largely surrounded by an infinity pool, which appears to spill over the edge of the building and nearly blends with the sea in the distance. This ethereal combination of water and glass, seen at its height in this space, challenges the senses while providing an observatory, or belvedere, of a most extraordinary kind.

Water/Cherry

Kengo Kuma and Associates
Near Tokyo (JP), 2012

Situated within a national park on private land, the Water/Cherry villa is an original response to the client's request for a modern reinterpretation of traditional Japanese residential architecture. In this project, architect Kengo Kuma sought to dissolve the boundaries between architecture and nature, a hallmark of his work as a whole, especially the coastal Water/Glass house (see p. 362). With Water/Cherry, Kuma embraced a very different setting and adopted a palette of natural, character-filled materials. Rather than design one dominant family dwelling, Kuma created a sequence of complementary pitched-roof pavilions as well as a series of gardens, pools of water, and green rooms between them. Covered walkways connect the pavilions and offer a series of viewing platforms for appreciating these outdoor elements, which have been landscaped in an elegant Japanese style. The villa includes a range of twenty-first-century reinterpretations of Japanese vernacular ingredients, such as the tea ceremony room and *onsen* (a hot-spring bath). Like other parts of the villa, the bedrooms connect with gardens and other outdoor spaces via sliding glass walls that readily disappear. *Tatami* mats, custom seating, and low tables, also inspired by traditional designs, add texture and warmth to this fresh Japanese home.

Soft & Hairy House

Ushida Findlay Architects
Tokyo (JP), 1994

Defined by its original, experimental work, architecture practice Ushida Findlay was founded by Scottish architect Kathryn Findlay (1953–2014) and her then husband, Eisaku Ushida, from Japan, in 1986. For this project in Tokyo, the architects intended to make a "soft and hairy house," quoting the Surrealist Salvador Dalí on the future of architecture. The poured concrete walls of the Soft and Hairy House have a semiorganic quality that comes partly from the pink pigment used in the mix and partly from how they are softened by integrated planting in the courtyard and on the roof. A surreal element is introduced by a spherical blue pod, which pushes outward from the house and into the courtyard, holding the egg-shaped bathroom within. Inside, Ushida Findlay used partially diaphanous, billowing sheets of canvas to disguise the ceilings and banks of fitted storage units. The living room features lustrous marble floors, a teal-hued leather semicircular sofa, created by a series of stuffed tubular forms sewn together, and custom curved shelving for books. Findlay said the design process was "like a worm eating through an apple" and was an attempt to "materialize the dream" in the manner of Dalí.

Rishikesh House

Rajiv Saini + Associates
Rishikesh (IN), 2010

In 1995 architect Rajiv Saini established his own Mumbai, India–based design studio—notable for creating serene and uncluttered spaces—whose commissions have included hotels, restaurants, and resorts. The studio has also designed numerous inventive new houses, including this striking vacation home in the city of Rishikesh, in northern India, where the Himalayan foothills can be seen in the distance. Saini's clients had acquired a tranquil site on the edge of a verdant plain close to the banks of the Ganges River. The river influenced how Saini positioned the house and inspired the architect to capture some of the natural dynamism of the waterway. Access to the single-story house of concrete and stone is via a sunken channel to the rear of the building that leads toward an entrance court. The drama of the house only reveals itself as one steps into the main lobby and catches an initial glimpse of the river vista. To one side of this lobby is a sculpted pavilion that contains the formal dining room, an enigmatic space at the heart of the house. Defined by the arrangement of curving latticed screens of timber and glass, the room looks across an internal garden and into the sitting room beyond.

Monapesy Manor

Jean-Louis Deniot
Chhatarpur (IN), 2008

One of Jean-Louis Deniot's most ambitious early projects was not in his native France (see p. 249) but in India. Nasreen and Moin Qureshi invited Deniot to design a new home on a parcel of former farmland in Chhatarpur, just south of New Delhi. The challenge was to create a residence with the rounded character of a nineteenth-century neoclassical villa, along with gardens to suit. Deniot drew inspiration from not only period French architecture, but also the work of the British architect Edwin Lutyens, who navigated the borderland between neoclassicism and Arts and Crafts, veering toward the former during his time in India. There are occasional touches of Art Deco in Deniot's design too, as seen in the central hallway, with its sweeping staircase and ironwork balustrade. One of the most inviting spaces is the winter garden room, which also serves as a music room, with a grand piano in one corner. Deniot covered the walls and ceiling with a diamond-pattern latticework over mirrored panels, creating layers of optical delight, complemented by the sequence of French doors overlooking the garden itself. A jute rug floats on the marble floor, while the centerpiece is a custom, velvet-upholstered octagonal borne whose central backrest is topped by a planter with a flamboyant array of palm fronds.

Farm House India

Shalini Misra
Near Delhi (IN), 2019

Interior designer Shalini Misra grew up in Kolkata, India, and studied at the School of Planning and Architecture in Delhi, India. She studied further in New York, Pittsburgh, and London, where she settled down and established her own design studio. Yet Delhi still pulled on her heartstrings, and eventually Misra and her husband, Rajeev, decided to build an escapist new home near the city with sweeping gardens designed, in part, by landscape architect and cultural theorist Charles Jencks (1939–2019). Misra designed the curvaceous two-story house using brick, expanses of glass, and a mosaic of green tiles to help the building blend into the treescape and grounds. The interiors offered a golden opportunity to collaborate with a number of gifted Indian artisans and manufacturers, including furniture makers and lighting designers. A key living space is the garden room, which projects outward from the front of the house and offers views of the gardens through expansive banks of glass. GamFratesi for Thonet cane sofas and armchairs are upholstered in a suitably horticultural green that shines out against a more neutral backdrop of gray flooring and a silver-toned rug that anchors the seating zone. A custom timber shelving unit to one side offers a home to ceramics and other treasures, while the custom coffee table is by Delhi-based furniture makers Mike and Preeti Knowles. A sheltered brick outdoor space is crowned by a patinated brass chandelier, called Flutter, by Umut Yamac.

Bruce House

Liza Bruce & Nicholas Alvis Vega
Jaipur (IN), 2000

Fashion designer Liza Bruce, on her and her husband's multiple adventures in residential interior design, once said, "It is the making of a house that interests us." She and her artist husband, Nicholas Alvis Vega, have made homes in England, Italy, Morocco, and India, where they created a palatial residence full of color, pattern, and drama. Bruce and Vega, who is the son of an architect, were first seduced by Jaipur during a tour of India with friends. A year later they found a vacant apartment on one floor of a late nineteenth-century mansion designed by the British architect Samuel Swinton Jacob (1841–1917) for a prominent official in the service of the maharaja of Jaipur. The long-neglected apartment came with ten spacious rooms and a roof terrace. Bruce and Vega took a characteristically exuberant and expressive approach to the interiors, which they layered with a vibrant palette of colors, including lilac for the loggia and a startling pink for the main salon. Here Vega painted floral patterns in white onto this raspberry base layer, tying in with the whites used for the window frames and other architectural detailing. The integrated window seats around the edge of the salon are padded with silk cushions made from vintage saris, while rugs and other textiles also help soften the space.

Diya House

SPASM Design Architects
Near Ahmadabad (IN), 2014

When the Patel family commissioned SPASM Design Architects to design the Diya House, near Ahmadabad, India, they requested a substantial home and to preserve the sapota, neem, and mango trees that already inhabited this parcel of former farmland. The Mumbai-based firm, led by principals Sangeeta Merchant and Sanjeev Panjabi, began the project by documenting these trees and figuring out how to integrate the gardens and landscape with 15,000 sq. ft. (1,393.5 sq. m) of living space. The two-story house was constructed with walls of rammed earth, as well as a coating of Corten steel for the upper level. Courtyards, planters, and an infinity pool were woven into the overall design; a number of carefully preserved trees now grow through the building itself. The central living room has floor-to-ceiling glass walls, which connect with the open-air gardens to one side and a more sheltered courtyard to the other. The room features beautifully crafted natural materials, such as earthen walls, stone floors, and timber ceilings. Much of the furniture, including the brass-and-wood display shelf, is custom designed by SPASM; the vibrant red upholstery of the swing sofa, suspend by thick leather straps, makes it an arresting centerpiece within a setting rich with neutral tones.

Villa Sarabhai

Le Corbusier
Ahmadabad (IN), 1956

Villa Sarabhai in Ahmadabad was part of a stellar sequence of mid-century Indian projects by Le Corbusier (1887–1965), which also included Villa Shodhan (1957) in the same city, as well as an epic commission to design the new provincial center of Chandigarh (1960). Manorama Sarabhai commissioned Villa Sarabhai as part a 22-acre (9 hectares) compound that also featured a baronial mansion belonging to her family, which had made its wealth in the textile industry. Sometimes described as a "modern palace," Villa Sarabhai was designed to almost disappear within the lush surrounding landscape—the roof of the main villa is covered with a garden with a grass lawn and flowers, and a slide extends from the roof into the swimming pool. Inside, the character of the house is partly defined by the use of key materials, including concrete, black local stone for the floors, teak, and cedar for the joinery, and terra-cotta bricks for a series of vaulted roofs in the Catalan style. These vaults create a powerful rhythm within the villa, which is also lifted by the use of vivid colors, such as the walls painted in blocks of yellow, blue, and red. The vaults help define various zones within the fluid sequence of living spaces, where areas for dining and relaxation sit alongside one another, as well as flowing out into the gardens.

Asha Parekh Residence

Nari Gandhi
Mumbai (IN), c. 1962

The Indian film actress Asha Parekh was at the height of her success in Hindi cinema during the Sixties and Seventies, appearing in about fifty films during those two decades alone. In the early Sixties, Parekh acquired a site in the desirable Mumbai neighborhood of Juhu (now known as the "Beverly Hills of Bollywood"), partly on account of its long, sandy beaches. Parekh turned to the architect Nari Gandhi (1934–1993) to design the house and its interiors. After studying architecture in Mumbai, Gandhi had spent five years in America working with Frank Lloyd Wright and embraced the American master's devotion to a contextual and organic form of architectural design. On his return to India, Gandhi received a wave of residential commissions, including the Juhu residence for Parekh. Gandhi designed her house with a structural framework of concrete and stone and a dramatic semicircular facade. Inside, his use of curvaceous forms continued, combined with a free-flowing approach to the main living spaces. The most cinematic part of the house is certainly the sitting room, where double-height areas are punctuated by a sculptural, seemingly floating mezzanine supported by stone pillars. A crescent-shaped buttercup-yellow sofa forms a kind of theater in the round here, as well as framing a room within a room.

Palmyra House

Studio Mumbai
Palmyra (IN), 2007

Architect Bijoy Jain of Studio Mumbai studied and worked in America for many years, including a stint in the firm Richard Meier & Partners, before returning to his native India and committing himself to projects that are contextually sensitive and sustainable, and fuse modern forms with local materials. Situated within a coconut plantation on the coast to the west of Mumbai, the Palmyra House was created to provide an escape from urban living. The design shows respect for the beauty of the surroundings, particularly the palm trees, which were preserved as much as possible. Jain designed two wooden pavilions facing the sea, parallel to one another, with a long

swimming pool between them. One of these pavilions contains the double-height living room, a library, and—on an upper level— the primary suite, while the other holds the kitchen/dining area plus guest bedrooms. The minimally furnished interiors feature swaths of teak, with low-slung rattan armchairs arranged on polished concrete floors. Each pavilion has a light and semitransparent quality; the louvers were handcrafted from wood from a native palm species. Constant connections between inside and outside space also help to reinforce the highly organic character of the project.

Aamby Valley House

Opolis
Aamby Valley City (IN), 2016
···

The township of Aamby Valley City lies among the mountains in a rural district of Maharashtra, situated between Mumbai and Pune in India. The design of this modern house, by Sonal Sancheti of the Mumbai-based practice Opolis, makes the most of this hilltop location and the open views across the valley toward the Sahyadri mountain range. Careful consideration was given to reduce the weekend home's impact on the site. The placement of the gardens, water pools, and terraces is sensitively mapped to enhance the views. At its highest point, the taller central section of the house reaches three stories but multiple shifts in height, volume, and scale are provided by

the pavilion-like wings. The generous family living area sits at the center of the house hosting a dining area to one side and flowing out—via a wall of sliding glass—to the outside areas. Stone walls add natural texture while contrasting with the pale-terra-cotta tones of the tiled limestone floors. The central seating zone is alluded to by nine locally sourced, sculptural ceiling lights, along with choice furniture, which includes a pair of 1956 Charles and Ray Eames lounge chairs and ottomans with twin coffee tables, made of raw slabs of tree-trunk timber.

Pondicherry House

Niels Schoenfelder
Near Puducherry (IN), 2013

....

Designed to withstand extremes of wind and weather, architect Niels Schoenfelder's self-designed family home near Puducherry balances the need for protection from the elements and the desire to connect with an enticing tropical landscape. Two walls of the home are largely closed, while the others feature large banks of timber-framed windows that slide open to maximize connection with the outdoors. For the German-born Schoenfelder and his wife, Malavika Shivakumar, who also works in the design world, the house offers a weekend escape from their busy lives in Chennai. Close to the coast to the north of Puducherry, the site is alongside a resort that the architect designed. The simple geometry of the home imparts a strong sense of Modernist-inspired precision on the outside, but Schoenfelder used a softer touch within. He softened concrete surfaces by using timber joinery, expressive furniture, and fabrics from Vastrakala, the textiles company of which Shivakumar is a partner. The ground-floor seating area is a perfect example of this approach, with its built-in sofa with embroidered Vastrakala pillows, custom furniture—like the cocktail table made of reclaimed Anjan wood and milled steel—and a window wall to one side that slides open to connect with a spacious terrace.

Bawa House

Geoffrey Bawa
Colombo (LK), 1969

....

The influential Sri Lankan architect Geoffrey Bawa (1919–2003) created two homes for himself in Sri Lanka, which were vital in the development of his original take on Tropical Modernism. One was his countryside home in Bentota, known as Lunuganga (now an enticing hotel), and the other was Bawa's townhouse in Colombo. Like Lunuganga, the Colombo house evolved organically over a period of time. Bawa gradually acquired four small houses, along with a narrow lane, and incorporated these buildings into his design one by one. The residence's components all look inward, connecting with a series of courtyards, gardens, and terraces. Inside, Bawa characteristically combined the use of traditional and recycled materials with a modern approach to space and light. One of the most welcoming spaces is the upstairs sitting room: a large and open room, with light coming in from two directions. The design feeds off the textures of the reinvented building, with the rich patina of time exhibited on the plaster walls, complementing the mottled rugs. The furnishings mix traditional Sri Lankan and Western designs: a Saarinen coffee table is placed in the corner, for example, mixing with cane chairs and an intricate patchwork of Balinese wall-hangings, sourced by Bawa on a trip to Indonesia in the 1970s.

Daswatte House

Channa Daswatte
Sri Jayawardenepura Kotte (LK), 2005

··

After completing his architecture studies in Sri Lanka and England, Sri Lankan architect Channa Daswatte went to work with his mentor, Geoffrey Bawa (see p. 370), on the design of the Heritance Kandalama hotel (1995), considered a masterpiece. In the late 1990s, Daswatte teamed up with Murad Ismail, another architect from Geoffrey Bawa Associates, to found their own firm, MICD Associates, in Sri Jayawardenepura Kotte. Like Bawa, Daswatte has always been fascinated by the way that buildings and gardens interweave with one another. The complex fusion of indoor and outdoor space, as well as the natural and the artificial, lends his work not only character and delight. This is very much true of Daswatte's own self-designed home, a two-story pavilion surrounded by a generous garden in the Sri Jayawardenepura Kotte neighborhood of Madiwela, to the east of Colombo. Right at the heart of the residence is a sheltered loggia: an open-sided halfway point between indoors and out. This space is furnished simply, with a linen sheet draped over an extra-wide daybed and stacks of books on a tribal rug. A sequence of vertical, weather-worn louvered shutters, salvaged from a retreat that Bawa designed, the Bentota Beach Hotel (1969), offer a filtered view of the lush greenery beyond.

Sky Residence

David Collins
Bangkok (TH), 2010

··

The Irish interior designer David Collins (1955–2013) studied architecture in Dublin before founding his eponymous London studio in 1985. He was best known for designing elegant, enticing British restaurants and hotels, including glamorous yet relaxed interiors for Marco Pierre White, Gordon Ramsay, and Marcus Wareing. Later Collins began tackling residential commissions and working abroad. In a project in the MahaNakhon tower (now King Power Mahanakhon) complex in Bangkok, Collins designed a sumptuous apartment that encapsulates his holistic approach to highly tailored spaces, embracing every aspect of the interior architecture and furnishings, with an emphasis on fine craftsmanship. He drew inspiration from the colors and textures of Thailand, with allusions to traditional motifs and artisanal techniques seen in the rugs, curtains, and other elements, including the locally sourced artwork. Collins explored a palette of blue tones—his favorite color (and that of his childhood bedroom)—in the sitting room and adjoining dining room, the latter set in an alcove and principally intended for evening use. Here he adopted a much darker, richer range of tones in the custom wall paneling, indigo rug with geometric patterning, and lacquered navy-blue chairs, which Collins designed.

Tara House

Bruno de Caumont
Near Ho Chi Minh City (VT), 2019

French designer Bruno de Caumont began his career selling antiques in Paris, before moving toward interior decoration and eventually adding furniture design to his portfolio. His passion for traditional lacquerwork furniture in particular drew him to Vietnam, where he set up a factory producing his designs. The success of these collections and a growing love of the country led to de Caumont's decision to move his home to Ho Chi Minh City in 2011. He found a Fifties house and christened it La Villa Verte, reflecting his vibrant use of color for the interiors. Following a visit to La Villa Verte, physician Chanh Tran Tien and his wife Trang commissioned de Caumont to work on the restoration of their own country escape. Although the house was only built in the Nineties, it had been neglected and required a great deal of work. Color, naturally, plays an important part throughout, as seen in the mint-green living room, where high ceilings enhance the sense of drama. Much of the furniture, including the color-coordinated and double-aspect sofa, was designed by de Caumont. This is blended with antiques, ceramics, and art sourced in Vietnam and China. The lotus pots, for example, come from Le Cong Kieu Street, the antiques district, in Ho Chi Minh City, while twin pictures of Chinese nobles were sourced from a flea-market in Shanghai.

Lalaland

Valentina Audrito
Canggu, Bali (ID), 2011

....

The Italian architect Valentina Audrito
has lived and worked in Bali since the
Nineties. Along with her husband, Abhishake
Kumbhat, she founded the atelier Word
of Mouth, which designs houses, hotels,
and restaurants, as well as lighting and
collections of furniture, drawing on both
contemporary and vernacular influences.
Audrito's design of her own family's house—
affectionately known as Lalaland—was
based on three existing *joglo* pavilions. A
traditional Indonesian typology, this kind of
timber-framed pavilion features a distinctive, tentlike roofline. Audrito used the three
structures as the basis for a contemporary
home with a fluid relationship between
indoor and outdoor spaces. This *joglo* holds
the main living area, defined by the placement of the wooden pillars. The high ceilings provide room for one of Audrito and
Kumbhat's lighting installations—crafted
from pots and pans—suspended from the
ceiling, while fluid links to the adjoining
terraces draw in natural light. Hanging
potted plants enliven the family's custom
kitchen, which flanks the muted, airy living
area within the same sociable pavilion.

Seminyak Villa

Damien Dernoncourt & Nicolas Robert
Seminyak, Bali (ID), 2015

....

French entrepreneur Damien Dernoncourt
created this ecofriendly family home with
the help of designer and fellow Frenchman
Nicolas Robert. While living and working in
Hong Kong, Dernoncourt missed having a
garden of his own, so at Seminyak—a coastal
resort in the south of the island of Bali—he
wanted to create a constant sense of connection between inside and outside space.
Dernoncourt found a site occupied by an
artist's studio, with the original materials
recycled whenever possible. The new two-
story villa, shared with Dernoncourt's wife
and children, includes five bedrooms overlooking landscaped grounds that combine
native plants and the influence of tranquil
Japanese garden design. The pivotal space
in the house is the double-height living
room, which is the first point of arrival on
stepping through the vast double entry
doors. Various zones within the open space
are defined by shifts in floor level, ceiling
height, and placement of the furniture,
which mixes contemporary designs, such
as the striking coffee table made of petri-
fied wood and raku tiles, with antique finds,
including a fifteenth-century Javanese
bench. Twin steel staircases climb to a mezzanine gallery; here an oversized headboard
made of antique rice boxes provides privacy
for an adjoining bed and adds a splash
of color.

Umah Tampih

Cheong Yew Kuan
Near Ubud, Bali (ID), 2014

....

The Balinese words *umah tampih* translate as the "folding house." It is a suitably poetic way of describing this inventive modern home, which was partly inspired by Japanese origami and partly by an extraordinary natural setting. The house was commissioned by Polish photographer Jan Tyniec and his partner, the fashion designer Christyne Forti who asked architect Cheong Yew Kuan (see p. 376) sign a home for them near the town of Ubud. Perched on a hillside overlooking the forested valley below, Cheong has described the primary pavilion as a kind of ribbon, with an irregular and sculptural form. Made with a mixture of concrete and characterful terra-cotta bricks, the pavilion is open to either side at the center, where the main living area is situated. The living space is without walls or windows and opens itself to the tropical landscape, creating a halfway point between inside and outside. Here a long, integrated gray-upholstered sofa sits under an antique painted wooden Toraja panel, flanked by Batak statues. The dining area revolves around a kidney-shaped, timber-topped table. Tyniec has described this remarkable room as a kind of "gate" open to the natural world.

Architect's House

Cheong Yew Kuan
Ubud, Bali (ID), 2003

Born in Malaysia, architect Cheong Yew Kuan studied in Singapore before working with Australian architect Kerry Hill (1943–2018). While Cheong was still with Hill's practice, he was sent to Bali to work on designing the Amanusa Hotel and stayed on. During the Nineties he founded his own practice and spent five years working on another luxury landmark hotel, Begawan Giri. From the late Nineties onward, Cheong balanced hotel commissions with a number of residential projects in Bali, including remodeling one of the Batujimbar Pavilions originally designed by Geoffrey Bawa (1919–2003, see page 370). Chief among these projects was Cheong's own experimental home in Ubud, which comprises a series of terra-cotta-tile-clad pavilions within a landscaped compound of courtyards, terraces, and pools. With the benefit of a benign climate, the design of the house offers constant shifts between indoor and outdoor living. One of the greatest delights is the repeated use of water, as seen in the "water court," with its twin frangipani trees and ponds populated by ornamental fish and lily pads. Here and elsewhere, the moisture encourages moss and other plants to colonize the walls, making this contemporary home feel like a timeless garden temple.

Hornblow House

Elora Hardy
Near Ubud, Bali (ID), 2016

In 2010 designer Elora Hardy, who grew up in Bali, launched her eco-conscious design atelier, Ibuku, which specializes in using natural materials in innovative ways. One of Hardy's favorite materials is bamboo, which is indigenous, fast growing, and sustainable. Over recent years Hardy and her studio have been focused on the design and construction of Green Village, near the uplands town of Ubud in Bali. Sitting within the region's lush rainforest, this new community is made entirely of bamboo pavilions, which appear to float among the trees like sailing ships passing through the vegetation. British graphic designer David Hornblow and his family were seduced by Hardy's work and her ecovillage on a trip to Bali and decided to commission a house here, composed of three complementary pavilions. The main living area has the feel of a tree house, with its open balcony to one side looking out upon the forest canopy. The high bamboo ceiling adds to the sense of openness, while underfoot the kitchen floor is made of polished andesite river rock. Ibuku also designed the sofas and other furniture, which are softened with hand-loomed colorful textiles and cushions from the Indonesian island of Lombok.

Australasia

Australia (AU)

New Zealand (NZ)

Vanuatu (VU)

Stamp House

Charles Wright Architects
Cape Tribulation, Queensland (AU), 2013

The futuristic Stamp House has the look of an alien spacecraft landing in a tropical landscape of Queensland, Australia. With its six cantilevered wings spread out over the reflective surface of a lake, the building seems to hover and glide, full of dynamic, shape-shifting energy. Designed by architect Charles Wright for an adventurous family, the home is situated within a rainforest, with the Daintree Mountains visible in the distance. In this remote, beautiful setting, conditions are extreme. The tropical climate sometimes requires shelter, but other times invites open-air living. The Stamp House seeks a balance between these two requirements, expressed in a dramatic form. The projecting wings of the building offer enclosed retreats, including the family bedrooms and bathrooms. But the heart of the building is largely unenclosed, featuring a sculptural concrete roof canopy that partially protects the communal spaces, including the sitting room—punctuated by angular bright-orange banquettes paired with silver-upholstered ottomans—and the stainless-steel kitchen, with a cantilevered dining table off to the side. Flanked by twin gunmetal-colored pots, the swimming pool, right at the center, is bordered by a sunken garden and open to the sky.

Marie Short House

Glenn Murcutt
Kempsey, New South Wales (AU), 1975

The Marie Short House was acclaimed Australian architect Glenn Murcutt's first truly rural residential commission. It was an important and influential project on many levels, helping to refine Murcutt's idea of "touching the earth lightly." Murcutt spent about eighteen months studying the subtropical climate—particularly wind and weather conditions—before picking out the perfect spot for the house, which draws inspiration from the vernacular forms of barns and wool sheds. When the home, situated on farmland in northern coastal New South Wales, was put up for sale by his former client, Marie Short, in 1980, Murcutt bought it for himself. Naturally, he preserved the intent of the design, but he did extend each of the house's two interconnected volumes to create more space. Each single-story wing has a natural feel that comes from his extensive use of timber, as well as windows that frame views of the open countryside. The open-plan kitchen, dining area, and lounge spaces are warmed by the brush box floors and hoop pine ceilings and walls, as well as the joinery of the built-in kitchen. Much of the furniture here, and in the adjacent sitting room, is by the Finnish Modernist master Alvar Aalto and has a suitably organic and richly textured character.

Cove House
Reuben Lane & Brendan Wong
Sydney, New South Wales (AU), 1973/2015

After his studies in Australia, architect Reuben Lane (1933–2012) went to Brazil to work with his mentor, Oscar Niemeyer. Following time spent in the new capital, Brasília, and then in Europe, Lane returned to Australia with a love of curvaceous forms. One of Lane's best-known houses is the Cove House (a.k.a. the Breen House) in the Sydney suburb of Cronulla. Originally commissioned by the Breen family, the Sydney icon changed hands many times over the years, until eventually it was bought by interior designer Brendan Wong's client, who had long admired this futuristic waterside home. The client asked Wong to refresh and modernize the house, introducing luxurious materials including walnut, onyx, brass, shagreen, and silk, complemented by travertine flooring. The double-height living room, partially framed by a sweeping staircase to one side and sinuous, sculpted walls, is still one of the greatest glories of the house, featuring a beautifully curated collection by Wong of mid-century classics, including a sofa by Joaquim Tenreiro positioned under a Le Corbusier tapestry. A primary bedroom features twin Jorge Zalszupin armchairs on a Wong-designed silk rug; the rounded bathtub is by Marcio Kogan for Artedomus and is an ideal complement to the cloudlike Paola Navone bed.

Buhrich House II

Hugh Buhrich
Sydney, New South Wales (AU), 1972

....

Situated in the northern Sydney neighborhood of Castlecrag, Buhrich House II by Hugh Buhrich (1911–2004) is regarded as one of the finest mid-century Modern houses in Australia. The German-born architect and his wife, Eva, a writer, arrived in 1939 and settled in Castlecrag during the Forties, designing and building Buhrich House I in a linear Bauhaus style. During the early Sixties the Buhrichs bought a second parcel of land on the same street but with a view of Middle Harbour. Initially, the architect used the site as a kind of shipyard, building a yacht here, but by the early Seventies the couple's children had grown up, and they were ready for a fresh challenge. Buhrich House II had a smaller footprint but was full of fresh ideas. A key element of the design was a curvaceous ceiling made of cedar, its waves echoing the waters of Middle Harbour. The main living space was open plan with a sandstone wall and fireplace anchoring the seating zone, which had the best views; the dining area and compact custom kitchen were three steps up. Buhrich himself designed many pieces in this character-filled room, including the fitted leather sofa and a pair of reclining pony-skin chairs.

Harbour House

Kerry Phelan
Sydney, New South Wales (AU), 2012

....

Architectural and interior designer Kerry Phelan founded her own practice in 2010 after many successful years with Hecker, Phelan & Guthrie. With offices in both Melbourne and Sydney, as well as Hong Kong, there have been there have been restaurant and hotel projects, but also many private homes, including this substantial new family residence in the Sydney suburb of Bellevue. Here, Phelan's clients wanted to make the most of their art collection, including pieces by Anish Kapoor and others, but just as importantly they wanted to maximize connections to the gardens and the views out across Sydney Harbour. With this in mind, the inviting loggia toward the rear of the house could be described as the heart of the home. It is certainly the point where inside and outside living combine and fuse together within one elegant, sociable space. The loggia provides a fresh-air living and dining room, positioned centrally to face the gardens and pool. Travertine floors unify the space, while also being highly practical, and Sabi cane sofas by Paola Lenti add both texture and comfort. A wall-mounted Tracey Emin illuminated neon light installation, called *With You I Breathe* (2010), hovers on one wall, ensuring that art still has a place even in this summer lounge.

Italianate House

Renato D'Ettorre
Sydney, New South Wales (AU), 2018

It is no surprise that this substantial, late nineteenth-century Italianate house caught the eye of architect Renato D'Ettorre—an Italian who settled in Sydney during the Sixties—more than once. When his client approached him to update the building, which had served time as offices, and convert it back into a residence, D'Ettorre embraced the opportunity. He restored and converted the front portion of this elegant, three-story terraced house, while also renovating a former stable block to the rear as a guest lodge. The most dramatic part of the house is a new recycled-brick addition that D'Ettore designed to replace a jumble of spaces that had been added onto the back of the building at some point in its history. The double-height extension features a vaulted ceiling, in salvaged brick, that echoes arches elsewhere in the original architecture. This theatrical space offers a stage for the dining room, as well as a comfortable lounge area, making it a perfect space for entertaining. A slim mezzanine gallery at a high level holds a study, which appears to float overhead. A wall of glass doors can fold up to connect the addition to a courtyard garden, further increasing the sense of light and openness.

Marshall House

Bruce Rickard
Sydney, New South Wales (AU), 1967

Sydney architect Bruce Rickard (1929–2010) was also a much-respected landscape designer. His residential architecture showed a keen understanding of the surroundings, responding to a site rather than imposing upon it. This is true of both his own home in Wahroonga (1961), in Sydney's Upper North Shore, and this house in Clontarf, in the Northern Beaches region, originally built for Penny and Greg Marshall. The house has a respectful relationship with the sloping site and its gardens, layered with *Angophoras* and other indigenous plants. The principal living spaces are all at ground level, with the three bedrooms below. The residence is now home to design writers Karen McCartney and David Harrison, who furnished it in an era-appropriate style, with mid-century pieces by Poul Kjærholm (see p. 183), Eero Saarinen, Hans J. Wegner, and others. There is no front door; rather, a north-facing row of inviting glazed doors greets visitors and allows sunlight to penetrate the open-plan interior in the winter. Rickard used numerous simple, economical design strategies throughout the house—for example, to avoid having kitchen messes on view, he tucked the kitchen into a galley, flanked on one side by a textural recycled-brick wall, which houses a fireplace on the other.

Whale Beach House II

Burley Katon Halliday
Sydney, New South Wales (AU), 2009

Sited on a steep hillside at Whale Beach, this home by architecture and interior design firm Burley Katon Halliday forges a direct relationship with the open water. Known for its picturesque sandy beachscape, the neighborhood is on a peninsula in a Northern Beaches suburb of Sydney. In addition to requesting a strong sense of connection with the sea, architect Iain Halliday's clients also desired a low-maintenance design that echoed the minimalist concrete architecture of Tadao Ando (see p. 359), whose work they had admired during travels in Asia. Halliday designed an uncluttered home of four staggered levels, which step gradually down the hillside toward the water. The entrance is at the uppermost level, with two of the other floors devoted to bedrooms, while the main living area is at midlevel, an open-plan space holding the dining, living, and kitchen zones. Here a glass wall slides open to a spacious balcony with ocean views; a latticed brise-soleil to one side offers privacy from neighboring houses. The furniture includes cream Minotti sofas as well as two Poul Kjærholm chairs with rattan seats and backs, tying in with the organic textures of cane furniture out on the balcony.

Rosenberg House

Neville Gruzman
Sydney, New South Wales (AU), 1966/1983

In the semirural northern Sydney suburb of Turramurra, architect Neville Gruzman (1925–2005) had the opportunity to tackle projects involving the same home for two separate clients nearly twenty years apart. In the original commission, Gruzman combined his love of theatrical, glamorous spaces with his interest in Japanese design and architecture, particularly in terms of synergy between inside and outside space. He created a concrete-framed, glass-sided pavilion that visually connects with the grounds in a vivid, open way while working with the topography. Later, during the early Eighties, new owners asked Gruzman to restore and extend the house, adding an additional pavilion that steps further down the gentle slope of the hillside. Gruzman carefully updated the most flamboyant space in the house, the living room, where he combined a floating fireplace hood and chimney with a wraparound cantilevered stairway in concrete. These elements sit within a double-height atrium—flanked with bookshelves and sandy-toned brickwork—heightening the theatrical feel. Gruzman's integrated seating platforms with black leather cushions enhance the sense of clarity and cohesion here.

Palm Beach House

Tamsin Johnson
Sydney, New South Wales (AU), 2018

Australian interior designer Tamsin Johnson studied at the Inchbald School of Design in London, later founding her own atelier in Sydney in 2013. As well as many residential projects, her portfolio also encompasses fashion stores, restaurants, and the interiors of the Raes on Wategos hotel in Byron Bay—which has been described as the "design equivalent of a Tom Collins: fresh, strong, and a little bit sweet." Rather like Raes, Johnson's residential interiors tend to be light-filled, welcoming, and uplifting, particularly when it comes to coastal retreats such as the Palm Beach House—an escapist residence in Sydney's Palm Beach neighborhood on the Barrenjoey Peninsula. Here, Johnson was asked to reinvent an Eighties beach house, which enjoyed a spectacular waterfront location. The project encompassed the entirety of the substantial six-bedroomed property, along with the adjoining boathouse—one of the most engaging and escapist spaces. Here, the doors to the terrace fold back to create a vivid sense of connection with the water. There's a maritime blue-and-white theme, with sophisticated Francophile touches, including the Seventies French rattan sofa and an oak table by Guillerme et Chambron. The rattan floor lamp by Mario Lopez Torres, in the shape of a palm tree, introduces a more playful note.

Bondi Beach House

Richards Stanisich
Sydney, New South Wales (AU), 2018

The Sydney-based practice Richards Stanisich was founded in 2018 by Kirsten Stanisich and Jonathan Richards, who had previously worked together for ten years at SJB Architects. Together they have designed a number of restaurants, bars, and hotels as well as fresh and original beachside homes imbued with a quality of sophisticated simplicity, as seen in the Bondi Beach House. The design of the beach house at Bondi maximizes its elevated position facing the water, with the key living spaces, adjoining terraces, and garden all oriented toward the ocean. The ground-floor central hallway, with a sculptural spiral stairway to one side, flows through to a central seating area that leads—in turn—out onto the terrace, easily transitioning between inside and out. White walls and ceilings combine with pale-blue hexagonal floor tiles, while the pale-peach tones of the rug, which hosts the seating arrangement, also connect with the organic character of the rattan sofas and side tables. These naturals and neutrals fuse together within a space that is contemporary and characterful, yet still allows the ocean to take center stage.

Dinnigan Farmhouse

Collette Dinnigan
Milton, New South Wales (AU), 2005

Australian fashion designer Collette Dinnigan has increasingly turned her attention to interior design. Her projects have included hotels and resorts, such as her suites at Bannisters by the Sea at Mollymook Beach, New South Wales, as well as a number of private residences, including a series of homes for herself and her family. One of Dinnigan's long-term projects has been her farmstead at rural Milton, not far from Mollymook Beach. Her work has encompassed restoring the pastures and woodlands of this former dairy farm, as well as turning a barn into a welcoming entertaining space and converting a former stable building into a guest lodge. But the heart of family life is the old farmhouse, which Dinnigan has transformed into a retreat decorated with antiques from the local area, as well as items picked up on her travels; the light fittings are from Italy, for example, while the floors are recycled Danish cheese boards. White walls and exposed woodwork prevail in the calm living room, which looks out onto the adjoining veranda and across the paddocks. Built-in banquettes around the original fireplace form a cozier room within a room, where the red-and-white-ticking cushions and other occasional crimson notes stand out against the soothing background of neutrals.

Thornton Residence

Doherty Design Studio & Detail 9 Architects

Thornton, Victoria (AU), 2019

....

Situated around two hours drive northeast of Melbourne, Thornton is a rural enclave situated between the Cathedral Range State Park and Lake Eildon. The natural beauty of the surroundings and the easy distance to the city make the area a tempting location for weekend houses. Here, interior designer Mardi Doherty—who opened her own studio in Melbourne in 2014—and Detail 9 Architects collaborated on the design of this enticing country cabin. Tucked into its hillside site, the Thornton Residence is divided up into three interconnected pavilions, which can be opened up or closed down as required. The primary pavilion draws on the vernacular of agricultural sheds in its silhouette and open volume, while banks of glass offer a golden panorama of the mountain landscape. Alongside the view itself, the white-tiled fireplace forms a key element within Doherty's interiors. The fireplace is flanked by a low plinth holding a window seat to one side for appreciating the open views. Timber floors unify this "great room;" the overall palette is one of pale neutrals, with splashes of color shining out from the L-shaped blue sofa, echoed in the tones of the dining chairs and the diaphanous blue curtains.

Hill Plains House

Jerry Wolveridge & Christina Theodorou

Near Kyneton, Victoria (AU), 2010

....

This off-the-grid home combines innovative architecture with sophisticated interior design. The house sits alone on a ridge not far from the former gold-rush town of Kyneton, about an hour's drive from Melbourne. The residence looks out across this rural landscape, with Mount Macedon towering in the far distance and hardly a neighbor in sight. Drawing inspiration from the Australian farmstead vernacular, architect Jerry Wolveridge designed and built the single-story home for himself and his family using recycled blackbutt timber punctuated by picture windows. Energy self-sufficiency is ensured by a combination of photovoltaic cells on the roof, battery storage, solar thermal tubes for heating hot water, and a wood-burning stove for extra heating in the winter. Wolveridge and his architect partner, Christina Theodorou, codesigned the warm, richly textured interiors. At the center of the home is an open-plan space featuring a kitchen with a custom island bench accented with bright yellow panels—more workbench—a space for dining, and a welcoming seating zone arranged around a fireplace within a partition wall. Made of 1,650 stacked blocks of recycled timber, this wall forms a focal point and ties in well with the black-stained timber ceiling and the earthy tones of much of the furniture.

Boyd House II

Robin Boyd
Melbourne, Victoria (AU), 1958

Seen from the street, the facade of architect Robin Boyd's (1919–1971) house offers few clues about the multiple complexities and delights within. The site of Boyd's second family home was a slim parcel of land in the Melbourne suburb of South Yarra. A secret courtyard garden at the center of the plan became, in many ways, the heart of the home, introducing light, air, and bursts of greenery. It also acted as a peaceful interlude between the main, two-story portion of the house at one end and a single-story lodge for the children at the other. A long, slatted sloping timber ceiling supported by steel cables helps tie all of these elements together. This plan created a pleasing journey of discovery through the home. Inside, a stairway led down to the main living space, which looked out onto the secret garden and was just large enough for a seating area, dining zone, and—to the rear—a custom galley kitchen tucked under the stairs. Much of the furniture within this key family space was designed by Boyd himself, including the coffee table and the crimson sofa sitting by the custom fireplace, with its striking brass hood. Boyd's wife Patricia and interior designer Marion Hall Best (1905–1988) both contributed ideas for the interiors and the color palette.

Grounds House

Roy Grounds
Melbourne, Victoria (AU), 1954

In the mid-nineteenth century, prominent Australian architect Roy Grounds (1905–1981) became preoccupied with the expression of geometry, leading to a series of innovative projects. He designed the triangular Leyser House (1952) in Kew and the circular Henty House (1953) in Frankston, both in Melbourne. Naturally, his fascination with geometrical forms also fueled the design of his own house that he shared with his wife in Toorak, a suburb of Melbourne. The concept for the Toorak house was essentially to place a large, circular courtyard within a square building. The courtyard offers a sheltered outdoor sitting room and a garden, while drawing sunlight into all of the spaces arranged radially around it. Most of the living areas are open plan, with timber ceilings and custom joinery creating a sense of warmth and character. There are just two enclosed pods, featuring partition walls clad in slatted timber or cork. The key living spaces in the house—including areas for seating, dining, and sleeping—all flow around the courtyard. The house was sensitively restored by new owners in 2003. Grounds designed much of the furniture to be fixed, including the circular dining table and cabinetry, on which sits a 1966 sculpture by Norma Redpath. The zebra-skin rug is similar to one Grounds also kept.

South Yarra House II

Fiona Lynch
Melbourne, Victoria (AU), 2017

The spaces designed by Fiona Lynch are characterized, above all, by her passion for craft, elegant materials, and fine detailing. Since founding her own practice in Melbourne in 2013, Lynch has forged collaborative relationships with artisans, artists, and makers, enriching her residential commissions. One of Lynch's recent Melbourne projects is a terraced residence in the city's desirable South Yarra neighborhood, which sits alongside the Royal Botanic Gardens and the banks of the Yarra River. Here, Lynch was asked to redesign the interiors of a period home to create an engaging setting for her clients and their eclectic collection of contemporary art. The interconnected dining and living rooms feature pale walls and newly introduced stone fireplaces, along with wooden floors and custom furniture designs. In the living room, specifically, these include a set of painted oak display cabinets with brass shelves set on marble plinths, while a piece by the Australian artist eX de Medici hangs above the mantelpiece. Other pieces in this characteristically calm and ordered space include a supersized sofa in a gentle gray-blue tone and, more playfully, a Hans J. Wegner Flag Halyard chair with a woolly sheepskin, which sits on the pastel-pink rug.

Sorrento Beach House

Pandolfini Architects
Sorrento, Victoria (AU), 2019

Melbourne-based architect Dominic Pandolfini studied at the city's RMIT University before joining the offices of Wood Marsh Architecture, where Roger Wood and Randal Marsh became mentors. In 2012, Pandolfini decided to open his own practice with a concentration on residential work. Pandolfini's focus on materiality, and the intrinsic character of noble materials, is much in evidence in the design of the Sorrento Beach House where the concentration on brick and timber gives the house a rich Scandinavian flavor. Situated in the coastal town of Sorrento, on the Mornington Peninsula, the beach house was designed as a series of interlinked pavilions arranged around a central courtyard, which hosts terraces, a garden, and a swimming pool. The primary pavilion, which holds the light-filled kitchen, dining area, and living room, is a soothing space, featuring a tall, double-sided fireplace in white brick. This forms a partial partition between the kitchen/dining area at one end of the space and the seating zone at the other. Significantly, the entire pavilion is unified by a calm, neutral palette accompanied by predominantly natural materials. Pale-blue notes appear periodically, as seen in the fluted joinery of the kitchen units and the gray-blues of the upholstery seen within the seating zone by the fire.

Franklin Road House

Katie Lockhart Studio & Jack McKinney Architects
Auckland (NZ), 2020

....

Known for its picturesque period build-ings, Ponsonby is one of the most desirable and creative residential neighborhoods in the New Zeland city of Auckland. Planning controls protect the heritage of its many Edwardian villas, so when Jack McKinney Architects and interior designer Katie Lockhart were asked to provide further living space for their clients, they added to the rear garden. The clients themselves had been inspired during a trip to Sri Lanka by the work of architect Geoffrey Bawa (see p. 370) and were keen to create a space that, like so much of Bawa's work, employs organic and textural materials. Inside, the dramatic, double-height living space features a low window framing an edited glimpse of the gardens and swimming pool, while additional light comes from a skylight set high in the vaulted roof. This soothing space serves as a living room, dining area, and kitchen, unified by a terra-cotta-tiled floor, earthy plastered walls, and elegantly detailed joinery for the kitchen units and integrated storage. The polished but organic furniture is partly sourced by Lockhart from Japan. Another Bawa-esque touch can be seen in the integrated planter set into the floor, bringing a touch of the garden deep into the home itself.

Tamarind

Burley Katon Halliday
Paradise Cove (VU), 2016

....

Around three hours away from Australia by plane, the South Pacific nation of Vanuatu consists of a cluster of around eighty small picturesque islands. The country made a great impression upon Elizabeth Jones, owner of a Sydney-based homeware store Arida, when she first visited with her husband Michael. So much so that eventually the couple decided to buy a home on the main island (known as Efate) within a few miles of the capital Port Vila. Here, the couple bought around 5 acres (2 hectares) of land by the beach, including an existing house known as Tula, built during the Eighties. The family asked Australian architect Iain Halliday of Burley Katon Halliday to update and extend the main house, while also reinventing two small structures on the site as guest cottages. The cottage, called Tamarind, features a sweeping veranda with a circular *nakamal*—a traditional gathering place—attached which is topped with a palm thatch roof installed by locals. Monochrome cushions clad with African mud-cloth textiles decorate the crisp white sofas, complemented by a striped stool in similar tones from Orient House. The smooth concrete floors and a high-pitched ceiling, combined with the ocean vista, add to the relaxed atmosphere.

Timeline

1947

Casa Barragán (MX)
Luis Barragán 144

Maison Jean Cocteau (FR)
Madeleine Castaing & Jean Cocteau 269

Kaufmann Desert House (US)
Richard Neutra & Marmol Radziner 48

1948

Palazzo Venier dei Leoni (IT)
Peggy Guggenheim 297

1949

Eames House (US)
Charles & Ray Eames 34

Glass House (US)
Philip Johnson 72

Dawnridge (US)
Tony Duquette 25

1950

Farnsworth House (US)
Ludwig Mies van der Rohe 65

Villa Santo Sospir (FR)
Madeleine Castaing, Jean Cocteau &
Francine Weisweiller 277

1951

Casa de Vidro (BR)
Lina Bo Bardi 174

Casa das Canoas (BR)
Oscar Niemeyer 164

1953

Miller House (US)
Eero Saarinen & Alexander Girard 66

Villar Perosa (IT)
Marella Agnelli & Stéphane Boudin 282

1954

Brody Residence (US)
A. Quincy Jones & William Haines 29

Maison Prouvé (FR)
Jean Prouvé 268

Farnley Hey (UK)
Peter Womersley 193

Grounds House (AU)
Roy Grounds 394

1955

Villa Fornasetti (IT)
Piero Fornasetti 293

La Reinerie (FR)
Serge Royaux & Cristóbal Balenciaga 272

1956

Villa Sarabhai (IN)
Le Corbusier 367

1957

Witthoefft House (US)
Arthur Witthoefft 81

Vreeland Apartment (US)
Billy Baldwin 85

Kenaston House (US)
E. Stewart Williams 50

High Sunderland (UK)
Peter Womersley & Bernat Klein 188

1958

Frank House (US)
Andrew Geller 118

Gunnløgsson House (DK)
Halldor Gunnløgsson 183

Wild Bird (US)
Nathaniel Owings & Mark Mills 22

Boyd House II (AU)
Robin Boyd 392

Number 31 (IE)
Sam Stephenson 187

1959

Maison Louis Carré (FR)
Alvar Aalto 269

Avery Row (UK)
Nancy Lancaster & John Fowler 213

1960

Mollino Apartment (IT)
Carlo Mollino 283

Stahl House (US)
Pierre Koenig 40

Astor Apartment (US)
Sister Parish & Albert Hadley 85

1961

Pinto Coelho Residence (ES)
Duarte Pinto Coelho 237

Esherick House (US)
Louis Kahn 120

1962

Dragon Rock (US)
Russel Wright & David Leavitt 78

Kjærholm House (DK)
Hanne & Poul Kjærholm 183

Asha Parekh Residence (IN)
Nari Gandhi 367

Kennedy Private Quarters (US)
Sister Parish & Stéphane Boudin 123

1963

La Ricarda (ES)
Antoni Bonet 242

Sørensen House (DK)
Friis & Moltke Architects & Vivian
Bigaard Sørensen 182

Ahm House (UK)
Povl Ahm & Jørn Utzon 200

Erskine House (SE)
Ralph Erskine 180

Villa Windsor (FR)
Stéphane Boudin 252

1964

Frey House II (US)
Albert Frey 44

Mogensen House (DK)
Borge Mogensen 187

Villa Namazee (IR)
Gio Ponti 323

Strick House (US)
Oscar Niemeyer & Michael Boyd 38

1965

Housden House (UK)
Brian Housden 206

Mathsson House (SE)
Bruno Mathsson 181

Maison Bordeaux-Le Pecq (FR)
Claude Parent 249

Rainer House (AT)
Roland Rainer 282

1966

Sunnylands (US)
A. Quincy Jones & William Haines 49

Gwathmey House (US)
Charles Gwathmey 114

1967

Marshall House (AU)
Bruce Rickard 386

Vergiate Villa (IT)
Enrico Baj 286

Risom Summer House (US)
Jens Risom 73

House in Patmos (GR)
John Stefanidis 309

Kappe Residence (US)
Ray Kappe 34

1968

Casa Tabarelli (IT)
Carlo Scarpa & Sergio Los 284

Blackbirds (UK)
George Buzuk 219

Elrod House (US)
John Lautner & Arthur Elrod 44

Cuadra San Cristóbal (MX)
Luis Barragán 145

Casa Tomie Ohtake (BR)
Ruy Ohtake 168

Springs House (US)
Ward Bennett 116

1969

Bawa House (LK)
Geoffrey Bawa 370

Casa Sotto Una Foglia (IT)
Gio Ponti & Nanda Vigo 296

Geller House II (US)
Marcel Breuer 112

Casa Masetti (BR)
Paulo Mendes da Rocha 174

Dr. Rogers House (UK)
Richard Rogers 203

Villa Spies (SE)
Staffan Berglund 181

1970

Palevsky House (US)
Craig Ellwood 45

Siegel House (UK)
David Shelley 195

Colombo Apartment IV (IT)
Joe Colombo 292

Capel Manor House (UK)
Michael Manser 216

1971

Casa Millán (BR)
Paulo Mendes da Rocha 170

The Factory (ES)
Ricardo Bofill 241

Villa Fiorentina (FR)
Billy Baldwin 278

Rams Residence (DE)
Dieter Rams 226

Missoni House (IT)
Rosita Missoni & Enrico Buzzi 286

Barton Court (UK)
Terence Conran 201

Buhrich House II (AU)
Hugh Buhrich 384

Can Lis (ES)
Jørn Utzon 244

1973

Panton House (CH)
Verner Panton 278

Aulenti Apartment (IT)
Gae Aulenti 287

Villa Savoia (CH)
Jacques Lopez 279

Rhydoldog Manor (UK)
Laura Ashley 192

1974

Casa de Verano (ES)
Ricardo Bofill 239

Douglas House (US)
Richard Meier 64

Samuel Apartment (FR)
Henri Samuel 264

Du Toit House (ZA)
Pius Pahl 347

1975

Nakashima Guesthouse (US)
George Nakashima 119

Marie Short House (AU)
Glenn Murcutt 382

Calvin Klein Residence (US)
Joe D'Urso 96

Casa Milan (BR)
Marcos Acayaba 173

1976

Putman Apartment (FR)
Andrée Putman 257

Ekensberg (SE)
Lars Sjöberg 180

Hopkins House (UK)
Michael & Patty Hopkins 204

1977

Ford Estate (US)
Darren Brown & Welton Becket & Associates 51

1978

Hunting Lodge (UK)
John Fowler & Nicholas Haslam 221

Hadley Apartment (US)
Albert Hadley 98

Les Jolies Eaux (VC)
Oliver Messel 153

Beekman Place Townhouse (US)
Paul Rudolph 100

1979

Eppich House (CA)
Arthur Erickson & Francisco Kripacz 16

The Grove (UK)
David Hicks 198

1980

Alidad Apartment (UK)
Alidad 202

1982

Collett House (UK)
Anthony Collett 207

RRL Ranch (US)
Ralph Lauren 57

Baratta Duplex (US)
Anthony Baratta 134

1983

Rosenberg House (AU)
Neville Gruzman 387

1984

Casa Senosiain (MX)
Javier Senosiain 142

1985

Koshino House (JP)
Tadao Ando 359

Casa Arcadia (MX)
Alix Goldsmith Marcaccini 142

Blass Apartment (US)
Bill Blass & MAC II 93

La Torre (IT)
Renzo Mongiardino 303

1986

Citterio Apartment (IT)
Antonio Citterio 292

1987

Fadillioglu House (TR)
Zeynep Fadillioglu Design 320

1988

Kasteel Van's-Gravenwezel (BE)
Axel Vervoordt 223

Château de Champgillon (FR)
Christian Louboutin & Bruno Chambelland 273

1989

Water Island House (US)
Jed Johnson & Alan Wanzenberg 117

Palais Bulles (FR)
Antti Lovag & Pierre Cardin 275

Sheats-Goldstein House (US)
John Lautner 40

La Datcha (FR)
Pierre Bergé & Jacques Grange 248

1990

Tarlow House (US)
Rose Tarlow 41

Grange Apartment (FR)
Jacques Grange 261

1991

Windy Gates Farm (US)
Keith McNally & Ian McPheely 68

Lugano House (CH)
Renzo Mongiardino & Studio Peregalli 281

1992

Sills House (US)
Stephen Sills & James Huniford 80

Château du Champ de Bataille (FR)
Jacques Garcia 248

1993

High Desert House (US)
Kendrick Bangs Kellogg & John Vugrin 52

Wolf Loft (US)
Vicente Wolf 110

1994

Versace Mansion (US)
Gianni Versace 134

Mindel Apartment (US)
Lee Mindel 84

Soft & Hairy House (JP)
Ushida Findlay Architects 363

1995

Water/Glass (JP)
Kengo Kuma and Associates 362

Ungers House III (DE)
Oswald Mathias Ungers 226

Paper House (JP)
Shigeru Ban 362

Château de Wideville (FR)
Valentino Garavani & Henri Samuel 250

1996

Maison Emery (BE)
Agnès Emery 224

Méchiche Apartment (FR)
Frédéric Méchiche 260

Round Hill Residence (JM)
Ralph Lauren 150

1997

Tunca House (TR)
Asli Tunca & Carl Vercauteren 322

La Colina (DO)
Bunny Williams & John Rosselli 151

Darryl Carter's Townhouse (US)
Darryl Carter 123

Skylands (US)
Martha Stewart 68

Casa Legorreta (MX)
Ricardo Legorreta 143

1998

Riad Emery (MA)
Agnès Emery 338

Malator House (UK)
Future Systems 193

Indian Bean (US)
Rodman Primack 124

1999

Fighine (IT)
David Mlinaric & Hugh Henry 300

Pawson House (UK)
John Pawson 206

2000

Villa Mabrouka (MA)
Yves Saint Laurent, Pierre Bergé &
Jacques Grange 333

Majorca House (ES)
Ágatha Ruiz de la Prada 245

Gibbs Residence (MA)
Christopher Gibbs 330

Tangala (ZM)
Giles & Bella Gibbs & Fred Spencer 345

Casa Nina (PT)
Jacques Grange 236

Dar El Sadaka (MA)
Jean-François Fourtou 339

Bruce House (IN)
Liza Bruce & Nicholas Alvis Vega 366

Redd House (US)
Miles Redd 108

2001

Casa Luna (MX)
Manolo Mestre 141

Maison Loum-Martin (MA)
Meryanne Loum-Martin 335

2002

Garouste Residence & Studio (FR)
Elizabeth Garouste 252

Holm & Becker House (DK)
Jacob Holm & Barbara Bendix Becker 186

Maison Deniot (FR)
Jean-Louis Deniot 249

Garcia House (US)
John Lautner, Marmol Radziner &
Darren Brown 29

Great (Bamboo) Wall (CH)
Kengo Kuma and Associates 354

Daouk Villa (LB)
May Daouk 316

2003

Architect's House (ID)
Cheong Yew Kuan 376

2004

Liaigre House (BL)
Christian Liaigre 152

House for a Photographer (ES)
Carlos Ferrater 244

Karan Apartment (US)
Donna Karan & Bonetti/Kozerski
Architecture 104

2005

Nile Riverboat (EG)
Christian Louboutin 344

Nairobi House (KE)
Maia Geheb & Rob Burnet 344

Villa D (MA)
Studio KO 341

Motta Farmhouse (BR)
Carlos Motta 168

Daswatte House (LK)
Channa Daswatte 371

Dinnigan Farmhouse (AU)
Collette Dinnigan 390

Saladino Villa (US)
John Saladino 23

Aspen Chalet (US)
Pauline Pitt 57

Nest House (JP)
Keisuke Maeda/UID 359

Rebecchini Apartment (IT)
Livia Rebecchini 303

Castillo Duplex (ES)
Lorenzo Castillo 237

Maison Habis (LB)
Pascale Habis 317

2009

Packham House (UK)
Richard Dewhurst & Jenny Packham 210

Tsai Residence (US)
Ai Weiwei & HHF Architects 75

Casa Iporanga (BR)
Arthur Casas 175

Whale Beach House II (AU)
Burley Katon Halliday 386

Baudoux Apartment (FR)
Florence Baudoux 255

Armani House (FR)
Giorgio Armani 275

Bloom House (US)
Greg Lynn & Jacklin Hah Bloom 32

Blake Residence (US)
Joseph Minton 63

Ourika Valley House (MA)
Liliane Fawcett & Imaad Rahmouni 342

Wood Patchwork House (RU)
Peter Kostelov 230

Yovanovitch Apartment (FR)
Pierre Yovanovitch 268

Integral House (CA)
Shim-Sutcliffe 19

Hable Smith House (US)
Susan Hable Smith 128

Château du Grand-Lucé (FR)
Timothy Corrigan 271

White O (CL)
Toyo Ito 175

Ludes House (BL)
Wolfgang Ludes 153

Amagansett House (US)
Yabu Pushelberg 113

Usine Gruben (CH)
Antonie Bertherat-Kioes 280

Ajioka House (US)
Buff & Hensman & Commune 35

Redecke-Montague House (MA)
Chris Redecke & Maryam Montague 340

Sky Residence (TH)
David Collins 371

Connecticut House (US)
India Mahdavi 70

Casa Grecia (BR)
Isay Weinfeld 169

Hill Plains House (AU)
Jerry Wolveridge 391

Adler-Doonan House (US)
Jonathan Adler & Gray Organschi 117

Kenzo Apartment (FR)
Kenzo & Ed Tuttle 259

Newson-Stockdale Apartment (UK)
Marc Newson & Squire and Partners 202

Páros House (GR)
Mark Gaudette & Ioannis Mamoulakis 308

Chalet La Transhumance (FR)
Noé Duchaufour-Lawrance 273

Serifos House (GR)
Paola Navone 308

Patrizia Moroso House (IT)
Patricia Urquiola 296

Maison Raya Raphaël Nahas (LB)
Raëd Abillama Architects 318

Rishikesh House (IN)
Rajiv Saini + Associates 364

Casa Cartagena (CO)
Richard Mishaan 160

Stilin Loft (US)
Robert Stilin 106

Bergamin House (BR)
Sig Bergamin 162

Maison Pasti (MA)
Umberto Pasti & Roberto Peregalli 330

Hagan House (US)
Victoria Hagan & Ray Pohl 69

VDC Residence (BE)
Vincent Van Duysen 225

Casa Na Areia (PT)
Aires Mateus 236

Las Vegas House (US)
Atelier AM & William Hablinski
Architecture 58

**Kent Reservoir/Dinos Chapman
House (UK)**
Brinkworth 218

Easton & Steinmeyer House (US)
David Easton 59

Dumfries House (UK)
David Mlinaric & Piers von
Westenholz 190

Izba Apartment (RU)
Denis Perestoronin 231

Drake House (CA)
Ferris Rafauli 18

Casa Torres (BR)
Guilherme Torres 169

Rivoli Apartment (FR)
Isabelle Stanislas 259

Residência BV (BR)
Jacobsen Arquitetura 166

Prairie House (US)
Madeline Stuart & Lake|Flato
Architects 20

Paris Apartment (FR)
Mathias Kiss 262

Kiely House (UK)
Orla Kiely 204

Manhattan Townhouse (US)
Sheila Bridges 87

Westcliff Poolhouse (ZA)
Silvio Rech + Lesley Carstens 346

Little Venice House (UK)
Studio Mackereth 209

Saint Moritz House (CH)
Studio Peregalli 280

Haenisch House (US)
Trip Haenisch 28

Lalaland (ID)
Valentina Audrito 373

Yabu Pushelberg House (CA)
Yabu Pushelberg 19

Rhinebeck Cottage (US)
Zack McKown & Calvin Tsao 79

2012

Paraty House (BR)
Alberto Pinto 165

Ashley Hicks Country House (UK)
Ashley Hicks 197

Fendi Apartment (IT)
Carla Fendi & Cesare Rovatti 304

Therasia House (GR)
Costis Psychas 309

Klein Residence (US)
David Piscuskas 130

Station House (US)
Federico de Vera 79

Sidorov Dacha (RU)
Gabhan O'Keeffe 231

Karoo Homestead (ZA)
Gregory Mellor 349

Derian Residence (US)
John Derian 112

Beldi House (MA)
Julie & Alex Leymarie 340

Water/Cherry (JP)
Kengo Kuma and Associates 363

Harbour House (AU)
Kerry Phelan 384

Pineapple Hill (BS)
Miles Redd 147

Spello Loft (IT)
Paola Navone 302

Rogers House (US)
Peter Rogers & Chuck Palasota 125

Frey Apartment (FR)
Pierre Frey & Marika Dru 265

The Observatory (ZA)
Rory Sweet & Silvio Rech + Lesley
Carstens 346

Apartment Haussmannian (FR)
Sarah Lavoine 253

Cloudline (US)
Toshiko Mori 77

Opus Apartment (HK)
Yabu Pushelberg 356

2013

Highlowe (BS)
Alessandra Branca 146

Southside Home (HK)
André Fu 357

Aparicio House (US)
Carlos Aparicio 135

Stamp House (AU)
Charles Wright Architects 382

Ojai House (US)
Commune 24

Houston House (US)
Fern Santini & Paul Lamb 59

Riad Méchiche (MA)
Frédéric Méchiche 335

Ezer Apartment (TR)
Hakan Ezer 322

McNally House (UK)
Keith McNally & Ian McPheely 196

Kemp House (UK)
Kit Kemp 210

Curtis House (US)
Lee Ledbetter & Nathaniel Curtis 125

Catalan House (ES)
Michèle van Hove & Nicolas
Vanderbeck 238

Houston House (US)
Miles Redd 61

Pondicherry House (IN)
Niels Schoenfelder 370

Solo House (ES)
Pezo von Ellrichshausen 243

Greenwich Village Residence (US)
Rafael de Cárdenas 90

Weishaupt House (US)
Stephan Weishaupt & Martin
L. Hampton 132

Mispelaere House (IT)
Yvan Mispelaere & Stéphane
Ghestem 298

Khoury Penthouse (LB)
Bernard Khoury / DW5 314

Romanek House (US)
Brigette Romanek 31

Casamota (DO)
Carlos Mota & Weetu 151

Umah Tampih (ID)
Cheong Yew Kuan 374

Gurney House (UK)
Claud Cecil Gurney 203

Schloss Untersiemau (DE)
Gert Voorjans 227

Elkann Apartment (IT)
Lapo Elkann & Studio Natalia Bianchi 290

Moby House (US)
Moby 35

Berkus-Brent Duplex (US)
Nate Berkus & Jeremiah Brent 101

Pennoyer & Ridder House (US)
Peter Pennoyer & Katie Ridder 75

Van de Weghe Townhouse (US)
Annabelle Selldorf & D'Apostrophe
Design 91

Diya House (IN)
SPASM Design Architects 366

Saronno Apartment (IT)
Studio Catoir 287

Guadalajara House (MX)
Alejandra Redo 141

Dowe-Sandes House (MA)
Caitlin & Samuel Dowe-Sandes 337

Maison Gemmayze (LB)
Carole Schoucair 316

Casa Guava (DO)
Celerie Kemble 150

Seminyak Villa (ID)
Damien Dernoncourt & Nicolas
Robert 373

Ansty Plum (UK)
David Levitt & Sandra Coppin 222

Casa Comprida (MZ)
Designworkshop & Interdeco 345

Val d'Orcia Farmhouse (IT)
Elodie Sire & Matteo Pamio 299

Hong Kong House (HK)
Fiona Kotur 354

Schafer House (US)
Gil Schafer 67

Guadagnino Apartment (IT)
Luca Guadagnino 295

Hunt Apartment (US)
Holly Hunt 65

Reed Apartment (UK)
Jonathan Reed 211

Park Avenue Apartment (US)
Kelly Behun 88

Hoppen House (UK)
Kelly Hoppen 205

**Tsarkoe Selo Chinese Village
Pavilion (RU)**
Kirill Istomin 230

Rossferry (BB)
Kit Kemp 154

Lagerqvist Beach House (SE)
Kristin Lagerqvist 182

Hong Kong Apartment House (HK)
Mattia Bonetti 355

Cabana Penaguião (BR)
Mónica Penaguião 165

Spetses House (GR)
Nikos Moustroufis & Isabel López-
Quesada 306

Casa Reyes (MX)
Pedro Reyes 145

Rocky Mountain Ski Retreat (US)
Peter Marino 54

Redzepi House (DK)
René & Nadine Redzepi 186

Cove House (AU)
Reuben Lane & Brendan Wong 383

Aspen Ski House (US)
Shawn Henderson & Scott Lindenau 56

Peter's House (DK)
Studio David Thulstrup 184

Oldham Residence (US)
Todd Oldham 119

Great Abaco House (BS)
Tom Scheerer 146

2016

Casa Anderson (BR)
Wilbert Das 160

Firestone Estate (US)
William Pereira & Sam Cardella 50

Tamarind (VU)
Burley Katon Halliday 398

Lagoon Lodge (MA)
Danny Moynihan, Katrine Boorman &
Fabrizio Bizzarri 334

West Chelsea Apartment (US)
Deborah Berke Partners 86

Hornblow House (ID)
Elora Hardy 377

Robshaw House (US)
John Robshaw 69

Terrenia (BS)
Lulu de Kwiatkowski 148

Villa Grigio (US)
Martyn Lawrence Bullard 48

Zorkendorfer House (US)
McLean Quinlan & Joanne
Zorkendorfer 58

Aamby Valley House (IN)
Opolis 369

River House (US)
Studio Sofield 92

2017

Trammell Shutze House (US)
Tammy Connor 126

Round Hill (US)
Tommy Hilfiger & Martyn Lawrence
Bullard 72

Sui Apartment (US)
Anna Sui 94

Prince Faisal's Majlis (SA)
Christopher Hall 325

Steinman House (US)
Craig Ellwood & Michael Boyd 24

Short Hills (US)
Fawn Galli 122

Casa Paloma (ES)
Faye Toogood 247

South Yarra House II (AU)
Fiona Lynch 395

Gazebo (MA)
Veere Grenney 331

Avenue Montaigne Apartment (FR)
Joseph Dirand 258

Upper East Side Apartment (US)
Virginia Tupker 86

Casa Wilbert (BR)
Wilbert Das 164

2018

Smit House (MA)
Willem Smit 333

Casa La Huerta (ES)
Anders Hallberg & Moredesign 245

Hendifar-Anderson Apartment (US)
Apparatus 102

Cindy Sherman Penthouse (US)
Billy Cotton & Cindy Sherman 82

Casa Tosca (MA)
Castellini Baldissera 332

Walter Segal House (UK)
Walter Segal & Faye Toogood 212

Butterfly House (US)
Frank Wynkoop & Jamie Bush 23

Casa Grande (MX)
Ken Fulk & Victor Legorreta 140

Henson House (US)
Mutuus Studio 37

Aldridge & Followill House (US)
Pierce & Ward 124

Little Holmby (US)
Reath Design & McKuin Design 41

Italianate House (AU)
Renato D'Ettorre 385

Bella Freud Apartment (UK)
Retrouvius, Piercy&Company &
Bella Freud 214

Bondi Beach House (AU)
Richards Stanisich 390

Beyond (ZA)
SAOTA 347

Palm Beach House (AU)
Tamsin Johnson 388

2019

Tara House (VT)
Bruno de Caumont 372

Milano Jenner (IT)
Dimorestudio 288

Thornton Residence (AU)
Doherty Design Studio & Detail 9
Architects 391

Turenne (FR)
Humbert & Poyet 267

Mjölk Country House (CA)
John & Juli Daoust Baker &
Studio Junction 20

Furlotti House (US)
Osmose Design 21

Sorrento Beach House (AU)
Pandolfini Architects 395

Collector's House (US)
Peter Pennoyer 67

Farm House India (IN)
Shalini Misra 365

Ridge Mountain House (US)
Steven Ehrlich 46

Floral Court (UK)
Studio Ashby 212

Sand House (BR)
Studio MK27 & Serge Cajfinger 161

2020

Bavarian Dacha (DE)
Studio Peregalli 228

Northern California Estate (US)
Studio Shamshiri, Commune &
Mark Hampton 21

Franklin Road House (NZ)
Katie Lockhart Studio & Jack McKinney
Architects 396

100 UN Plaza (US)
Leyden Lewis 90

Gyedong Hanok Residence (KR)
Teo Yang Studio 358

Gstaad Chalet (CH)
Thierry Lemaire 279

Belnord Residence (US)
Anna Karlin 93

Bibliography

Roberta de Alba, **Paul Rudolph: The Late Work**. New York: Princeton Architectural Press, 2003.

Luigi Alini, **Kengo Kuma: Works & Projects**. Milan: Electa, 2005.

Roman Alonso et al., **Commune**. New York: Abrams, 2014.

Fernando Álvarez et al., **Antoni Bonet: La Ricarda**. Barcelona: COAC, 1997.

Emilio Ambasz & Shigeru Ban, **Shigeru Ban**. London: Laurence King, 2001.

Tadao Ando, **Tadao Ando: Houses & Housing**. Tokyo: Toto Shuppan, 2007.

Jean-Louis André, **Intérieur Extérieur: Les Architectes et Leur Maison**. Paris: Éditions du Chene, 1999.

Paul Andreas & Ingeborg Flagge, **Oscar Niemeyer: A Legend of Modernism**. Basel: Birkhauser, 2003.

Peter Andrews et al., **The House Book**. London: Phaidon, 2001.

Amy Astley, **Architectural Digest: AD at 100**. New York: Abrams, 2019.

Mauro Baracco & Louise Wright, **Robin Boyd: Spatial Continuity**. Abingdon: Routledge, 2017.

Armelle Baron, **Axel Vervoordt: Timeless Interiors**. Paris: Flammarion, 2007.

Luis Barragán & René Burn, **Luis Barragán**. London: Phaidon, 2000.

Haig Beck & Jackie Cooper, **Glenn Murcutt: A Singular Architectural Practice**. Melbourne: Images Publishing Group, 2002.

Pierre Bergé et al., **Maison Jean Cocteau**. Paris: Somogy Art Publisher, 2010.

Lina Bo Bardi et al., **Lina Bo Bardi**. Milan: Instituto Lina Bo e P. M. Bardi/Edizioni Charta, 1994.

Nate Berkus, **The Things That Matter**. New York: Spiegel & Grau, 2012.

Werner Blaser, **Eduardo Souto de Moura: Element Stone**. Basel: Birkhäuser, 2003.

Botond Bognar, **Kengo Kuma: Selected Works**. New York: Princeton Architectural Press, 2005.

Christoph Bon et al., **Lunuganga**. Singapore: Marshall Cavendish Editions, 2007.

Anne Bony, **Alberto Pinto: Signature Interiors**. Paris: Flammarion, 2016.

Hamish Bowles et al., **Vogue Living: Houses, Gardens, People**. New York: Alfred A. Knopf, 2010.

Michael Boyd (ed.), **Making LA Modern: Craig Ellwood**. New York: Rizzoli, 2018.

Dominic Bradbury, **The Iconic House: Architectural Masterworks Since 1900**. London: Thames & Hudson, 2009.

Dominic Bradbury, **The Iconic Interior: 1900 to the Present**. London: Thames & Hudson, 2012.

Dominic Bradbury, **Interior Design Close Up**. London: Thames & Hudson, 2015.

Kay Breslow, **Charles Gwathmey & Robert Siegel: Residential Works, 1966-77**. New York: Architectural Book Publishing Company, 1977.

Mel Byars, **The Design Encyclopedia**. London: Laurence King, 2004.

Barbara-Ann Campbell-Lange, **John Lautner**. Cologne: Taschen, 2005.

Marco Casamonti (ed.), **Kengo Kuma**. Milan: Motta Architettura, 2007.

Mirabel Cecil & David Mlinaric, **Mlinaric on Decorating**. London: Frances Lincoln, 2008.

Pippo Ciorra & Florence Ostende (eds.), **The Japanese House: Architecture & Life After 1945**. Venice: Marsilio Editori, 2016.

Arnt Cobbers, **Marcel Breuer**. Cologne: Taschen, 2007.

Jill Cohen et al., **House & Garden's Best in Decoration**. New York: Condé Nast Books/Random House, 1987.

Aline Coquelle, **Palm Springs Style**. Paris: Assouline, 2005.

Terence Conran & Stafford Cliff, **Terence Conran's Inspiration**. London: Conran Octopus, 2008.

Giovanna Crespi (ed.), **Oswald Matthias Ungers: Works & Projects, 1991-98**. Milan: Electa, 1998.

Adèle Cygelman, **Palm Springs Modern**. New York: Rizzoli, 1999.

Colin Davies, **Key Houses of the 20th Century: Plans, Sections and Elevations**. London: Laurence King, 2006.

Colin Davies, Patrick Hodgkinson & Kenneth Frampton, **Hopkins: The Work of Michael Hopkins & Partners**. London: Phaidon, 1995.

Kim Dirckinck-Holmfeld, **The Utzon Library**. Copenhagen: Danish Architectural Press, 2004.

Cristina Donati, **Michael Hopkins**. Milan: Skira, 2006.

Diane Dorrans Saeks, **Jean-Louis Deniot Interiors**. New York: Rizzoli, 2014.

Joachim Driller, **Breuer Houses**. London: Phaidon, 2000.

Dorothy Dunn, **The Glass House**. New York: Assouline, 2008.

Emily Evans Eerdmans, **The World of Madeleine Castaing**. New York: Rizzoli, 2010.

Paul Eishenhauer (ed.), **Wharton Esherick: Studio and Collection**. Atglen: Schiffer Publishing, 2010.

Arthur Erickson, **The Architecture of Arthur Erickson**. London: Thames & Hudson, 1988.

Frank Escher (ed.), **John Lautner: Architect**. London: Artemis, 1994.

Antonio Esposito & Giovanni Leoni, **Eduardo Souto de Moura**. Milan: Electa, 2003.

Meredith Etherington-Smith, **Axel Vervoordt: The Story of a Style**. New York: Assouline, 2002.

Franck Ferrand, **Jacques Garcia: Decorating in the French Style**. Paris: Flammarion, 1999.

Marcus Field, **Future Systems**. London: Phaidon, 1999.

Charlotte & Peter Fiell, **Design of the 20th Century**. Cologne: Taschen, 1999.

Stephen Fox et al., **The Architecture of Philip Johnson**. New York: Bullfinch, 2002.

Kenneth Frampton & David Larkin (eds.), **The Twentieth Century American House**. London: Thames & Hudson, 1995.

Françoise Fromonot, **Glenn Murcutt: Buildings & Projects, 1962-2003**. London: Thames & Hudson, 2003.

Masao Furuyama, **Tadao Ando**. Cologne: Taschen, 2006.

Paul Goldberger & Jospeh Giovannini, **Richard Meier: Houses & Apartments**. New York: Rizzoli, 2007.

Jennifer Golub, **Albert Frey: Houses 1 & 2**. New York: Princeton Architectural Press, 1999.

Wendy Goodmand & Hutton Wilkinson, **Tony Duquette**. New York: Abrams, 2007.

Alastair Gordon, **Beach Houses: Andrew Geller**. New York: Princeton Architectural Press, 2003.

Alastair Gordon, **Weekend Utopia: Modern Living in the Hamptons**. New York: Princeton Architectural Press, 2001.

Mark Hampton, **Legendary Decorators of the Twentieth Century**. London: Robert Hale, 1992.

Alan Hess, **The Architecture of John Lautner**. London: Thames & Hudson, 1999.

Alan Hess, **Oscar Niemeyer Houses**. New York: Rizzoli, 2006.

David Hicks, **Style & Design**. London: Viking, 1987.

David Hicks, **Living With Design**. London: Weidenfeld & Nicholson, 1979.

Ashley Hicks, **David Hicks: A Life of Design**. New York: Rizzoli, 2008.

Thomas S. Hines, **Richard Neutra and the Search for Modern Architecture**. New York: Rizzoli, 2005.

Jan Hochstim, **Florida Modern**. New York: Rizzoli, 2004.

Karen Howes, **Vacation Homes**. London: Merrell, 2007.

James Huniford, **At Home**. New York: Monacelli, 2020.

Neil Jackson, **Craig Ellwood**. London: Laurence King, 2002.

Neil Jackson, **Pierre Koenig**. Cologne: Taschen, 2007.

Kit Kemp, **A Living Space**. London: Hardie Grant, 2012.

Orla Kiely, **Home**. London: Conran Octopus, 2013.

Martin Kieren, **Oswald Matthias Ungers**. London: Artemis, 1994.

Gloria Koenig, **Albert Frey**. Cologne: Taschen, 2008.

Gloria Koenig, **Charles & Ray Eames**. Cologne: Taschen, 2005.

Mateo Kries & Alexander von Vegesack (eds.), **Joe Columbo: Inventing the Future**. Weil am Rhein: Vitra Design Museum, 2005.

Markku Lahti, **Alvar Aalto Houses**. Helsinki: Rakennustieto Oy, 2005.

Adam Lewis, **Billy Baldwin: The Great American Decorator**. New York: Rizzoli, 2009.

Adam Lewis, **The Great Lady Decorators: The Women Who Defined Interior Design, 1870-1955**. New York: Rizzoli, 2010.

Jacques Lucan et al., **The Function of the Oblique: The Architecture of Claude Parent and Paul Virilio, 1963-69**. London: AA Publications, 1996.

Esa Laaksonen & Ásdis Ólafsdóttir (eds.), **Alvar Aalto Architect: Maison Louise Carré, 1956-63**. Helsinki: Alvar Aalto Foundation, 2008.

Barbara Lamprecht, **Richard Neutra**. Cologne: Taschen, 2006.

Andres Lepik, **O. M. Ungers: Cosmos of Architecture**. Berlin: Hatje Cantz, 2006.

Adam Lewis, **Albert Hadley: The Story of America's Preeminent Interior Designer**. New York: Rizzoli, 2005.

Lisa Lovatt-Smith, **The Fashion House: Inside the Homes of Leading Designers**. London: Conran Octopus, 1997.

Thomas Luntz, **Liaigre**. Paris: Flammarion, 2007.

Thomas Luntz, **Liaigre: 12 Projects**. Paris: Flammarion, 2014.

Greg Lynn, **Form**. New York: Rizzoli, 2008.

Robert McCarter, **Aalto**. London: Phaidon, 2014.

Robert McCarter, **Breuer**. London: Phaidon, 2016.

Robert McCarter, **Louis Kahn**. London: Phaidon, 2005.

Karen McCartney, **50/60/70 Iconic Australian Houses**. Sydney: Murdoch Books, 2007.

Karen McCartney, **Superhouse**. Melbourne: Lantern, 2014.

Peter McMahon & Christine Cipriani, **Cape Cod Modern**. New York: Metropolis Books, 2014.

Matilda McQuaid, **Shigeru Ban**. London: Phaidon, 2003.

George H. Marcus & William Whitaker, **The Houses of Louis Kahn**. New Haven: Yale University Press, 2013.

Anne Massey, **Interior Design of the 20th Century**. London: Thames & Hudson, 1990.

Patrick Mauriès, **Fornasetti: Designer of Dreams**. London: Thames & Hudson, 1991.

Jayne Merkel, **Eero Saarinen**. London: Phaidon, 2005.

Detlet Mertins, **Mies**. London: Phaidon, 2014.

Danielle Miller, **New Paris Style**. London: Thames & Hudson, 2012.

Henrik Sten Møller & Vibe Udsen, **Jørn Utzon Houses**. Copenhagen: Living Architecture, 2007.

Martina Mondadori Sartoga, **Renzo Mongiardino: A Painterly Vision**. New York: Rizzoli, 2017.

Tony Monk, **The Art & Architecture of Paul Rudolph**. London: Wiley-Academy, 1999.

Alison Morris, **John Pawson: Plain Space**. London: Phaidon, 2010.

Michael Müller, **Børge Mogensen**. Berlin: Hatje Cantz, 2016.

John V. Mutlow, **Ricardo Legorreta Architects**. New York: Rizzoli, 1997.

Marilyn & John Neuhart, **Eames House**. Hoboken: Ernst & Sohn, 1994.

Oscar Niemeyer, **The Curves of Time: The Memoirs of Oscar Niemeyer**. London: Phaidon, 2000.

William Norwich (ed.), **Interiors: The Greatest Rooms of the Century**. London: Phaidon, 2019.

Helen O'Hagan, Kathleen Rowold & Michael Vollbracht, **Bill Blass: An American Designer**. New York: Abrams, 2002.

Olivia de Oliveira, **Subtle Substances: The Architecture of Lina Bo Bardi**. Barcelona: Gustavo Gili, 2006.

Michael J. Ostwald, **Ushida Findlay**. Barcelona: 2G/GG Portfolio, 1997.

John Pardey, **Jørn Utzon Logbook Vol. III: Two Houses on Majorca**. Copenhagen: Edition Bløndal, 2004.

Richard Pare, **Tadao Ando: The Colours of Light**. London: Phaidon, 1996.

Pierre Passebon, **Jacques Grange Interiors**. Paris: Flammarion, 2009.

John Pawson, **John Pawson**. Barcelona: Gustavo Gili, 1998.

Clifford A. Pearson (ed.), **Modern American Houses: Fifty Years of Design in Architectural Record**. New York: Abrams, 2005.

Ruth Peltason & Grace Ong-Yan (eds.), **Architect: The Pritzker Prize Laureates in Their Own Words**. London: Thames & Hudson, 2010.

Nils Peters, **Jean Prouvé**. Cologne: Taschen, 2006.

Mario Piazza, **Abitare: Fifty Years of Design**. New York: Rizzoli, 2010.

Daniele Pisani, **Paulo Mendes da Rocha**. New York: Rizzoli, 2013.

Gennaro Postiglione et al., **One Hundred Houses for One Hundred Architects**. Cologne: Taschen, 2004.

Kenneth Powell, **Richard Rogers: Complete Works**. Vols. 1-3. London: Phaidon, 1999-2006.

Catherine Prouvé & Catherine Coley, **Jean Prouvé**. Paris: Galerie Patrick Seguin, 2008.

Paige Rense (ed.), **Architectural Digest: Designers' Own Homes**. Los Angeles: Knapp Press, 1984.

David Robson, **Geoffrey Bawa: The Complete Works**. London: Thames & Hudson, 2002.

David Robson, **Beyond Bawa: Modern Masterworks of Monsoon Asia**. London: Thames & Hudson, 2007.

Graziella Roccella, **Gio Ponti**. Cologne: Taschen, 2009.

Timothy M. Rohan, **The Architecture of Paul Rudoph**. New Haven: Yale University Press, 2014.

Joseph Rosa, **Albert Frey: Architect**. New York: Rizzoli, 1990.

Joseph Rosa, **Louis Kahn**. Cologne: Taschen, 2006.

Paul Rudolph & Sibyl Moholy-Nagy, **The Architecture of Paul Rudolph**. London: Thames & Hudson, 1970.

Margaret Russell, **Designing Women: Interiors by Leading Style-Makers**. New York: Stewart, Tabori & Chang, 2001.

Witold Rybczynski, **Home: A Short History of an Idea**. New York: Penguin, 1987.

John Saladino, **Style by Saladino**. London: Frances Lincoln, 2000.

John Saladino, **Villa**. London: Frances Lincoln, 2009.

Laura Sartori Rimini & Roberto Peregalli, **The Invention of the Past: Interior Design and Architecture of Studio Peregalli**. New York: Rizzoli, 2011.

Fritz von der Schulenburg & Karen Howes, **Luxury Minimal**. London: Thames & Hudson, 2012.

Grant Scott & Samantha Scott-Jeffries, **At Home With The Makers of Style**. London: Thames & Hudson, 2005.

Julius Shulman, **Modernism Rediscovered**. Cologne: Taschen, 2016.

Pierluigi Serraino, **Eero Saarinen**. Cologne: Taschen, 2006.

Geoffrey Serle, **Robin Boyd: A Life**. Melbourne: Melbourne University Press, 1995.

Stephen Sills, **Stephen Sills: Decoration**. New York: Rizzoli, 2013.

Stephen Sills, James Huniford & Michael Boodro, **Dwellings: Living with Great Style**. New York: Little Brown, 2003.

Michael S. Smith, **Houses**. New York: Rizzoli, 2008.

Elizabeth A. T. Smith, **Case Study Houses**. Cologne: Taschen, 2006.

Félix Solaguren-Beascoa, **Arne Jacobsen: Approach to His Complete Works**. Copenhagen: Danish Architectural Press, 2002.

James Steele, **Charles and Ray Eames: Eames House**. London: Phaidon, 1994.

James Steele & David Jenkins, **Pierre Koenig**. London: Phaidon, 1998.

John Stefanidis, **Living by Design**. London: Weidenfeld & Nicholson, 1997.

Tim Street-Porter, **The Los Angeles House**. London: Thames & Hudson, 1995.

Tim Street-Porter, **Hollywood Houses**. London: Thames & Hudson, 2004.

Tim Street-Porter, **Palm Springs: Modernist Paradise**. New York: Rizzoli, 2018.

Deyan Sudjic, **Future Systems**. London: Phaidon, 2006.

Deyan Sudjic, **John Pawson: Works**. London: Phaidon, 2005.

Rose Tarlow, **The Private House**. New York: Clarkson Potter, 2001.

Angelika Taschen (ed.), **Living in Argentina**. Cologne: Taschen, 2008.

Sophie Tasma-Anargyos, **Andreé Putman**. London: Laurence King, 1993.

Brian Brace Taylor, **Geoffrey Bawa**. London: Thames & Hudson, 1986.

Suzanne Trocmé, **Influential Interiors**. London: Mitchell Beazley, 1999.

Keiko Ueki-Polet & Klaus Klemp (eds.), **Less and More: The Design Ethos of Dieter Rams**. London: Gestalten, 2009.

Livio Vacchini et al., **Craig Ellwood: 15 Houses**. Barcelona: 2G/Gustavo Gili, 1999.

Maritz Vandenberg, **Farnsworth House: Mies van der Rohe**. London: Phaidon, 2003.

Alexander von Vegstack, **Jean Prouvé: The Poetics of Technical Objects**. Weil am Rhein: Vitra Design Museum, 2004.

Wilfried Wang & Alvaro Siza, **Souto de Moura, Gustavo Gili**. Barcelona: Gustavo Gili, 1990.

Kelly Wearstler, **Hue**. Pasadena: Ammo Books, 2009.

Andrew Weaving, **Sarasota Modern**. New York: Rizzoli, 2006.

Michael Webb, **Modernist Paradise: Niemeyer House/Boyd Collection**. New York: Rizzoli, 2007.

Alan Weintraub & Alan Hess, **Casa Modernista: A History of the Brazilian Modern House**. New York: Rizzoli, 2010.

Richard Weston, **The House in the Twentieth Century**. London: Laurence King, 2002.

David Whitney & Jeffrey Kipnis (eds.), **Philip Johnson: The Glass House**. New York: Pantheon Books, 1993.

Hutton Wilkinson, **More is More: Tony Duquette**. New York: Abrams, 2009.

Leslie Williamson, **Handcrafted Modern**. New York: Rizzoli, 2010.

Leslie Williamson, **Modern Originals**. New York: Rizzoli, 2014.

Vicente Wolf, **Lifting the Curtain on Design**. Monacelli, New York, 2010.

Vicente Wolf, **Learning to See**. New York: Artisan, 2002.

Russel Wright, **Good Design is for Everyone—In His Own Words**. Garrison: Manitoga/Russel Wright Design Centre/Universe, 2001.

Herbert Ypma, **Maison: Christian Liaigre**. London: Thames & Hudson, 2004.

Federica Zanco (ed.), **Luis Barragán: The Quiet Revolution**. Milan: Skira, 2001.

Claire Zimmerman, **Mies van der Rohe**. Cologne: Taschen, 2006.

Index

Picture Credits

Adam Štěch: 296B; Adrian Gaut, Courtesy of Anna Karlin: 93T; Alessandra Ianniello / Living Inside: 316B; Alessandro Paderni, Courtesy of Moroso: 296T; Alexandre Bailhache: 24T; Alexey Knyazev, Courtesy of Peter Kostelov: 230B; Andrea Ferrari, Courtesy of Dimorestudio: 288-289; Andrea Ferrari: 308T; Andrea Papini / House of Pictures: 182T; Andrew Rowat: 20T; Anson Smart: 388-389, 398-399; Armando Salas Portugal © Barragán Foundation, Switzerland / DACS 2021: 144; Björn Wallander / OTTO: 57B, 90T, 146B, 147T, 147B, 265T; Chris Everard: 200T; Chris Tancock: 193T; Corbis / Tom Sibley / Getty Images: 85B; Courtesy of Arquitectura Orgánica: 143; Courtesy of Laura Ashley: 192T, 192B; Courtesy of Todd Oldham Studio: 119T; Dan Marshall: 203T; Dan Piassick: 62-63; Danilo Scarpati: 285; Darren Bradley: 40T, 40B, 44B; Dave Lauridsen: 21T; David Straight, Courtesy of Katie Lockhart Studio: 396-397; Deidi von Schaewen: 256-257, 367B; Derek Swalwell: 391T; Derry Moore: 190-191, 213, 308B; Don Freeman: 92, 117B; Douglas Friedman / Trunk Archive: 30-31, 140, 150B, 151B; Douglas Friedman, Courtesy of Martyn Lawrence Bullard Design: 48B; Durston Saylor, Architectural Digest © Condé Nast: 150T; DW5 Bernard Khoury / Photo by Ieva Saudargaite: 314-15; Edmund Sumner / VIEW: 145B, 360-361; Eirik Johnson: 72B; Engin Aydeniz: 322T; Enrico Cano: 368; Eric Boman: 334B; Eric Piasecki / OTTO: 125B, 270-271; Eric Sander, Courtesy of Studio Jacques Garcia: 248T; Ezra Stoller / Esto: 22, 112B; Fabrizio Bergamo, Courtesy of Antonio Citterio Patricia Viel: 292T; Felix Forest, Courtesy of Richards Stanisich: 390T; Fernando Guerra, Courtesy of Studio MK27: 161T, 161B; Filippo Bamberghi: 286T; Florian Böhm: 226B; Floto Warner / OTTO: 73T, 73B; fotografieSCHAULIN / Kerstin Rose medienservice: 243T; François Dischinger / Trunk Archive: 102-103; François Halard / Trunk Archive: 344T; François Halard, Courtesy of Kelly Wearstler Studio: 42-43; François Halard, Courtesy of Vincent Van Duysen: 225; Frédéric Ducout: 363T; Fritz von der Schulenburg / The Interior Archive: 93B, 198T, 198B, 199, 223, 230T, 252T, 261, 303T, 309T; Gaëlle Le Boulicaut: 153T, 186T, 236T; GAP Interiors / House and Leisure / Photography by Micky Hoyle & David Ross / Styling by Retha Erichsen: 347T; GAP Interiors/Chris Tubbs: 245B; Gianni Franchellucci: 279T; Gieves Anderson / Trunk Archive: 86T; Gio Ponti Archives: 323B; Grant Harder: 16-17; Greg Cox / Bureaux: 245T, 345B, 346T, 346B, 347T; Guido Taroni: 330T, 333T; Henry Bourne, Courtesy of Toogood: 212T; Hiroyuki Hirai: 362T; Horst P. Horst / Condé Nast via Getty Images: 278T; Ingalill Snitt: 180T; Ignazia Favata / Studio Joe Colombo: 292B; Iwan Baan: 175B; Jacques Dirand / The Interior Archive: 249T; Jason Schmidt: 18, 70-71; Jean-François Jaussaud / Luxproductions, Courtesy of Thierry Lemaire: 279B; Joshua McHugh: 20B, 117T; Julius Shulman © J. Paul Getty Trust / Getty Research Institute, Los Angeles (2004.R.10): 29T; Justin Alexander: 385; Laure Joliet / This Represents: 41B; Leonardo Finotti: 170-171; Leslee Mitchell: 124B; Leslie Williamson: 181B, 282T, 283, 287B; Leyden Lewis Design Studio: 90B; Lindman Photography: 180B, 187T; Luke White / The Interior Archive: 231B; Manolo Yllera: 237T; Marc Serota / Getty Images: 134B; Maree Homer, Courtesy of Brendan Wong Design: 383T, 383B; Marina Melia / Villa Santo Sospir © DACS / Comité Cocteau, Paris 2021: 276-277; Mark Luscombe-Whyte / The Interior Archive © Fondation Le Corbusier (F.L.C.) / ADAGP, Paris and DACS, London 2021: 367T; Mark Luscombe-Whyte / The Interior Archive: 41T, 50T, 84, 98, 141T, 142, 143T, 143B, 207T, 207B, 260, 273T, 317, 322B, 324-325, 330B, 332, 365T, 365B; Mark Roskams: 134T; Martin Morrell / OTTO: 258; Matěj Činčera (OKOLO): 284; Matthieu Salvaing: 252B; Michael Freeman: 363B; Michael Sinclair: 214-215; Michael Weber, Courtesy of André Fu Studio: 357; Michael Wee: 387, 394T, 394B; Miguel Flores-Vianna / The Interior Archive: 94-95; Mikael Olsson for T Magazine - New York Times: 294-295; Mitsumasa Fujitsuka, Courtesy of Kengo Kuma & Associates: 362B; Ngoc Minh Ngo: 165B; Nikolas Koenig / OTTO: 130-131; Oberto Gili: 72T, 238B, 250-251, 280B, 282B, 303B, 304-305; Pascal Chevallier / WiB Agency: 248B; Patrick Bingham-Hall: 382T; Paul Massey / Livingetc © Future Plc: 186B; Paul Raeside / OTTO: 196T, 196B; Per-Erik Uddman / TT News Agency / PA Images / Alamy Stock Photo: 181T; Pernille Loof / Trunk Archive: 148-149; Peter Aaron / OTTO: 96-97, 100, 116B; Peter Krasilnikoff, Courtesy of Studio David Thulstrup: 184, 185T, 185B; Philip Durrant, Courtesy of Studio Ashby: 212B; Photographix / Sebastian Zachariah: 364T; Pieter Estersohn / Art Department: 58T, 65B, 68T, 69T, 75T, 87, 125T; Prue Roscoe / Taverne Agency: 373B; Rachael Smith: 222T, 222B; Ray Wilson, Courtesy Peggy Guggenheim Collection Archives; 297T; Ricardo Bofill Taller de Arquitectura: 240-241; Richard Powers. Courtesy of Fawn Galli: 122; Richard Powers © Fonds Prouvé, ADAGP, Paris and DACS, London 2021: 268B; Richard Powers © Ludwig Mies van der Rohe / DACS 2021: 65T; Richard Powers © Oscar Niemeyer / DACS 2021: 38-39, 164B; Richard Powers, Courtesy of Yabu Pushelberg: 356T, 356B; Richard Powers: 19T, 19B, 23T, 23B, 24T, 24B, 25T, 25B, 26-27, 28T, 28B, 29B, 32-33, 34T, 35T, 36-37, 44T, 45T, 45B, 46-47, 49T, 49B, 50B, 51T, 51B, 52T, 52B, 53, 56T, 56B, 59B, 64, 66T, 66B, 69B, 74T, 74B, 75B, 76-77, 79T, 79B, 80T, 80B, 81T, 81B, 88-89, 101T, 101B, 104T, 104B, 105, 108T, 108B, 109, 113T, 113B, 114-115, 116T, 118T, 118B, 119B, 120, 121T, 121B, 126T, 126B, 127, 128T, 128B, 129, 132-133, 135T, 135B, 141B, 160B, 164T, 165T, 166-167, 168T, 168B, 169T, 169B, 172-173, 174T, 174B, 175T, 182B, 183T, 187B, 194-195, 197T, 197B, 201, 202B, 203B, 204B, 204T, 208-209, 210T, 211T, 211B, 218T, 218B, 219T, 219B, 224T, 224B, 226T, 238T, 239T, 239B, 242T, 242B, 243B, 244T, 244B, 249B, 253, 254-255, 259B, 259T, 262T, 262B, 263, 265B, 268T, 269T, 269B, 273B, 274T, 274B, 275B, 275T, 280T, 287B, 293T, 293B, 297B, 298T, 298B, 299T, 299B, 300, 301T, 301B, 302, 306-307, 320-321, 333B, 335T, 335B, 336-337, 338, 339, 340B, 340T, 341T, 341B, 342T, 342B, 343, 364B, 366B, 369, 370T, 371T, 371B, 372, 373T, 374-375, 376T, 376B, 382B, 384B, 384T, 386T, 386B, 390B, 391B, 392T, 392B, 393; Robert Emmett Bright: 264; Robert Knudsen / White House Photographs / John F. Kennedy Presidential Library and Museum, Boston: 123T; Robert Polidori: 99; Robert Rieger: 228-229; Roger Davies / OTTO: 35B, 54-55, 57T, 59T, 160T; Roger Guillemot / EdiMedia Art Archive / World History Archive: 272; Rory Gardiner, Courtesy of Pandolfini Architects: 395B; Sharyn Cairns: 395T; Shim Yun Suk (Studio Sim), Courtesy of Teo Yang Studio: 358T, 358B; Simon Brown / The Interior Archive: 205, 348-349; Simon Brown, Courtesy of Firmdale Hotels: 154-155, 210B; Simon Upton / The Interior Archive: 67B, 68B, 123B, 162-163, 202T, 206T, 220-221, 231T, 237T, 281T, 281B, 290-291, 331T, 331B, 334T, 354B, 354T, 355T, 355B, 366T; Solvi dos Santos / Hemis: 323T; Stephen Kent Johnson. Styled by Michael Reynolds: 112T; Stephan Julliard / Tripod Agency / Styling by Sarah de Beaumont: 316T, 318-319; Stephen Kent Johnson / OTTO: 21B, 82-83, 106-107, 124T, 286T, 377; Stephen Silverman © Barragán Foundation, Switzerland / DACS 2021: 145T; Tara Wing, Courtesy of Manitoga, Russel Wright Design Center: 77; The Lunuganga Trust: 370B; The Modern House / Photo by Jonathan Gooch: 216-217; The Modern House / Photo by Taran Wilkhu: 188-189, 206B; The Mustique Company: 153B; Thomas Hoepker / Magnum Photos: 85T; Thomas Loof / Trunk Archive: 60-61, 183B, 236B; Tim Beddow / The Interior Archive: 0345T, 344B; Tim Crocker: 193B, 200B; Tim Street-Porter: 34B; Tim Van de Velde, Courtesy of Gert Voorjans: 227T, 227B; Tobias Harvey: 246-247; Todd Eberle, Courtesy of Selldorf Architects: 91; Trevor Tondro / OTTO: 58T; Verner Panton Design AG; 278B; Vicente Wolf: 110-111; William Abranowicz / Art + Commerce: 152, 309B; William Waldron / OTTO: 67T, 146T, 151T; William Waldron, Courtesy of Deborah Berke Partners: 86B.

Front cover images (T to B): William Waldron / OTTO; Richard Powers; Todd Eberle. Courtesy of Selldorf Architects. Back cover images (T to B, L to R): Richard Powers © Ludwig Mies van der Rohe / DACS 2021; Douglas Friedman. Courtesy of Martyn Lawrence Bullard Design; Björn Wallander / OTTO; Douglas Friedman / Trunk Archive.

Every reasonable attempt has been made to identify owners of copyright. Errors and omissions notified to the Publisher will be corrected in subsequent editions.

Author Acknowledgments

Phaidon Press Limited
2 Cooperage Yard
London E15 2QR

Phaidon Press Inc.
65 Bleecker Street
New York, NY 10012

phaidon.com

First published 2021

© 2021 Phaidon Press Limited

ISBN 978 1 83866 306 3

A CIP catalogue record for this book
is available from the British Library
and the Library of Congress.

Commissioning Editor: Virginia McLeod
Project Editor: Belle Place
Production Controller: Lily Rodgers
Design: Pentagram

Printed in Italy

The publisher would like to thank
the following for their contributions to
the making of this book: Vanessa Bird,
Lisa Delgado, Holly Pollard, and
Isabella Ritchie.

The author would like to express his sincere thanks to Virginia McLeod, Emilia Terragni, Belle Place, and the rest of the publishing team at Phaidon for their much valued support during the research, development, and production of this book. Special thanks are also due to picture researcher Milena Harrison-Gray, copy editors Lisa Delgado and Isabella Ritchie, together with Michael Bierut and Laitsz Ho at Pentagram for their work on the graphic design of the *Atlas*.

My gratitude is also due to the many photographers who have helped to make this book possible, especially my long-standing travel companion and colleague Richard Powers, who was instrumental in the evolution of many of the featured house stories. Particular thanks are also due to Mark Luscombe-Whyte, Simon Upton, Fritz von der Schulenburg, Karen Howes, Danielle Miller, Karen McCartney, Rachael Smith, William Norwich, my agent Carrie Kania, and my very patient family, Faith, Florence, Cecily, Noah, and Elsie Bradbury.

Above all, the author and publishers would like to thank all of the featured designers, architects, and creative innovators who have contributed to this project, together with the many home owners around the world who have kindly opened their doors to so many inspirational spaces. We are deeply grateful to you for sharing your work and the dream rooms seen within these pages.